Queer Theory in Film & Fiction

AFRICAN LITERATURE TODAY 36

Guest Editor: John C. Hawley
Editor: Ernest N. Emenyonu
Assistant Editor: Patricia T. Emenyonu

Associate Editors: Adélékè Adéẹ̀kọ́
Madhu Krishnan
Pauline Dodgson-Katiyo
Stephanie Newell
Oha Obododimma
Vincent O. Odamtten
Kwawisi Tekpetey
Iniobong I. Uko
Wangui wa Goro

Reviews Editor: Obi Nwakanma

JAMES CURREY

GUIDELINES FOR SUBMISSION OF ARTICLES

The Editor invites submission of articles on the announced themes of forthcoming issues. Submissions will be acknowledged promptly and decisions communicated within six months of the receipt of the paper. Your name and institutional affiliation (with full mailing address and email) should appear on a separate sheet, plus a brief biographical profile of not more than six lines. The editor cannot undertake to return materials submitted, and contributors are advised to keep a copy of any material sent. Articles should be submitted in the English Language.

Length: Articles should not exceed 5,000 words.

Format: Articles should be double-spaced, and should use the same type face and size throughout. Italics are preferred to underlines for titles of books. Articles are reviewed blindly, so do not insert your name, institutional affiliation and contact information on the article itself. Instead, provide such information on a separate page.

Style: UK or US spellings are acceptable, but must be used consistently. Direct quotations should retain the spellings used in the original source. Check the accuracy of citations and always give the author's surname and page number in the text, and a full reference in the Works Cited list at the end of the article. Italicize titles of books, plays and journals. Use single inverted commas throughout except for quotes within quotes which are double. Avoid subtitles or subsection headings within the text.

Citations: Limit your sources to the most recent, or the most important books and journals, in English. Cite works in foreign languages only when no English-language books are available. Cite websites only if they are relatively permanent and if they add important information unavailable elsewhere.

For in-text citations, the sequence in parentheses should be (Surname: page number). No year of publication should be reflected within the text. All details should be presented in the Works Cited list at the end of the article. Consistency is advised. Examples:

Cazenave, Odile. *Rebellious Women: The New Generation of Female African Novelists*. Boulder, CO: Lynne Rienner Publishers, 2000.

Duerden, Dennis. 'The "Discovery" of the African Mask.' *Research in African Literatures*. Vol. 31, No. 4 (Winter 2000): 29-47.

Ukala, Sam. 'Tradition, Rotimi, and His Audience.' *Goatskin Bags and Wisdom: New Critical Perspectives on African Literature*. Ed. Ernest N. Emenyonu. New Jersey: Africa World Press, 2000: 91-104.

Ensure that your Works Cited list is alphabetized on a word-by-word basis, whether citations begin with the author's name or with an anonymous work's title. Please, avoid footnotes or endnotes. Do not quote directly from the Internet without properly citing the source as you would when quoting from a book. Use substantive sources for obtaining your information and depend less on general references.

Copyright: It is the responsibility of contributors to clear permissions.

All articles should be sent to the editor, Ernest N. Emenyonu, as an e-mail attachment (Word)
Email: eernest@umflint.edu
African Literature Today
Department of Africana Studies
University of Michigan-Flint
303 East Kearsley Street
Flint MI 48502 USA
Fax: 001-810-766-6719

Books for review to be sent to the Reviews Editor. Reviewers should provide full bibliographic details, including the extent, ISBN and price:
Obi Nwakanma, University of Central Florida, English Department, Colburn Hall, 12790 Aquarius Agora Drive, Orlando, FL 32816, USA
Obi.Nwakanma@ucf.edu

AFRICAN LITERATURE TODAY

ALT 1-14 BACK IN PRINT. See www.jamescurrey.com to order copies
ALT 1, 2, 3, and 4 Omnibus Edition
ALT 5 The Novel in Africa
ALT 6 Poetry in Africa
ALT 7 Focus on Criticism
ALT 8 Drama in Africa
ALT 9 Africa, America & the Caribbean
ALT 10 Retrospect & Prospect
ALT 11 Myth & History
ALT 12 New Writing, New Approaches
ALT 13 Recent Trends in the Novel
ALT 14 Insiders & Outsiders

Backlist titles available in the US and Canada from Africa World Press and in the rest of the world from James Currey, an imprint of Boydell & Brewer
ALT 15 Women in African Literature Today
ALT 16 Oral & Written Poetry in African Literature Today
ALT 17 The Question of Language in African Literature Today
ALT 18 Orature in African Literature Today
ALT 19 Critical Theory & African Literature Today
ALT 20 New Trends & Generations in African Literature
ALT 21 Childhood in African Literature
ALT 22 Exile & African Literature
ALT 23 South & Southern African Literature
ALT 24 New Women's Writing in African Literature
ALT 25 New Directions in African Literature

Recent and forthcoming* titles
African Literature Today continues to be published as an annual volume by James Currey (an imprint Boydell & Brewer since 2008).
North and South American distribution:
Boydell & Brewer Inc., 68 Mount Hope Avenue, Rochester, NY 14620-2731, US
UK and International distribution:
Boydell & Brewer Ltd., PO Box 9, Woodbridge IP12 3DF, GB
Nigeria edition (ALT 24–33): HEBN Publishers Plc
ALT 26 War in African Literature Today
ALT 27 New Novels in African Literature Today
ALT 28 Film in African Literature Today
ALT 29 Teaching African Literature Today
ALT 30 Reflections & Retrospectives in African Literature Today
ALT 31 Writing Africa in the Short Story
ALT 32 Politics & Social Justice
ALT 33 Children's Literature & Story-telling
ALT 34 Diaspora & Returns in Fiction
ALT 35 Focus on Egypt
ALT 36 Queer Theory in Film & Fiction
ALT 37 (November 2019)*

Queer Theory in Film & Fiction

AFRICAN LITERATURE TODAY 36

EDITORIAL BOARD

Editor: *Ernest N. Emenyonu*
University of Michigan-Flint

Assistant Editor: *Patricia T. Emenyonu*
University of Michigan-Flint

Associate Editors: *Adélékè Adéèkó*
Ohio State University

Madhu Krishnan
University of Bristol

Pauline Dodgson-Katiyo
Anglia Ruskin University

Stephanie Newell
Yale University

Oha Okododimma
University of Ibadan

Vincent O. Odamtten
Hamilton College, New York

Kwawisi Tekpetey
Central State University

Iniobong I. Uko
University of Uyo

Wangui wa Goro
Independent scholar

Reviews Editor: *Obi Nwakanma*
University of Central Florida

James Currey
is an imprint of
Boydell & Brewer Ltd
www.jamescurrey.com
and of
Boydell & Brewer Inc.
www.boydellandbrewer.com

Our Authorised Representative for product safety in the EU is
Easy Access System Europe - Mustamäe tee 50, 10621 Tallinn, Estonia,
gpsr.requests@easproject.com

© Contributors 2018
First published 2018

All Rights Reserved. Except as permitted under current legislation
no part of this work may be photocopied, stored in a retrieval system,
published, performed in public, adapted, broadcast, transmitted,
recorded or reproduced in any form or by any means, without the
prior permission of the copyright owner

British Library Cataloguing in Publication Data
A catalogue record for this book is available from the British Library

ISBN 978-1-84701-184-8 hardback
ISBN 978-1-84701-185-5 paperback

The publisher has no responsibility for the continued existence or accuracy of URLs
for external or third-party internet websites referred to in this book, and does not
guarantee that any content on such websites is, or will remain,
accurate or appropriate

Contents

Notes on Contributors — x

EDITORIAL ARTICLE
Desiring Africans: An Introduction
JOHN C. HAWLEY — 1

ARTICLES
Visual Activism: A Look at the Documentary *Born This Way* — 7
UNOMA AZUAH

African Queer, African Digital: Reflections on Zanele — 17
Muholi's *Films4peace* & Other Works
NAMINATA DIABATE

To Revolutionary Type Love: An Interview with — 38
Kawira Mwirichia, Neo Musangi, Mal Muga,
Awuor Onyango, Faith Wanjala & Wawira Njeru
NG'ANG'A MUCHIRI

Liminal Spaces & Conflicts of Culture in South African — 52
Queer Films: *Inxeba (The Wound)*
GRANT ANDREWS

Gay, African, Middle-Class & Fabulous: — 67
Writing Queerness in New Writing
from Nigeria & South Africa
SHOLA ADENEKAN

The City as a Metaphor of Safe Queer Experimentation — 82
in Monica Arac de Nyeko's 'Jambula Tree'
& Beatrice Lamwaka's 'Pillar of Love'
EDGAR NABUTANYI

Homosexuality & the Postcolonial Idea: Notes from　　96
Kabelo Sello Duiker's *The Quiet Violence of Dreams*
IVES S. LOUKSON

A Warm, Woolly Silence: Rethinking Silence through　　110
T.O. Molefe's 'Lower Main' & Monica Arac de Nyeko's
'Jambula Tree'
ROBERT LARUE

Breaking/Voicing the Silence: Diriye Osman's *Fairytales*　　123
for Lost Children
ASUNCIÓN ARAGÓN

Reading for Ruptures: HIV & AIDS, Sexuality & Silencing　　135
in Zoë Wicomb's 'In Search of Tommie'
LIZZY ATTREE

Queer Temporalities & Epistemologies: Jude Dibia's　　151
Walking with Shadows & Chinelo Okparanta's
Under the Udala Trees
KERRY MANZO

Dilemma of an African Woman Faced with Bisexuality:　　165
A Reading of Armand Meula's *Coq mâle, coq femelle*
STELLA ONOME OMONIGHO

FEATURED ARTICLES
African Oral Literature & the Environment　　175
NDUBUISI OSUAGWU

'From the Street to the World of Art': Writing Women's　　188
Liberation in Nawal El Saadawi's *Zeina*
SIMONE A. JAMES ALEXANDER

LITERARY SUPPLEMENT
Pregnancy in the Time of Ebola (Short story)　　211
M'BHA KAMARA

Okonkwo's Revenge (Short story)　　220
PEDE HOLLIST

Guilt (Short story) 232
CHIOMA DURUAKU

TRIBUTE
Ben Obumselu (1930–2017): Pioneer African Literary Critic 241
ISIDORE DIALA

REVIEWS
Ezra Chitando & Adriaan van Klinken, eds, *Christianity* 246
and Controversies over Homosexuality in Contemporary
Africa; and Adriaan van Klinken & Ezra Chitando, eds,
Public Religion and the Politics of Homosexuality in Africa
JOHN C. HAWLEY

Chantal Zabus, *Out in Africa: Same-Sex Desire in* 249
Sub-Saharan Literatures & Cultures
JOHN C. HAWLEY

Unoma Azuah, *Blessed Body: The Secret Lives of* 252
Nigerian Lesbian, Gay, Bisexual & Transgender
INIOBONG I. UKO

Chimamanda Ngozi Adichie, *Dear Ijeawele, or* 259
a Feminist Manifesto in Fifteen Suggestions
NONYE C. AHUMIBE

Razinat T. Mohammed, *The Travails of a First Wife* 263
NONYE C. AHUMIBE

Efe Farinre, *Folk Tales are Forever* 268
NONYE C. AHUMIBE

M. J. Simms-Maddox *Priscilla: Engaging in the* 271
Game of Politics
PETROLINA IFEOMA KPANAH

Uzodinma Iweala, *Speak No Evil* 274
OBI NWAKANMA

Notes on Contributors

Shola Adenekan is a researcher and tutor in African literature and cultures at the University of Bremen, Germany. His monograph, *African Literature in the Digital Age: Class and Sexual Politics in New Writing from Nigeria and Kenya* is forthcoming. Adenekan is also a journalist and the publisher of Thenewblackmagazine.com

Grant Andrews is a lecturer at the University of the Witwatersrand School of Education. His research interests include masculinities and queer representations in South African literature and film.

Asunción Aragón is Senior Lecturer of English at the University of Cadiz (Spain) where she teaches African Literature, Multiculturalism and Gender Studies. Her research focuses on African literature, its diaspora, and the intersections of gender, sex and race.

Lizzy Attree has a PhD from SOAS, University of London. Her collection of interviews with the first African writers to write about HIV and AIDS from Zimbabwe and South Africa was published in 2010. She has taught at Rhodes University, South Africa and Kings College, London. She was the Director of the Caine Prize from 2014 to 2018 and is the co-founder of the Mabati Cornell Kiswahili Prize.

Unoma Azuah is an LGBT activist, a poet, a writer and a College Professor. Recently, she concluded a book project on the lives of gay Nigerians entitled *Blessed Body: The Secret Lives of LGBT Nigerians*. She teaches writing at the Illinois Institute of Art, Chicago, Illinois.

Naminata Diabate is Assistant Professor of Comparative Literature at Cornell University. A scholar of sexuality, race, biopolitics and postcoloniality, Naminata's research primarily explores African, African

American, Caribbean, and Afro-Hispanic literatures, cultures and film She completed her book manuscript: *Naked Agency: Genital Cursing and Biopolitics in Africa*, and is currently working on the second book *African Sexualities and Pleasures under Neoliberalism*.

Isidore Diala is currently Professor of African Literature in the Department of English and Literary Studies, Imo State University, Owerri, Nigeria. Isidore Diala was Professor Ben Obumselu's undergraduate student at Abia State University, Uturu, Nigeria. Diala edited *The Responsible Critic: Essays on African Literature in Honor of Professor Ben Obumselu* (2006) and is working on a compendium of Obumselu's articles titled *The Intellectual Muse: Ben Obumselu on African Literature*.

John C. Hawley is Professor of English at Santa Clara University, editor of several books on the intersection of queer and postcolonial theories, and author of several articles on African novelists.

Pede Hollist is an Associate Professor of English at The University of Tampa, and Fulbright Scholar 2017–18. His novel, *So The Path Does Not Die*, was named the 2014 African Literature Association Creative Book of the Year. His recent published short stories include 'Payout by the Liberty Expressway' in *Ake Review* 2017; 'The Tale of the Three Water Carriers', long-listed for the 2015 Short Story Day Prize, and 'Song of a Goat', anthologized in *Lusaka Punk* 2015. 'Foreign Aid' was shortlisted for the 2013 Caine Prize.

Simone A. James Alexander is Professor of English, Africana Studies, and Women and Gender Studies, and Director of Africana Studies at Seton Hall University, New Jersey, where she teaches and researches in the areas of Postcolonial literature, African American, African and Caribbean literature, and women writers. Her book, *African Diasporic Women's Narratives: Politics of Resistance, Survival and Citizenship*, reprinted in May 2016 won the 2015 College Language Association Creative Scholarship Award and received Honorable Mention by the African Literature Association. She is also the author of *Mother Imagery in the Novels of Afro-Caribbean Women* and co-editor of *Feminist & Critical Perspectives on Caribbean Mothering*.

Mohamed Kamara is Associate Professor of French at Washington and Lee University, Virginia. He teaches French and Francophone literatures and cultures, including eighteenth-century French literature by women. He has published articles on Léopold Sédar Senghor and human rights, French colonial education, Abdelkébir Khatibi, Birago Diop, on the teaching of the Francophone African novel, as well as on the plays of the Sierra Leonean playwright, Yulisa Amadu Maddy. Mohamed is currently working on a book-length study of French colonial education in sub-Saharan Africa.

Ives S. Loukson is writer and PhD student at the University of Bayreuth. His research interest includes postcolonial theory, South African literature, and Francophone literature.

Robert LaRue is an Assistant Professor in the Department of English at Moravian College. Currently, his work addresses the presence and roles of politics within postcolonial queer expressions.

Kerry Manzo (pronouns: they/them/their) is a doctoral candidate at Texas Tech University. Their dissertation examines the impact of counterpublics on the emergence of African modernist and LGBTI literature.

Ng'ang'a Muchiri PhD is an Assistant Professor of English at the University of Nebraska-Lincoln. He teaches courses on African and Caribbean literature. His current book project is titled, *Writing Land, Righting Land: Literature's Influence on African Property Rights*.

Edgar Fred Nabutanyi is a Lecturer in the Department of Literature, Makerere University. While his teaching interests are in Critical Theory and Media Studies, his research interest is in how vulnerable and minority subjectivities subvert public discourses for self-enunciation.

Stella Onome Omonigho is a Senior Lecturer in the Department of Foreign Languages at the University of Benin. Among her publications is a play titled *Ada, l'histoire d'une orpheline*, published by l'Harmattan in Paris.

Ndubuisi Osuagwu teaches African literature in the Department of English and Literary Studies, University of Calabar, Nigeria. He has a special interest in the oral forms of the literature.

Chioma Toni-Duruaku teaches in the Department of Humanities, Federal Polytechnic Nekede Owerri, Nigeria. Her interest in creative writing has brought forth many Short Stories including 'No More Mutiny in Paradise', 'Miss Courtesy', and 'The All-Sufficient Grace' as well as many poems, among which is 'Ode to Chinua Achebe' published in the African Literature Association Publication *Chinua Achebe (1930–2013): A Tribute*. Chioma is also an attorney, with a specialization in Alternative Dispute Resolution. Positively guiding youths, giving hope to the less privileged and working for a better world are her interests.

Editorial

Desiring Africans: An Introduction

JOHN C. HAWLEY

> Do not get tempted into that. You are young people. If you go that direction, we will punish you severely ... It is condemned by nature. It is condemned by insects and that is why I have said they are worse than pigs and dogs.
>
> Robert Mugabe, in the mining town of Shurugwi, 2011

In his well-received *Desiring Arabs* (2007), Joseph A. Massad extends the argument made by his mentor, Edward Said, in *Orientalism* (1978) that documents how orientalist writing was dehumanising and racist – an analysis of colonial discourse that postcolonial theorists have extended far beyond the Arab world. But Massad also broadens Michel Foucault's history of sexuality to demonstrate how colonial systems helped (mis)shape internalised conceptions of sexuality throughout the postcolonial world. He presents a wide array of Arabic writing from the nineteenth century to show the changes in the understanding of sexual practice that were influenced by European values, and in the process criticises the West for what amounts to a system of bait-and-switch: imposing Victorian standards on what had been stereotyped by them as the licentious Orient, and then in our time amassing their cultural troops to condemn what they now view as a sexually backward postcolony that needs 'civilising' yet again. Rayyan Al-Shawaf summarises Massad's approach as follows (and one might reasonably substitute the word 'African' for 'Arab' in this description, as I will argue in what follows):

> Arab cultural traditions have always included a measure of tolerance for same-gender sex practices, without recognizing a separate socio-sexual categorization for those who engage in such practices. Recently, however, there has been an attempt by certain Westerners and Westernised Arabs to universalize arbitrary and exclusivist sexual identities, including heterosexuality and (more problematically) homosexuality. This initiative has caused a backlash in Arab countries against those who identify themselves as homosexual – an identity associated by many Arabs with

1

> Western cultural imperialism – but also against people who engage in same-gender sex without considering themselves homosexual. (Al-Shawaf 'Review of *Desiring Arabs*': 103)

Many others who are interested in postcolonial theory as it intersects with gender analysis can appreciate Massad's sensitivities (see, for example, Hawley *Postcolonial, Queer* and *Postcolonial and Queer Theories*) without agreeing with his politics, particularly in the arena of LGBTQ futures in Africa. As Al-Shawaf argues: '*Desiring Arabs* is not a work of history, but an intellectual polemic' (104), evidenced in such emotionally charged statements as the following: 'the Gay International [whatever that is] is destroying social and sexual configurations of desire in the interest of reproducing a world in its own image, one wherein its sexual categories and desires are safe from being questioned' (Massad: 189). Massad goes on to warn, ominously, that the apparent successes being racked up by this strangely powerful consortium will be 'not the creation of a *queer* planet … but rather a *straight* one' (190, original emphasis). Massad reasons that Western gay rights activists are insisting on a binary world: heterosexual and homosexual: 'by inciting discourse about homosexuals where none existed before, the Gay International is in fact *heterosexualizing* a world that is being forced to be fixed by a Western binary' (188, original emphasis). Al-Shawaf, in arguing against the hysteria of this position, notes correctly that the Western world Massad describes here has become much less binary, and much more queer – as, in fact, has the African continent.[1]

What has not changed, though, is the need for visibility and for free speech for non-normative sexual expression. When Massad argues that these 'Westernised' postcolonial subjects, in echoing their European and American masters by demanding a *public* space for queer sexual expression, are in fact responsible for the oppression that ensues, he seems to have aligned himself with some very shady characters, indeed. 'This new situation', Massad writes, 'may very well bring about their social and physical death from which the Gay International claims it is trying to save them in the first place' (376). Such a cynical framing of the movement for human rights seems to echo not only those who have wondered why 'those people' can't just support the heterosexual world in public and carry on their 'perverted' lives in the privacy of their bedrooms: it also seems to suggest that LGBTQ folks are *asking for* whatever violence is dished out by a self-righteous and intolerant world. Far better, one assumes, to maintain a nativist agenda that many have characterised as patriarchal and notably binary.

Editorial. Desiring Africans: An Introduction

It comes perhaps as little surprise, therefore, that a Pew Research study in 2013 confirmed that Sub-Saharan African and Muslim-majority countries are perceived as being the least accepting of gays – in the world. In his speech before the United Nations on September 28, 2015, Robert Mugabe represented his nation with these notable words: 'We equally reject attempts to prescribe "new rights" that are contrary to our values, norms, traditions, and beliefs. We are not gays!' (see Laing 'Mugabe Calls David Cameron "Satanic" for Backing Gay Rights'). In such an important forum, and coming from a former revolutionary leader, these words are practically a shout of defiance as things fall apart.

In their two recently edited collections of essays on the intersection of Christianity, politics and homosexuality in Africa, Ezra Chitando and Adriaan van Klinken point out that these debates are relatively recent. This could be used to argue that forms of non-normative sexuality have always been tacitly accepted in most African societies or, conversely, that 'gays' and 'lesbians' are only in the recent decades coming out of the closet. In any case, readers of those essays will stipulate with Neville Hoad that

> Africa is hardly a stable signifier, especially on a terrain of sexuality ... with [the continent's] resistance to any singularity, it's unevenly shared colonial and postcolonial histories and its array of sexual and cultural norms and forms that crosscut and confound an already significant variety of nation-states with something as amorphous and contested as the idea of 'queer'. (Afterword: Out of Place, Out of Time': 188)

But Chitando and van Klinken point to three historical events in recent years as helping move the issue forward from the back burner: 'the controversy within the Anglican Communion, the rise of Pentecostalism and the impact of HIV' (*Christianity and Controversies over Homosexuality in Contemporary Africa*: 10). They conclude their second volume with the September 2015 'Elmina Consultation Statement', formulated in Ghana, which says, in part:

> We call upon our faith communities to make either public commitment or private arrangement to serve as places of sanctuary for those who live under the threat of violence for working on behalf of the gospel. We understand this group to include LGBTI people, women and men living with HIV, ethnic, racial and religious minorities .. and those who are potential victims of gender violence ...

> [We call upon the Church] to curb anti-gay and anti-transgender violence, discrimination, and marginalization; to build relationships with and learn from African Anglican scholars who are already offering biblical

interpretations that affirm the dignity and humanity of LGBTI people; and 'to pray for the safety of our LGBTI sisters and brothers, their families and communities, and for the scholars and activists who tirelessly work on their behalf.' (Chitando and van Klinken: 200)

Pushing back against the notion that homosexuality is a colonial import is a growing number of writers, including Bernardine Evaristo ('How far back can homosexuality be traced in Africa? You cannot argue with rock paintings'), Sylvia Tamale ('The mistaken claim that anything is un-African is based on the essentialist assumption that Africa is a homogeneous entity'), Brent Meersman ('Why is it only this so-called 'African' taboo on homosexuality that is suddenly being reclaimed as a cornerstone of African culture, when so many other customs are not?'), and Eusebius McKaiser ('Even assuming homosexuality does not predate colonialism, which it does, it would not follow that homosexuality should not be permitted here. Why should African beliefs and traditions not be subject to moral criticism and revision?').

Yet, as several of the essays in this collection discuss (Attree, Aragón, LaRue), societies like those of Zimbabwe, Uganda, Nigeria, etc., are notable for their increasingly frantic attempts to silence those who might contradict Mugabe's angry assertion. Recent documentaries like Noni Salma's *Veil of Silence* (2013) and Shaun Kadlec and Debb Tullmann's *Born This Way* (2013) push back with accounts of actual lives that give the lie to the attempt at erasure that is the heart of Mugabe's claim. Filmmakers like Kawira Mwirichia, Neo Musangi, Mal Muga, Awuor Onyango, Faith Wanjala and Wawira Njeru are creating an archive that suggests a hidden history that *will* become visible, despite the mandates of dictators. Films like *Inxeba*, *Dakan*, *Woubi Cheri*, and a burgeoning number of short stories and novels, make visible various alternative ways of conceiving of Africanness (see, for example, Hawley 'In Transition: Self-Expression in Recent African LGBTIQ Narratives'). Naminata Diabate begins her fascinating essay in this special issue of *African Literature Today* by quoting a defiant informant: 'Without a visual identity we have no community, no support network, no movement. *Making ourselves visible is a continual process*' (emphasis added). As Taiwo Osinubi recently observed, 'contemporary queer representations challenge cultures of unknowing and recalibrate the perception and perceptibility of queers' ('Queer Prolepsis and the Sexual Commons': ix). And a disruptive process it is, without a doubt. Osinubi argues that 'queer figures in the twenty-first-century cultural landscape do not stay on the fringes of the political community, lurk in shadows, nor communicate their presence obliquely' (ix). As a homely saw would have it, the squeaky wheel gets the oil (and, as Massad points out, the backlash).

Change is happily evident in the success this year of director Wanuri Kahiu's *Rafiki* ('friendship') in the Kenyan courts.

NOTES

1   Osinubi notes that 'critics of the Americanness or whiteness of queer studies forget the existence of similar critique within the Global North … In the concluding chapter to *Bodies That Matter*, Judith Butler argues that meanings of *queer* cannot be assumed: they must be re-articulated and redirected for use anew across different terrains and occasions (Butler 226-28)' (xiv).

WORKS CITED

Al-Shawaf, Rayyan. 'Review of *Desiring Arabs*'. *Dissent* (formerly *Democratiya*) Spring 2008. www.dissentmagazine.org/wp-content/files_mf/1389821516d12AlShawaf.pdf (accessed 13 February 2018).

Butler, Judith. *Bodies That Matter: On the Discursive Limits of Sex*. New York: Routledge, 1993.

Chitando, Ezra and Adriaan van Klinken, eds. *Christianity and Controversies over Homosexuality in Contemporary Africa*. New York: Routledge, 2016.

Evaristo, Bernardine. 'The Idea that African Homosexuality was a Colonial Import is a Myth'. *The Guardian* 8 March 2014. www.theguardian.com/commentisfree/2014/mar/08/african-homosexuality-colonial-import-myth (accessed 13 February 2018).

Hawley, John C. 'In Transition: Self-Expression in Recent African LGBTIQ Narratives'. *Journal of the African Literature Association* Vol. 11, No. 1 (2017): 120-34.

——*Postcolonial, Queer: Theoretical Intersections*. Albany, NY: State University of New York Press, 2001a.

——*Postcolonial and Queer Theories: Intersections and Essays*. Westport, CT: Greenwood, 2001b.

Hoad, Neville. 'Afterword: Out of Place, Out of Time'. *Research in African Literatures* Vol. 47, No. 2 (2016): 186-91.

Kahiu, Wanuri, dir. *Rafiki* (2018).

Laing, Aislinn. 'Mugabe Calls David Cameron "Satanic" for Backing Gay Rights'. *The Telegraph* 24 November 2011. www.telegraph.co.uk/news/politics/david-cameron/8912132/Mugabe-calls-David-Cameron-satanic-for-backing-gay-rights.html (accessed 13 February 2018).

Massad, Joseph A. *Desiring Arabs*. Chicago and London: University of Chicago Press, 2007.
McKaiser, Eusebius. 'Homosexuality un-African? The Claim is an Historical Embarrassment'. *The Guardian* 2 October 2012. www.theguardian.com/world/2012/oct/02/homosexuality-unafrican-claim-historical-embarrassment (accessed 15 February 2018).
Meersman, Brent. 'Homosexuality is African'. *Mail & Guardian* 26 March 2012. http://thoughtleader.co.za/brentmeersman/2012/03/26/homo sexuality is-african (accessed 15 February 2018).
Osinubi, Taiwo Adetunji. 'Queer Prolepsis and the Sexual Commons: An Introduction'. *Research in African Literatures* Vol. 47, No. 2 (2016): 7-23.
Salma, Noni, dir. *Veil of Silence*. Nigeria, Audacity Innovative, 2014.
Tamale, Sylvia. 'Homosexuality is not un-African'. *Al-jazeera America* 26 April 2014. http://america.aljazeera.com/opinions/2014/4/homo sexuality-africamuseveniugandanigeriaethiopia.html (accessed 15 February 2018).

Visual Activism

A Look at the Documentary *Born This Way*

UNOMA AZUAH

When I think of visual activism and the African LGBT community, I think of Neo Musangi of Kenya, a gender-nonconforming feminist academic, activist and performer. One of Neo's public performances called 'Time and Space' demonstrates gender fluidity. Neo gets to the centre of a public space with both male and female clothing. Neo performs each gender with a complete wardrobe. While this goes on, the audience, a variety of people, from civil servants and pedestrians, to passers-by, form a large crowd and surround Neo as Neo switches from male to female clothing. Each full display leaves the audience confused and wondering to which gender Neo belongs. Neo's visual activism forces live audiences to think about the blurred line between gender identities.

When I think of visual activism and the African LGBT community, I think of South Africa's Zanele Muholi and her long-term outstanding project called 'Faces and Phases'. This project consists of a photograph series created between 2007 and 2014. These portraits 'commemorate and celebrate lives of black queers'. The pictures are of mostly women Muholi met in her journeys all across South Africa. Her objective in these projects is to 'counter invisibility, marginality and systemic silence'. She seeks, instead, to include LGBT people at the forefront of South Africa's liberation narrative. In these series of photographs, Muholi's mission is to create an archive of 'visual, oral and textual materials that include black lesbians and the role they have played in our communities' (Muholi 'Faces and Phases').

When I think of visual activism and the African LGBT community, I think of the timeline for movies like *Dakan*, released in 1997, the first Sub-Saharan African feature film on a gay theme. I think of the documentary *Woubi Cheri*, another pioneer film from Ivory Coast, released in 1998. Then, 2001 was the Senegalese movie, *Karmen Geï*, a movie that dared to feature a lesbian protagonist. There is *Z-Yaanbo* from Burkina Faso, which was released in 2011, *Call Me Kuchu*, from Uganda, released in 2012. I think further about that country's David Kato who was right in the middle of this movie project when he was murdered. The film was nevertheless completed. Then there is *God Loves Uganda*, released in 2013 and *Veil of Silence*, released in 2014 when Nigeria was on the verge of enacting the anti-same-sex marriage law. The production and release of these visual representations of LGBT lives emerged from the restlessness of African LGBT activists who are tired of being weighed down and repressed by draconian anti-gay laws across Africa.

The urgency for African LGBT members to be heard and be seen is captured when Tullman, one of the producers of the documentary *Born This Way* spoke to a Cameroonian LGBT person. In her words: 'we are tired of Cameroon pretending that gay people don't exist. We are ready to step forward.' Additionally, the movie *Woubi Cheri* is described as a 'cry of protest against a society which refuses to see, let alone accept, homosexual relationships' (California Newsreel *Woubi Cheri*). The director of *Dakan*, Mohamed Camara made the movie *Dakan* 'to pay tribute to those who express their love in whatever way they feel it, despite society's efforts to repress it' (California Newsreel *Dakan*). The resolve to be acknowledged, to be heard and to be respected gave rise to these visual movements. In this pile of visual representation of LGBT Africans, human rights documentaries like *Born This Way* are changing lives.

Documentaries are tools of revolution; documentaries change lives and opinions. The renowned filmmaker, Sam Kauffman, affirms that 'the job of documentary filmmakers ... is to shed some light on a neglected people or issue' (Thurston 'Can a Film Change the World?'). The persecution of a sexual minority group is one such issue. To further show the power of documentaries, the sociologist John Abraham Stover adds that he believes 'quite strongly both as a sociologist and as an individual in the power of [documentaries] to change people's lives and shape public opinion' (Stover 'The Intersections of Social Activism, Collective Identity, and Artistic Expression in Documentary Filmmaking': 3). These words of affirmation speak to the importance of *Born This Way* in the way it portrays homosexual lives in Cameroon. Directed and produced by Shaun Kadlec and Debb Tullmann, the film traces the lives of four gay Cameroonians: Cedric, Gertrude, Pascaline and Esther. All are defendants in a legal action in which Alice Nkom, a famous Cameroonian gay rights attorney represents them. The film is impressive in many ways, not the least of which is its portrayal of the 'hustle' of gay life in the Cameroonian city of Douala against the general bustle of the urban scene. The documentary portrays the challenges of these four individual lives, inspiring respect and compassion for them – sometimes also shown by those around them.

There are three revolutionary scenes in this documentary. Because the scenes reveal how the activists in *Born This Way* confront and fight oppression, I call the scenes 'sites of resistance'; they represent a revolt and a social movement. The first site of resistance is the scene where Pascaline shares her sexual orientation with the taxi driver who is taking her to a safe space. The second site of resistance is the scene where Attorney Alice Nkom defends homosexuals as citizens who should not be criminalised. The third site of resistance is the scene where Gertrude 'comes out' to the mother superior that raised her as a child.

The site of resistance where Pascaline shares her sexual orientation with the taxi driver shows the importance of conversations and dialogues. The taxi driver finds the topic of homosexuality strange and far-fetched. However, his ability to initiate a moment of learning empowers Pascaline to open up to him. Her story wins over the taxi driver's heart. He ends up not being distant, indifferent or even hateful of such a strange sexual attraction; instead, he appreciates the knowledge.

The section where Attorney Alice Nkom defends homosexuals on Cameroonian national television in a country that has the highest rate of arrest of homosexual cases also reveals a moment of revolt. That instance of challenging the criminalisation of a group is a moment of 'revolution.' Homosexuality is a stigmatised word in Cameroon; hence, the television firm represents the state as a public sphere. It is one of the sites where LGBT advocacy faces the most resistance just as the spiritual also presents a daunting site. Nevertheless, the attorney creates a movement when she single handedly challenges the state and public site by daring to defend a marginalised group. The spiritual site, which is embodied in the scene where Gertrude 'comes out' to the mother superior symbolises the most brutal site of opposition. Religion is a well-known roadblock. For instance, scholars like Peter Geschiere have noted that 'Christian communities in Cameroon as well as the judiciary system persistently denounce homosexuality' (Lyonga 'The Homophobic Trinity': 56). In deconstructing these sites of resistance, de Ridder et al., in the article 'Towards a Pragmatic Approach to Resistance and Subversion in Media Research on Gay and Lesbian Identities', offer a framework that defines these three scenes by arguing:

> For social change to occur there needs to be a symbiosis between agency and structure. To this end, a dialectic approach is needed that bridges the gaps between, on the one hand, a ... project that creates awareness of norms, discourse and hegemony, and on the other, identity politics that have the potential to change laws and institutions. (de Ridder et al. 'Queer Theory and Change': 204)

The symbiotic relationship between Nkom as a guest at the Cameroonian television station and the television station itself makes it such that, while she fills in their time slot for that programme to be aired, she utilises that platform to attack homophobia and the injustice meted out to Cameroonian homosexuals. On Gertrude's side, she returns to the convent to show her appreciation for a mother superior who cared for her in place of her own mother. She shows the mother superior appreciation and affection, but she uses that opportunity to unmask herself by 'coming out' to her. That burden of secrecy she bore for a long time is lifted. In the case of Pascaline and the cab driver, by driving Pascaline he earns money, while Pascaline through his services gets to her safe-space destination. The dialectic approaches are evident in the tension or conflicts created within these scenes, even as we are made aware of the norms or laws that disenfranchise a marginalised group. Alice Nkom straddles the identity politics in the hope that the laws against homosexuals in Cameroon can be changed or dismantled.

Lundberg defines a social movement as 'a voluntary association of people engaged in concerted efforts to change attitudes, behavior and social relationships in a larger society' (quoted in Triangular Chair 'What is the meaning of the term Social Movement?'). These four people fight social injustice at their sites of resistance because their lives and their views are rejected in their community. This is consistent with the traits of any group that is likely to form a social movement: they have little chance of becoming integrated into the life of the community; they are marginalised, not fully accepted, isolated, and threatened by economic insecurity and loss of social status. These three scenes embody the marks of a social movement, which Anderson and Parker describe as a 'dynamic ...behavior, which progressively develops structure through time and aims at partial or complete modification of a social order' (*Sociology: Its Organization and Operation*). Pascaline, Gertrude and Alice Nkom form a social movement at these sites with their ability to counter dominant attitudes and cultural norms. They form a social movement that has created a shift in the prevalent homophobic prejudice in Cameroon.

When one looks at homosexuality and the multiple fronts from which it is being attacked, especially in Africa, it becomes interesting to note that before colonialists introduced sodomy laws, there existed, and still exist, non-heterosexual practices on the continent. However, recently, religious fundamentalists have promoted a serious wave of homophobia. Drawing upon history, there is a need for a new orientation of African governments on the subject of homosexuality. Hence, the emergence of gay-themed documentaries in Africa is especially welcome as a tactical strategy in the tackling of homophobia, notably those coming from Uganda, South Africa, Nigeria and Cameroon.

The documentary medium used to tell the Cameroonian LGBT story enhances its message and delivery. Some may argue that documentaries have no impact on the lives of LGBT Africans especially when these movies are shot by foreigners and featured mostly abroad. The issue of who shoots the movies may not be as significant as whose story is being told. Besides, the lives of LGBT Cameroonians and Africans in general are impacted even when such effect or progress may not always be so apparent because of setbacks and cases of violence. Nevertheless, the immediate impact of *Born This Way* can be seen through the lives of Cedric and other featured protagonists in this documentary. Cedric for example, got the opportunity to relocate to the US and work after the documentary gave him prominence. With his current position, he is able to assist the Cameroonian LGBT community. In his words:

> Today, I continue to help my former colleagues in Cameroon. I advise them on important matters and help write reports that aim to assist those still suffering the indignities heaped on them just for being gay. Despite the sadness that is always present, I plan to live a long … life so that I can play a role in changing the environment for LGBT people in not only Cameroon, but also anywhere we are persecuted for being born different from others. (Tchante 'African LGBT Activist Escapes Death Threat')

Pascaline was able to get support and funding for her legal battles. Incidentally, the prosecutions and convictions of LGBT people in Cameroon have dropped remarkably. The LGBT organisation Alternative Cameroon continues to provide legal, social and health services to the Cameroonian LGBT community including the incarcerated ones. *Born This Way* has given the oppression of the LGBT community in Cameroon global attention. When *Born This Way* was premiered in Berlin for the 63rd annual Berlinale, for instance, the Cameroonian Ambassador to Germany admitted as much: 'Documentary films can help to highlight marginalized populations, the disabled, native cultures or homosexuals' (Jacobs 'Born This Way in Berlin').

A good number of LGBT organisations in Africa like Alternative Cameroon and The Initiative for Equal Rights (TIERS) in Nigeria have started promoting and featuring LGBT movies in their community centres. In the case of Nigeria for instance, a TIERS administrator shared that the documentary they promoted called *Veil of Silence* stirred a lot of controversy and got many people talking when it was released in Lagos. A second documentary they promoted called *Hell or High Waters*, according to him, produced a tremendous response and excitement in the Nigerian LGBT community in Lagos. Beyond these reformist trends is also the fact that when African LGBT persons see people like themselves in movies and stories that recognise their lives, it motivates them to self-love and self-affirmation, the two crucial steps to paths that lead to fighting for self-rights. The transgender screenwriter and producer of *Veil of Silence*, Nigerian Noni Salma, adds her voice to the need for LGBT documentaries when she states that the use of

> documentaries as a tool for advocacy works ... From my experience working on my film *Veil of Silence*, I realized that the more visible LGBTIQ people are, the more normalized it can get. Because a film is visual, a relatable character becomes one the audience empathizes with regardless of sexual orientation or gender identity. Documentary films can show who we are, our complexity and our humanity. It is a great tool to starting conversations and building bridges. (Azuah 'Interview with Habeeb Lawal now known as Noni Salma')

The place of documentaries in educating, changing lives and effecting social changes cannot be overemphasised; visual stories are easily absorbed compared to textual representation. Documentaries have a reach that is greater than the printed word and is seen by a larger audience. Stewart Dunlop asserts: 'A visually recorded fact is invincible evidence and therefore has a greater power to move minds more than the written or the spoken word. This is how awareness can be created of social stigmas'. He goes on to say that, 'Documentaries can educate and inspire people into taking certain steps which would not have been possible otherwise. Lives are changed when people watch brave deeds or selfless serving of humanity and then decide to emulate the examples shown in the documentary.' In the same way, lives are seen being changed in *Born This Way*.

It is noteworthy that Gertrude's adopted mother, the nun, speaks to the need to respect all people's lives, even if some people do not accept all forms of sexuality. This is a progressive deviation from the position of the Church in Cameroon. When Gertrude and the nun tour the convent and Gertrude stumbles upon a gun, which at first startles her, the sister explains that it is just an air gun for scaring away the crows. It is striking here that the lives of these nuisance creatures are respected and spared, whereas homosexuals face violence and even death. The medium of documentary is one of the emerging forces pushing against the tide of homophobia as it applies to all African countries battling hate. Documentaries speak to the challenges faced by the African LGBT community as its members are stripped of their humanity.

In most African countries, Cameroon in particular, homosexuality is predominantly perceived as a malediction or disease that a person might have, causing them to be dishonoured, beaten, banned from participation in numerous spheres of human endeavour or even killed. Homophobic violence in Cameroon, as well as in many other regions of Africa such as Uganda or Kenya, is often sanctioned or ignored. The dangers of LGBT were manifested in Cameroon with the murder of Eric Ohena Lembembe, a journalist-activist, on 15 July 2013. He was found dead in his house, and according to Neela Ghoshal ('Processing the Murder of Eric Ohena Lembembe'), was killed specifically because of his sexual orientation.

After the Rwandan genocide in 1994, human rights violations in Africa became part of public consciousness. In the last couple of years, violence against the LGBT community in Cameroon has stirred debate about the place and responsibility of government on this topic and the urgent need for African leaders to take pragmatic steps to check violence, abuse, discrimination and injustice against the LGBT community. Tragedies such as the death of Lembembe, the destruction of an LGBT organisation's building through arson, the death threats received by lawyers defending these people, and the incessant torture and constant harassment perpetrated by police have individuals from certain quarters insisting that the issue of anti-LGBT violence continues to escalate, while pragmatic decisions that should be made to remedy the crisis are nearly non-existent.

One formidable strategy human rights activists continue to deploy to draw the attention of Africans in particular and the world at large to the humanitarian emergencies in the continent is the documentary film, an emerging genre complete with codes, conventions, and dominant motifs, which is a symbol of an increasingly post-literate world – a visual topography where both fiction and the real merge. Therefore, documentary film as a signifying practice has the capacity to create an ambiance where the African LGBT community can be given the opportunity to live peacefully among other Cameroonians regardless of their sexual orientation. The immense power of cinema in conferring identities emanates from the fact that it is so close to real life. As a signified practice, documentary film becomes a visual strategy to raise people's awareness of the discrimination faced by the LGBT community.

The resolution and eradication of homophobia in African countries like Nigeria, Uganda and Cameroon requires an urgent means of re-orientation and re-education. This could save lives; it could save many innocent gay men and women from jungle justice and from the risky sexual practices often forced upon them by the criminalisation of their sexual preferences. It could save a whole generation that is unjustly persecuted. What it would take is a multiplicity of mediums including textual and visual strategies. Movies especially can play a key role. They rouse more interest; they engage viewers longer. They stimulate curiosity and interest. They make the experience of accepting a narrative more active and real. People forget many things easily, but a visual experience can ensure that ideas and concepts are permanently etched in their minds. As a visual topography, documentary film has the power to engage in real social action and enacting real change, and a film such as Born This Way is able to provide hope and relief to many LGBT and make Cameroonian society understand that there are variations in the sexual orientation of people housed under a roof called a nation.

Despite the daily flow of anti-gay messages in Cameroonian society, many fearless activists and campaigners still fight for tolerance and better living conditions for the LGBT community. This brings to the fore the courageous battles engaged in by the prominent activist and lawyer Alice Nkom. She continues to dedicate her efforts in addressing the situation, having already been working in the field of human rights. Her support for gay rights indicates a path of hope and underpins a kind of promise.

Like other films on the subject, Born This Way enters into conversation with mounting opposition against LGBT, particularly in Cameroon, in the light of the increasing volume of discourse on LGBT communities in Africa. The visibility and narratives coming from them in this documentary have arguably achieved a nonpartisan dismissal of the idea that homosexuality and gender/sexual spectrums do not exist in the African continent. The characters in Born This Way are Cameroonians. They are not immigrants from foreign lands, neither are they aliens from outer space. The simple presence of the film within the Cameroonian filmscape illustrates LGBT orientations as borderless, unfixed from specific time or place, and renders their 'alienness' meaningless. Without any semblance of hatred or reprisal Cédric insists, 'We want to fight for the cause in our country we love. Why not be pioneers in this country?' (Duncan 'New Film Explores Homophobia and Hatred Towards LGBTI Community in Cameroon').

Despite the challenges LGBT communities encounter in Cameroon, one point is clear with the screening of *Born This Way*, there is still hope that the situation can improve. This film is a revolution in the Cameroonian film history because it emphasises the importance of coming out, taking a stand and constructing identity based on an 'unacceptable' sexual orientation where LGBT is taboo. The documentary aptly espouses the fact that the forces and structures that spread homophobia and ignorance may be international and rigid but the ties that bind LGBT people and their stories are universal. The production of more gay-themed documentaries like *Born This Way* will be the driving force of change in spite of the polarities they stir up. Such films will continue to inspire the quiet revolutions begun by activists like Nkom, Gertrude, Pascaline and Cédric, and hopefully motivate more African scriptwriters to engage this medium for a better world. Though these revolutionaries confront intense oppositions and divergences, they pave a path for the acceptance of homosexuals in Africa.

WORKS CITED

Anderson, W. and Parker, F. *Sociology: Its Organization and Operation*. Princeton, NJ: Van Nostrand, 1964.

Azuah, Unoma. 'Interview with Habeeb Lawal now known as Nons Salma', digital recording and transcript, 14 November 2016.

California Newsreel. *Dakan*. NewsReel.org, California, 1997. www.newsreel org/nav/title asp?tc=CN0024 (accessed 26 February 2018)

California Newsreel. *Woubi Cheri*. NewsReel org, California, 1998. http://newsreel.org/video/WOUBI-CHERI (accessed 26 February 2018)

De Ridder, Sander, Frederik Dhaenens and Sofie Van Bauwel. 'Queer Theory and Change Towards a Pragmatic Approach to Resistance and Subversion in Media Research on Gay and Lesbian Identities'. *Observatorio Journal* Vol. 5, No. 2 (2011): 197-215. https://biblio.ugent.be/publication/_212627 (accessed 5 February 2018).

Duncan, Jonathan. 'New Film Explores Homophobia and Hatred Towards LGBTI Community in Cameroon'. *Africa is a Country* 25 March 2014. http://africasacountry.com/2014/03/new-film-explores-homophobia-and-hatred-towards-lgbti-community-in-cameroon (accessed 27 February 2018).

Ghoshal, Neela. 'Processing the Murder of Eric Ohena Lembembe'. Human Rights Watch, 17 July 2013. www.hrw.org/news/2013/07/17/processing-murder-eric-ohena-lembembe (accessed 27 February 2018).

Jacobs, Rick. '*Born This Way* in Berlin'. *HuffPost Blog*. 12 February 2013. www.huffingtonpost.com/rick-jacobs/born-this-way-in-berlin_b_2668956.html (accessed 5 February 2018).

Kadlec, Shaun and Debb Tullmann, directors. *Born This Way*. 2013. French, English. United States, Cameroon. College and University Educational DVD.

Lyonga, Frida. 'The Homophobic Trinity: Pentecostal End-Time Prosperity Gospels as Contributors to Homophobia in Cameroon'. *Christianity and Controversies over Homosexuality in Contemporary Africa*. Eds Ezra Chitando and Adriaan van Klinken. Routledge, 2016.

Muholi, Zanele: 'Faces and Phases'. Michael Stevenson archive, 2010. http://archive.stevenson.info/exhibitions/muholi/facesphases.htm (accessed 5 February 2018).

Stover, John Abraham. 'The Intersections of Social Activism, Collective Identity, and Artistic Expression in Documentary Filmmaking'. eCommons: Dissertations, Loyola University, Chicago, IL 2012. https://ecommons.luc.edu/cgi/viewcontent.cgi?article=1395 &context=luc_diss (accessed 26 February 2018).

Tchante, Cédric. 'African LGBT Activist Escapes Death Threat'. HuffPost Blog, 21 April 2017. www.huffingtonpost.com/entry/african-lgbt-activist-esc_b_9750158.html (accessed 27 February 2018).Triangular Chair. 'What is the meaning of the term Social Movement?' http://triangularchair.wordpress.com/aboutsocial-movement (accessed 5 February 2018).

Thurston, Andrew. 'Can a Film Change the World?' *BU Today*. Boston University, 10 January 2013. www.bu.edu/today/2013/can-a-film-change-the-world (accessed 5 February 2018).

African Queer, African Digital

Reflections on Zanele Muholi's *Films4peace* & Other Works

NAMINATA DIABATE

'Without a visual identity we have no community, no support network, no movement. *Making ourselves visible is a continual process*' (2008, emphasis added). This quote by Joan E. Biren is the epigraph of Zanele Muholi's 2008 MFA thesis titled 'Mapping Our Histories: A Visual History of Black Lesbians in Post-Apartheid South Africa'.[2] Bringing an empowering visibility to LGBTQ people, building a support network, and constructing an archive through the visual are central goals in Muholi's vision and work. As a black lesbian from humble beginnings, Muholi hails from the country with the most progressive constitution regarding gender and sexual identities, and where, paradoxically, black lesbians and other racialised sexual minorities are more likely to suffer homophobic violence such as 'curative rape' and massacres.

All too often, these homophobic attacks against black lesbians are subsumed under the categories of enclosure, and even of erasure in a utopian yet doomed project of creating a radical sexual homogeneity. For a category of individuals whose sexual practices and gender identities suffer relentless attacks, both systemic and personal, survival can often and simply take the powerful form of signalling one's presence. Though problematic, visibility through the digital becomes an appealing mode of survival, and even of permanence and *ex-sistence* (Lacan *Ecrits*) – the privilege of stepping outside of one's condition in an act of examination. It is this battle against enclosure and the constant threat of erasure that Muholi is waging with her digitally accessible photography, short documentaries, and video installations.

I explore the extent to which the formulation of digitality as a mode of symbolic capture, and as a form of conversion of bodies into data for the global accumulation of capital, manifests itself in the African art context. As a way of contextualising my claim, I provide a brief political and cultural history of how African visual and digital arts depict the development of dissenting genders and sexualities.

This longstanding investment in visibility, first through the visual and now through the digital, becomes more urgent with the promise of democratised inclusion and freedom in the information age. Colin Koopman calls the age 'infopower', which he argues has displaced the current biopolitical era. In the second part of the essay, an exploration of digitality as a continuation of control society as formulated by Seb Franklin and other thinkers shows the limits of certain dissemination processes of artistic creations. In my discussion of the circulation of Zanele Muholi's 2004 photographic image 'Aftermath' and her 2013 four-minute piece for *films4peace* on hate crimes, I highlight the failed promises of digitality. When digitality is mediated through rhizomatic multinational corporations and coincides with the frenetic consumption of images, the otherisation of historically marginalised subjects persists and even flourishes. Ultimately, in exposing the dark side of digitality through contemporary African cultural products, I seek to question the celebration of digital democratisation and of its promises.

VISUAL ARTS AND QUEERNESS

Given the historical importance that the visual played in the othering processes of Africans during colonisation, several notable African visual artists have mobilised photography to counter if not to displace the available disempowering images of black African bodies.[3] More recently, photographs, art films, short documentaries and video installations by Zanele Muholi, Jean Brundrit, Ingrid Masondo, Sabelo Mlangeni and Lunga Kama have contributed significantly to the visibility of sexual minorities and to establishing their archives. More importantly, these artists enable the African debate regarding social justice, art, and the democratisation of digital access in the information age. This debate is even more crucial in relation to queer modes of (re)presentation because queer subjects are often exploited in political debates. Genderqueer people are more multiply marginalised than other segments of the population as they are often used as distracting strategies by ineffective postcolonial governments (Hoad *African Intimacies: Race, Homosexuality, and Globalization*), scapegoats by American evangelists (Gettleman 'Americans' Role Seen in Uganda Anti-Gay Push'), or as an endangered species that international gay and lesbian rights activists in a sort of White Saviour Industrial Complex invested in 'making a difference' (Cole 'The White-Savior

Industrial Complex'). For this group then, the promises of digitality as inclusion and equality has become a source of power.

Zanele Muholi is part of this larger artistic context, and her work on black lesbians emerged in that hopeful yet challenging era. From her first solo exhibition in 2004, Muholi has depicted the lives and loves of people who are black and lesbian, gay, bisexual, transgender and intersex (LGBTI), seeking to achieve 'black queer visibility' against the constraints of enclosure and erasure. The result is a growing archive that negotiates identity politics, establishing Muholi as an international activist.[4] Her persistent investment in a queer archive, paired with her ability to constitute subjects by bringing them into the space of appearance, has rendered her project generative in terms of its political implications. Foremost among the political implications is the formation of an alternative form of interaction, augmenting a sense of community despite the geographical separation of those who have been historically marginalised because of their genders and sexual practices. As she works to capture the reality of her model subjects, the artist carefully avoids the tempting trap of rendering violence in a pornographic light, which might unwittingly set the survivors up as the 'losers' and empower their perpetrators (Muholi in Garb 'Figures and Fictions: South African Photography in the Perfect Tense' 287). These statements highlight the artist's keen awareness of the gains and limits of (re)presentation.

However, the artist's empowering projects become debatable when thrust into the circuits of global capital expansion as aided by digitality. Muholi's art can be thought to escape the processes of control by postcolonial nation-states given their limited economic and technological advances. Her creations, however, cannot escape the negative effects of the digital revolution through their co-optation by corporations such as Pinterest and Puma, which are often motivated primarily by capitalist interests, as I explore with the digital circulation of her 2004 photographic image 'Aftermath' and the 2013 Puma-commissioned short art film. It is therefore necessary to expose the limits of digitality as a space of emancipatory representational forms.

DIGITALITY: PROMISES AND FAILURES

Digitality here should be understood in its two broadest senses, the first of which highlights its material aspect. Drawn from Nicholas

Negroponte's pioneering 1995 *Being Digital*, 'digitality' designates the ways in which digital devices have shaped the conditions of living, producing, and consuming. The ubiquity of the digital in our daily lives has led some to call us prosthetic beings. The art world has not escaped the digital invasion, so much so that designating a specific aesthetic endeavour as digital is an exercise in futility (Whitelaw 2000). Thus, I posit as 'digital' all works that require the medium of a computer or a smartphone for them to be disseminated, consumed and experienced.

Increasingly, Muholi's visual work is becoming digital, amplifying her ideological investments in recording and rendering legible queer practices. As a highly motivated artist who cultivates a partnership with her model subjects, to whom she refers as her 'people', Muholi demonstrates an awareness of the evolving nature of lesbianism and in so doing, notes the meaning of private lives in the digital age, saying: 'The young lesbians now, they are socialites, connected by the social medias and all of that. And they're free when it comes to photographs' (Human Rights Watch *Zanele Muholi, Visual Activist*). One of her model subjects, whose hair the artist is braiding, strengthens Muholi's observation about the freedom and attraction of being photographed, sharing: 'I was surprised, but at the same time it was fun! I had fun and I didn't know I was photogenic. So since then, I like to take myself pictures' (Human Rights Watch). The model's statement serves to challenge the argument of those who complain that Muholi exploits the images of her subjects.

Rendering the world recordable and knowable through the ease and speed with which it disseminates and archives news and artefacts carries important implications for the African context where the plunder of material resources and intangible assets has resulted in the fragility of lives and the ephemerality of artefacts (Mbembe 'African Contemporary Art: Negotiating the Terms of Recognition'). Dispersal and exchange of ideas and images via digitality might end up being more powerful than centuries-long aesthetic and political advocacy of a 'pan-African' project. As such, digitality seems like a panacea for an artistic endeavour invested in subcultural preservation and dissemination. In addition to the formation of strong alternative communities, digitality is also framed as the cure to African economic 'underdevelopment'.

Such a redemptive narrative could not have come at a better time. It arrived when African countries were slowly coming to terms with the devastating aftereffects of the Structural Adjustment Programs by

Bretton Woods financiers, practices that Judith Butler, in a different context, compellingly conceptualises as precarity, the politically induced effects of neo-liberal policies (*Frames of War: When Is Life Grievable?*). Over several years, the late Nelson Mandela celebrated the benefits of information sharing and digital advances. In 1995, a year after becoming president, Mandela declared in a speech: 'In the twenty-first century, the capacity to communicate will almost certainly be a key human right. Eliminating the distinction between the information-rich and information-poor is also critical to eliminating economic and other inequalities between North and South, and to improve the life of all humanity' (Wilson *The Information Revolution and Developing Countries*: 1).[5]

However, democratised digital access is accompanied by the imbrication and capture of all in global market processes, highlighting thus the dark side of digitality. That dark side results from the deleterious effects of neo-liberalism – the application of market principles to all aspects of life – which, as Michel Foucault explains, accompanies biopolitics for the production of docile bodies (*The Birth of Biopolitics*).[6] Thus, digital democratisation coincides with its fragility. It is fragile because its enabling conditions come with the imperative to capture, optimise, and filter, implicating unavoidably some forms of inclusion and exclusion. These aspects relate to the second definition of digitality as a condition of exclusion and as a metaphorical mode of 'capturing individual and social behaviors for the purpose of valorization' and of exploitation (Franklin *Control: Digitality as Cultural Logic*: 8). As such, digitality falls under what Giorgio Agamben calls 'apparatus'; that is 'anything that has in some way the capacity to capture, orient, determine, intercept, model, control, or secure the gestures, behaviors, opinions, or discourses of living beings' (*What is an Apparatus?* 14). As an expansion of conventional sites of capture such as prisons, psychiatric wards, schools and factories, Agamben adds metaphorical spaces of capture, including computers and cellular telephones (14). Once captured, beings and behaviours undergo a process of discretisation, what Gilles Deleuze calls 'dividuation', which moulds people into samples, data, markets, or 'banks' ('Postscript on the Societies of Control': 6). This transformation turns the captured into easily exploitable data for the global capitalist accumulation of profit.

The promises of digitality to end unfreedom, injustice and inequality are appealing because of the so-called rational nature of the digital-machine. Supposedly nonpartisan (attesting to the abandon with which we share our personal data on social media platforms), digital logic renders all affairs and objects equal. However, digitality banks on its hidden dark sides to increase the efficacy and rigour with which exploitation and exclusion are effected. Anybody that is impacted by digitality also suffers its negative impacts. But, these negative effects are more salient for queer subjects who may invest in the digital for visibility and survival. It is in this digital context and about these subjects that two of Muholi's powerful works on the devastation of homophobia, 'Aftermath' and the short contribution to *films4peace*, emerge. The choice of these two pieces rests on the ways in which, independently of the artist's goals, they have become readily available for voyeurism and imbricated in neo-liberal-biopolitical mechanisms of exploitative appropriation.

AFTERMATH': DOUBLE INSCRIPTION AND DIGITAL CAPTURE

'Aftermath' was first presented at the *Visual Sexuality: Only Half the Picture* exhibition in September 2004 in South Africa. It was part of a series of black and white photos portraying black women engaging in various sexual activities: strapping a dildo with a condom wrapped on it ('Dada' 2003), kissing ('Kiss' 2003), chest binding ('ID Crisis' 2003), and ('Pad on Plate' 2003 that features a soiled sanitary pad on a plate complete with cutlery). At the exhibition that brought the artist national recognition, several visitors felt outraged, and a student even demanded 'an apology for having to be put through such trauma' referring to 'Dada' (quoted in Godana 'Is Anybody Comfortable?').

'Aftermath' portrays a female's lower torso, thighs, knees, and hands covering her crotch in a modesty gesture, despite her wearing a charcoal-colour brief with the ubiquitously placed label 'Jockey' just below her belly button. A long and centipede-shaped skin scar runs vertically from the woman's right upper thigh to her knee.[7] The scar is the result of a corrective rape, which the subject suffered several years prior to the photo being taken. The photo was taken after the 17-year old woman underwent a second curative rape, which did not leave a bodily scar; but added an emotional scar to the skin one. The artist's powerful framing of the lower torso through a close-up shot highlights the unmistakable presence of the violent bodily inscription. The act of illuminating the aftereffects of corrective rape also invites unwanted scrutiny. Photography is then mobilised for the social and political role of archiving and of rendering visible in the form of exposure.

African Queer, African Digital: Zanele Muholi's Films4peace 23

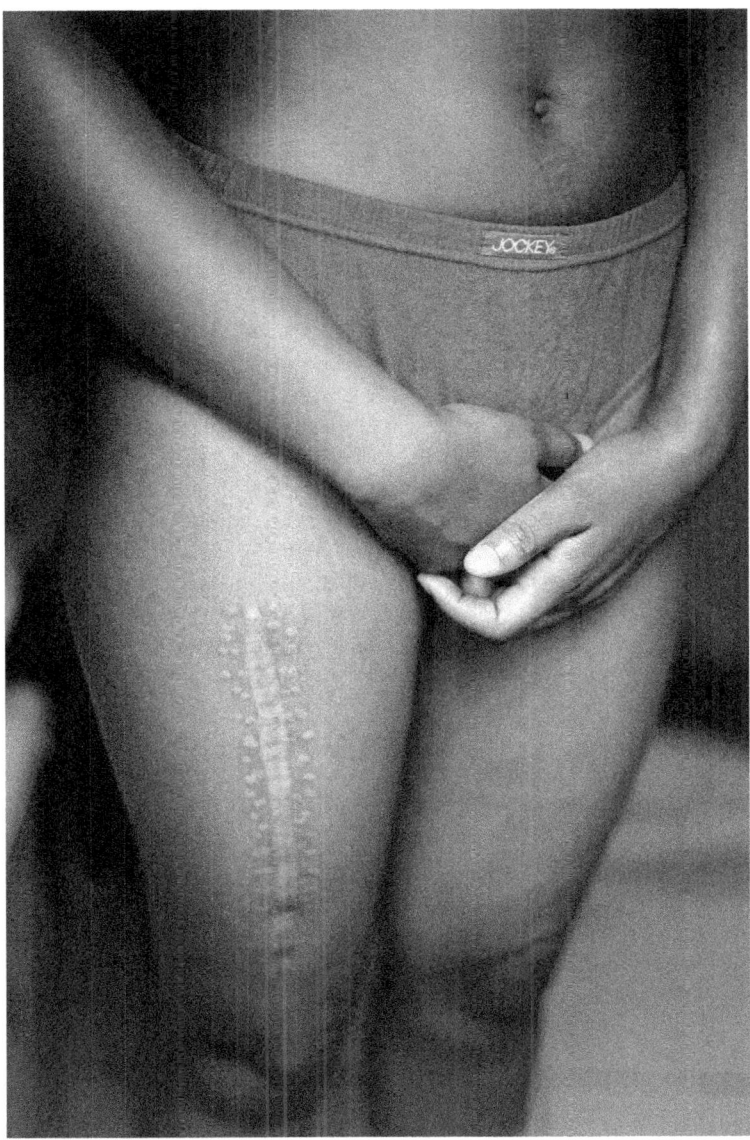

Figure: 1 *Aftermath*, 2004 Silver gelatin print. Full captions in separate document (© Zanele Muholi. Courtesy of Stevenson, Cape Town/Johannesburg and Yancey Richardson, New York)

The reception of Muholi's work has mainly been celebratory. The list of her different awards and accolades, corporate sponsorships, and the flurry of speaking engagements around the world attests to that laudatory mode. For instance, 'Aftermath' has received formidable scholarly attention with most interlocutors lauding the artist's vision for a black queer archive and courage to realise such a vision. Reporting on Muholi's first exhibition, Nonkululeko Godana (2004) similarly highlights the ways in which 'Aftermath' serves as a direct translation of Muholi's activism into documentary photography. More nuanced than Godana, Gail Smith argues that Muholi's 'photographs are not artistically or technically brilliant – and some are downright disturbing – but the exhibition, and the response to it, show some movement towards addressing the staggering absence of "out and proud" lesbians in South African society' ('Outlaw Culture'). These evaluations are representative of the dozens of articles and book chapters that celebrate Muholi's myriad activist achievements. I seek not to undermine Muholi's achievements; but rather to trouble facile narratives of digital dissemination as promising terrain for democracy and freedom. The laudable readings become highly problematic with the unrestrained and uncontrolled digital circulation of the image. Indeed, through digital presence, the photograph and its subject become doubly inscribed, bodily and digitally.

'Aftermath' exposes the constant fear and the resilience of lesbian lives, which are markedly vulnerable to rape. Not only do these rapes consist of the intention to erase certain allegedly undesirable sexual practices and identities, but they also constitute forms of inscription. The large physical scar is a form of inscription, a form of what Christine Braunberger has called in a different context, that of tattoos, 'bodily excess' ('Revolting Bodies: The Monster Beauty of Tattooed Women'). Here, the scar is an excess because two different entities coexist on the survivor's material body and perhaps her psyche: the subject herself and the presence of another – her violator who inscribes his eternal presence. The scar simultaneously belongs and does not belong to the survivor because it strikingly defines her image while ensuring the present absence or the absent presence of the assaulter.

Although a marker of healing and of closure, this scar 'as a trace of corporeal writing, marks the place of a previous incision or injury. A sign of what no longer is. It also is a deep historical marker. The scar occurs as a double gesture' (Richter: *Thought-Images: Frankfurt School Writers' Reflections from Damaged Life*). This scar serves as a reminder of danger and of vulnerability because it is both a memory and a palimpsest of shattered dreams, vulnerable presence and uncertain future. The scar also attests to the authority of the violator and of his power of inscription, of insertion, of labelling and even of branding. With this bodily marking, the assaulter has violently inserted himself into his victim's life. Given the location of the scar, perhaps, the assaulter's goal was inscription – re-inscription if we follow Sara Ahmed and Jackie Stacey in their analysis of skin (*Thinking Through the Skin*) – rather than the threat to his victim's life. As such, the scar becomes the trace of an already lasting assault and violation.

The bodily inscription is compounded by an even more pervasive inscription and capture, digital that is. From its original exhibition in the gallery in South Africa, 'Aftermath' is now digitally available on Stevenson's website, Muholi's official art gallery. However, an online search in August 2016 indicated that 'Aftermath' was also available on course websites and on major social media platforms, including Facebook and Pinterest. This digital inscription with its ensuing re-objectifying process may commodify the original subject, thus putting pressure on Muholi's attempt to rearticulate the goals behind her archiving of this scar.

When presented in the 2004 exhibition, the image was framed by the caption: 'Many lesbians bear the scars of their difference, and those scars are often in places where they can't be seen' (quoted in Gunkel *The Cultural Politics of Female Sexuality in South Africa*: 1). Then, the caption provided the artist's desired framework from which to make sense of this scar, which meant to uncover the inscriptive nature of curative rape. However, the caption disappears in subsequent online presentations of the image. Without the caption, the image is exposed, making the scar vulnerable to multiple and even subversive readings. These can range from an accident to violence by others or by the self, none of which is necessarily related to homophobia. Although exposed, the scar still withholds its multi-layered history, proving the fantastical nature of the statement that suggests that one photograph is worth one thousand words. Here, we are in the terrain of a 'contamination' narrative whereby the image as intended by the artist carries possibly emancipatory aspect. But, as 'Aftermath' circulates moving away from its originary intention, it gets contaminated by Pinterest in a kind of corporate imbrication.

To digitally compile an archive is also to run the risk of subjecting the experiences so archived to measurement, judgement, or stereotype. As the image travels through the floodlights and the dungeons of digitality, depending on one's perspective, the subject in 'Aftermath becomes a type and even an archetype, especially for those in search of exotic images of an othered queer sexuality, of an identity that is multiply queered by variables of economic status, postcoloniality, gender, and race. The idea of the image serving as the archetype of black lesbianism is already inscribed in the anonymity that the subject enjoys (Thomas 'Zanele Muholi's Intimate Archive'). Such preserved anonymity through the covering of her genitalia, breasts, and most importantly, her face while archiving her experience turns the woman into 'an allegorical figure, standing for those in the state of similar aftermaths' (Van Der Vlies 'Art as Archive': 99).

The inscription and the capture of 'Aftermath' on Pinterest, for instance, with its wider circulation and filtering have made the subject in the image less and less legible without the caption. On Pinterest, the world's largest catalogue of ideas and images curated by users, people can find recipes, parenting hacks, style inspiration and other ideas. The company is valued at $5 billion. Although unpacking Pinterest's distribution of profits is beyond the scope of this article, I wonder if Muholi or the subject in the image have benefited from the presence of her artwork or of their image on Pinterest.

My analysis of the capture and circulation of 'Aftermath' carries important implications for scholars who are quick to celebrate Muholi's perceived resistance to exotic eroticism and to framing. Indeed, my argument problematises both Pumla Dineo Gqola's hopeful interpretation of Muholi's work as resisting 'precisely such endeavours to name, tame and classify' ('Through Zanele Muholi's Eyes': 83) and Desiree Lewis's celebratory argument that Muholi unsettles the codes of ethnography and of exotic erotica ('Against the Grain: Black Women and Sexuality'). Undoubtedly these celebratory readings are consistent with certain historical, technological and ideological trends. However, they need revising to reflect the current development on the failures of digitality as democratising and emancipatory. If a caption-free 'Aftermath' is subject to exploitation because filtered and captured by the mechanisms of digitality, a commissioned piece by Puma – the 2013 short film – might serve corporations in questionable ways.

FILMS4PEACE: QUEER DEATH, DEFIANCE AND EXTRACTED VALUE

In turbulent economic times, intangible assets, mostly reputation, become winning strategies for corporations. That appealing reputation

African Queer, African Digital: Zanele Muholi's Films4peace 27

is often built through a much-admired and cost-effective strategy, philanthropic action. And it is in this business of building reputation that Puma, the German multinational company that designs and manufactures athletic goods, invested in *films4peace*. Not surprisingly, Mark Coetzee, the curator of the series explains the company's rationale: 'PUMA.Peace wishes to contribute to making the world a better place. A world that is safer, more peaceful and more creative. We are honoured that so many amazing and high profile museums, galleries and online partners have joined us in this important initiative' (Artlyst *Films4peace* 'Short Film Commissions Screened For World Peace Day').

According to their website, from 2011 to 2013 the company celebrated World Peace Day each 21 September, by releasing arts films. Puma invited some of the world's most innovative artists from 13 countries to visually interpret the subject of peace. Their commissioned art films should answer the question: 'What does peace mean to you?' A total of 23 invited artists created 23 short art films.[8] In the interest of making the films accessible to as wide an audience as possible, they had to be dialogue-free and short. For three successive years, the commission released seven, ten, and six short films, as broadly as possible in more than 120 live and virtual platforms, with the goal of effecting 'positive social change and broaden[ing] the discussions around peace globally' (*films4peace*). The lofty and certainly laudable goal of globally broadening the discussion around peace presupposes that the largest number of people will watch the films so that positive social change can be effected.

In the last year of the series, 2013, Muholi contributed the 3:55-minute film on hate crimes, particularly the devastation of corrective rape. and the possibility of living a thriving life in its aftermath. Since being uploaded on 19 September 2013 to Puma's YouTube, the film has recorded 1,353 views and 41 shares. For those familiar with the politics of numbers on YouTube, 1,353 views does not indicate a particularly successful engagement with viewership.[9] Perhaps the marginal public enthusiasm for Puma's series explains why the series was cancelled after three years.

Muholi's short piece opens with three shots of white screens with credits in the chronological order: Puma, *films4peace*, and Zanele Muholi. From that soundless, calm, and surreal white scene follows a black screen and the viewer is immediately confronted head-on in an eye-level, medium close-up shot with adult black feet on a dirt road.

The determined male and female steps are even more convincing

Figure 2 Screen Capture, Short film for peace by Zanele Muholi, published 19 September 2013 (*films4peace* website)

with the loud and heavy sounds of their footsteps. Their dusty and battered shoes range from plastic, knee-high boots to sandals and athletic shoes. The following low-angle still camera shows a single, long line of adults passing by on a dirt road. Although the faces of the figures are unavailable to the viewer, their body language is solemn and dignified. With the establishing, extreme wide shot, the line of mourners, some carrying crosses, are still walking caught between the whitish sky, a range of mountains, and trees on their right hand side and a seemingly manicured grass on their left. As the viewer takes in the scenery and its different protagonists: landscape, sky, grass and humans, the soundtrack changes from the footsteps to a sombre female funeral dirge while the shots fluctuate between the walking feet, the mourners walking past open and dirt graves, some marked with name plates and crosses. Several scenes provide different angles from which to make contact with the mourners: head-on, backside and sideways.

The film unfolds by setting up a smooth transition between day and night and the endless stream of mourners through which we might apprehend the ubiquity of deaths and of community support. The smooth transition between the last two shots gives a natural feel to the

African Queer, African Digital: Zanele Muholi's Films4peace 29

Figure 3 Screen capture. Short film for peace by Zanele Muholi, published 19 September 2013 (© Zanele Muholi. Courtesy of Stevenson, Cape Town/ Johannesburg and Yancey Richardson, New York)

Figure 4 Screen capture. Short film for peace by Zanele Muholi, published 19 September 2013 (© Zanele Muholi. Courtesy of Stevenson, Cape Town/ Johannesburg and Yancey Richardson, New York)

passage of time and of the alternating nature of birth and death, day and night, hatred and love.

The story links two intimately connected settings: a large burial ground with multiple open dirt graves that are frequently visited by mourners, and a murder site located in a remote dry land with shrubs. Two minutes into the film, the murder site – where the body is found – is introduced with two walking males who come upon a half-clothed female body lying face up with her hands and feet spread out. Several eye-level angle shots show the remaining and tattered clothes on the body and even a skull sitting next to it, suggesting the rampant violent nature of the area. After the discovery of the body, several individuals gather around it, grieving the lost life as the viewer hears screaming female voices.

Then one sees hands cordoning off the area with police tape, marking the existence and even the intervention of the state in this drama of violence. Given the failure of the state to fulfil its basic functions and affirmative obligations – education, medical services, security, and other necessaries of life – often, its existence needs to be showcased. A close-up panning shot of the body highlights the victim's hands, face, feet, belly, and other body parts. Following an unsettling shot of the corpse, a group of young black males and females encircle the murder site, several of them planting in it red candles.

In the last low-medium shot, a panning camera movement frantically seeks to capture the standing group from the back while the sun picks through the spaces between them. To end, the white screen with credits appears.

A crucial question that haunts this film is 'why does the artist feature queer death in a corporate series on peace?' For those unfamiliar with Muholi's work, it may be unclear how this film is about queer death. The only sentence framing the film on YouTube, 'South African artist Zanele Muholi explores hate crimes and the end of a life in her short film for Puma's *films4peace*', gives a hint. Although useful, the category 'hate crimes' is still vague and inclusive. But, the half-nakedness and the face-up position of the body powerfully suggest that the 'female' body has suffered sexual violence, pointing towards the specific category of corrective rape. Muholi's close interest in black lesbianism and of its fate in South Africa strengthens the suggestion of a queer life cut short. Multiple answers are possible to the crucial question, and I suggest that, for Muholi, peace cannot be imagined and even conceived without taking stock of the predicament and of the precariousness of life of certain segments of the population, in this

African Queer, African Digital: Zanele Muholi's Films4peace   31

Figure 5 Screen capture. Short film for peace by Zanele Muholi, published 19 September 2013 (© Zanele Muholi. Courtesy of Stevenson, Cape Town/ Johannesburg and Yancey Richardson, New York)

Figure 6 Screen capture. Short film for peace by Zanele Muholi, published 19 September 2013 (© Zanele Muholi. Courtesy of Stevenson, Cape Town/ Johannesburg and Yancey Richardson, New York)

Figure 7 Screen capture. Short film for peace by Zanele Muholi, published 19 September 2013 (© Zanele Muholi. Courtesy of Stevenson, Cape Town/Johannesburg and Yancey Richardson, New York)

Figure 8 Screen capture. Short film for peace by Zanele Muholi, published 19 September 2013 (© Zanele Muholi. Courtesy of Stevenson, Cape Town/Johannesburg and Yancey Richardson, New York)

case, queer subjects. As such, the discussion of peace goes hand in hand with the discussion of homophobia and other hate crimes.

Foregrounding queer death to spark discussions about queer life, Muholi's film represents an assertion of queerness against the imposition of a heterosexual denial of queerness. This assertion takes multiple forms: a visual rebuttal of the 'un-Christian' nature of queerness and the grievability of queer life through the formation of a caring community. The ubiquity of conventional Christian tropes of redemption and peace, candles and crosses, serves to resist the argument that same-sex sexuality is un-Christian, rendering the film not only assertive but also utterly defiant. The Christian tropes also suggest tolerance of all as well as respect for earthly human life – of which the victim was denied. The formation of a caring community to which the queer life was dear and recognised as grievable constitutes one of the film's formidable messages of 'peace'. If the killer refused to recognise this life as human and therefore as worthy of living, the community bestowed humanity on the lost life by mourning it. Here, we are in the Butlerian terrain of grievability because lives that are not recognisable are also not grievable: 'They cannot be mourned because they are always already lost or, rather, never "were"' (Butler: 33). With its multitude of defiant stands, this film resists being read as a pornography of violence. Certainly, it is an archive of pain, to borrow Christopher Colvin's phrase ('Trauma'), but it is equally an archive of defiance.

That this unsettling film ends on a scene with young men and women bearing witness to brutal end of a queer life is a mostly conventional trope of hope for the future. The young ages of these actors suggests their innocence, as they are still uncontaminated by the corruption of minds, by the incomprehensible intolerance for the different other. Upon these actors is bestowed the commendable project of building a society unpolluted by hatred of all kinds. The last shot reminds the viewer of a better day to come, suggesting the power of the light of hope to displace the forces of darkness. Although invigorating, this teleological approach to human affairs through the lens of the feel-good trope carries multiple complicating concerns, especially the widely adored inspirational assurance 'it gets better' (IGB).[10] The inspirational ending of the film resonates with the anticipated Hollywood happy ending so all viewers can go home comforted by the fantasy that order and goodness have been established. However, the feel-good ending often fails to interrogate and confront the larger systemic configurations – education, unemployment, etc. –

that lead to hate crimes such as corrective rapes.

The inspirational yet debatable ending aims to make the piece palatable to a global audience, thus converging with Puma's goal of inspiring. As such, the film falls into a certain safe yet sterile neoliberal template. Further, the emphasis on shoes and feet in the film may work to centre Puma, known for its athletic shoes. Although the shoes are unmarked, one cannot but interrogate their heavy presence. Could this movie about the cycles of life and death, of hatred and love as the community comes together to remember those who have passed on make sense without the multiple scenes that prominently include shoes? I would speculate that given its financial support to the project, Puma found creative ways to be incorporated surreptitiously into the film's narrative.

Through the lens of digitality as continuation of control emerges the most unsettling aspect of Muholi's collaboration with Puma. This reflection on peace through curative rape inserts the victim into the circuits of capital expansion. In her death, the figure becomes metaphorically valuable because, when she was alive, she was too poor and perhaps too remotely located to be any use to global capitalism. Although non-exploitable to global capitalism when alive, in death the victim is captured and subject to exploitation under the mutating logic of capital. Muholi's collaboration with Puma shows how the gain of visibility, in the activist vision, has been eroded by corporate mediation, exploitation or even seizure.

CONCLUSION

Muholi's particular archive of work, its disseminations, and its celebratory receptions constitute a response to queer invisibility and enclosure. However, in representing violence against lesbian bodies with the goal of curtailing such violence, the digital capture and the dispersal of the photographic image and the short film offer the violated queer body as both capital and object. This development shifts understandings of artistic interventions as opportunities for participating in positive social change.

My analysis may be read as 'paranoid' because of the way in which it may appear to overestimate the reach of global capitalism. My reflection, however, should be the starting point for a more compelling exploration of the promises of digitality, especially in its relation to artistic renderings of queerness. Ultimately, this analysis of the darker sides of the digital revolution suggests the imperative for artists to negotiate with greater clarity with local and global forces of commodification and control.

NOTES

1 I thank Michal Raizen, Kate McCullough, and Lucinda Ramberg for their rigorous comments on a previous draft of this article.
2 Biren is an internationally acclaimed documentary artist whose photographic and film work has focused on queer people and practices for more than three decades.
3 David Goldblatt, Pieter Hugo, Berni Searle, Rotimi Fani-Kayode, Andrew Dosunmu, Oladélé Ajiboyé Bamgboyé and Tracey Rose, among others. For more on this, see Hayes 'Power, Secrecy, Proximity' and Richards 'Aftermath: Value and Violence in Contemporary South African Art'.
4 Among Muholi's remarkable works are her portraiture 'Faces and Phases' (2006-15) a growing collection series of living portraits, ZaVa (2013), Brave Beauties (2006-10), Being (2007), Only Half the Picture (2006), Somnyama Ngonyama, Hail the Dark Lioness (2017); her video performance (2017), What Don't You See When You Look at Me? (2008: 4:13 min.), and her documentaries: Difficult Love (48 min., commissioned by the South African Broadcast Corporation, 2010), We Live in Fear (2013, 11:23 min., commissioned by Human Rights Watch); and her short films Enraged By A Picture (2005, 17 min.) and the 2013 Puma-commissioned art film for films4peace (2013: 3:18 min.).
5 Three years later, Mandela strengthened his position, calling for greater investment in the expansion of telecommunication networks (1998).
6 As a form of power that emerged toward the end of eighteenth century, biopolitics broadly designates the imbrication of life processes into political calculations in the name of the enhancement of the life of the population. However, within biopolitics resides an aporia because it endows some lives with legal and political prerogatives, while disallowing others. The disallowed lives often are those that have been historically marginalised on the basis of race, sexual practices, postcoloniality and gender and that have little to no access to conventional sites of knowledge production.
7 The story behind the image speaks of the intimacy that Muholi fosters with her subjects. For instance, she explains that 'Aftermath' was taken two days after the 17-year-old girl in the image had been raped by a male 'friend' aiming to 'show her that she is not a man' (Muholi in Godana: 91). The subject reportedly called Muholi two hours after the second rape incident to confide in her.
8 These artists include familiar names such as Isaac Julien (UK), Noriko Okaku (Japan), Terence Nance and Hank Willis Thomas (USA), Magali

Charrier (France), Peterson Kamwathi (Kenya), Yang Fudong (China), Nandipha Mntambo (Swaziland), Max Hattler (Germany), Zanele Muholi (South Africa), Janet Biggs (USA), Ergin Çavuşoğlu (Bulgaria), Gregory Crewdson and Costanza Theodoli-Braschi (USA and UK), Tom Gran and Kayleigh Gibbons (UK), Joe Lawlor and Christine Molloy (Ireland), Michael Nyman (UK), Jacco Olivier (Netherlands) and Bill Porter (UK). Of the 13 countries, three are African: Swaziland, South Africa and Kenya

9 Note that Beyonce's *Lemonade*, uploaded in December 2016, has recorded 52,441,924 views.

10 In 2010, Jasbir Puar, Tavia Nyong'o, and others levelled a similar critique at Dan Savage's viral video campaign 'It Gets Better' to end queer youth suicides.

WORKS CITED

Agamben, Giorgio. *What is an Apparatus? And Other Essays*. Translated by David Kishik and Stefan Padatella. Stanford, CA: Stanford University Press, 2009.

Ahmed, Sara and Jackie Stacey, eds. 'Introduction'. In *Thinking Through the Skin*. New York, NY: Routledge, 2002: 1-17.

Artlyst. 'Films4Peace Short Film Commissions Screened For World Peace Day'. 10 September 2012. www.artlyst.com/news/films4peace-short-film-commissions-screened-for-world-peace-day (accessed 1 March 2018).

Braunberger, Christine. 'Revolting Bodies: The Monster Beauty of Tattooed Women'. *NWSA Journal* Vol 12 No. 2 (2000): 1-23.

Butler, Judith. *Frames of War: When Is Life Grievable?* New York, Verso, 2009.

Cole, Teju. 'The White-Savior Industrial Complex'. *The Atlantic*. 21 March 2012.

Colvin, Christopher. 'Trauma'. In *New South African Keywords,* eds Nick Shepherd and Steven Robins. Athens, OH, Ohio University Press, 2008: 223-34.

Deleuze, Gilles, 'Postscript on the Societies of Control'. *October* Vol. 59 (1992): 3-7.

Fani-Kayode, Rotimi. 'Traces of Ecstasy (1992)'. In *Reading the Contemporary: African Art from Theory to the Marketplace*, eds Olu Oguibe and Okwui Enwezor. London: The MIT Press and Institute of International Visual Arts, 1999: 276–81.

Foucault, Michel. *The Birth of Biopolitics: Lectures at the Collège de France, 1978-1979*, ed. Michel Senellart, translated Graham Burchell. Picador, 2010 [2004].

Franklin, Seb. *Control: Digitality as Cultural Logic*. Boston: MIT Press, 2015.

Garb, Tamar. 'Figures and Fictions: South African Photography in the Perfect Tense'. In *Figures and Fictions: Contemporary South African Photography*, eds Tamar Garb; Martin Barnes. Göttingen: Steidl; London: V&A, 2011: 11-85.

Gettleman, Jeffrey. 'Americans' Role Seen in Uganda Anti-Gay Push'. *The New York Times*. 3 January 2010.

Godana, Nonkululeko. 'Is Anybody Comfortable?' *This Day*, 6 September 2004.

Gqola, Pumla Dineo. 'Through Zanele Muholi's Eyes: Re/imagining Ways of Seeing Black Lesbians'. In *Zanele Muholi: Only Half the Picture*, eds Zanele Muholi and Sophie Perryer. Cape Town: Michael Stevenson 2006.

Gunkel, Henriette. *The Cultural Politics of Female Sexuality in South Africa*. New York: Routledge, 2010.

Hayes, Patricia. Power, Secrecy, Proximity: A Short History of South African Photography'. *Kronos* No. 33 (2007): 139-62.

Hoad, Neville Wallace. *African Intimacies: Race, Homosexuality, and Globalization*. University of Minnesota Press, 2007.

Human Rights Watch. *Zanele Muholi, Visual Activist*. Katherine Fairfax Wright, Malika Zouhali-Worrallo and Zanele Muholi. 2013. www.youtube.com/watch?v=9aiufq04dp0 (accessed 1 March 2018).

Lacan, Jacques. *Ecrits: The First Complete Edition in English*, trans. Bruce Fink. New York: Norton, 2012 [1966].

Lewis, Desiree. 'Against the Grain: Black Women and Sexuality'. *Agenda* Vol. 2, No. 63 (2005): 11-24.

Mbembe, Achille, interviewed by Vivian Paulissen. 'African Contemporary Art: Negotiating the Terms of Recognition'. *Africultures*. 1 December 2009. http://africultures.com/african-contemporary-art-negotiating-the-terms-of-recognition-9030 (accessed 13 February 2016).

Muholi, Zanele. Faces and Phases'. *Transition* 107 (2012):113–24.

——*Isilumo Siyaluma*. Cape Town: Blank Projects, 2011.

——'Faces and Phases'. Munich: Prestel, 2010.

——*Only Half the Picture*. Cape Town: Michael Stevenson, 2006.

Negroponte, Nicholas. *Being Digital*. New York: Vintage Books, 1995.

Richards, Colin. 'Aftermath: Value and Violence in Contemporary South African Art'. In *Antinomies of Art and Culture: Modernity, Postmodernity, Contemporaneity*, eds Terry Smith, Okwui Enwezor and Nancy Condee. Durham, NC: Duke University Press, 2008: 250-89.

Richter, Gerhard. *Thought-Images: Frankfurt School Writers' Reflections from Damaged Life*. Stanford, CA: Stanford University Press, 2007.

Smith, Gail. 'Outlaw Culture'. *Mail & Guardian*, 8 September 2004.

Thomas, Kylie. 'Zanele Muholi's Intimate Archive: Photography and Post-Apartheid Lesbian Lives'. *Safundi: The Journal of South African and American Studies* Vol. 11, No. 4 (2010) 421-36.

Van Der Vlies, Andrew. 'Art as Archive: Queer Activism and Contemporary South African Visual Cultures'. *Kunapipi* Vol. 34, No. 1 (2012): 94-116.

Whitelaw, Mitchell. 'The End of New Media Art?' *Realtime* No. 38 (2000): 7. www.realtimearts.net/article/issue38/5413 (accessed 25 July 2018).

Wilson, Ernest J. III. *The Information Revolution and Developing Countries*. Cambridge, MA: MIT Press, 2004.

To Revolutionary Type Love

An Interview with Kawira Mwirichia, Neo Musangi, Mal Muga, Awuor Onyango, Faith Wanjala & Wawira Njeru

NG'ANG'A MUCHIRI

In June 2017, the Goethe-Institut in Nairobi, Kenya hosted an exhibition titled *To Revolutionary Type Love*. Created by artist Kawira Mwirichia, the project celebrates queer love, globally. Mwirichia focused on the *kanga*, a ubiquitous fashion item for women across East Africa. In addition, Mwirichia curated photography by Mal Muga, Neo Musangi, Maganga Mwagogo, Wawira Njeru, Awuor Onyango and Faith Wanjala. I had an insightful conversation with this group of visual artists on various topics including artists as archivists, where they source their inspiration, and the global photography canon.

Ng'ang'a Muchiri (NM): How did the project come about?

Kawira Mwirichia: There were a series of inspirations. I'd gone to a friend's wedding and saw the laying down of *kangas* to receive the bride, and it hit me that this is a gesture that us queers in Kenya would not experience. I feel like it's a very profound, very emotive gesture because it's you and your lover being honoured by the community, so you're being accepted; you're being celebrated and so I wanted to do that for the queer community. From that intention, it sort of grew into what it is now, and it's going to keep going.

NM: I think that's a great point of departure because the *kanga* ritual for the bride is such a common act, and yet it is so common but completely unavailable to a certain segment of Kenyans.

Kawira Mwirichia: I feel like the absence of loving gestures can be just as damaging. I think it takes away from an individual. For instance if you grow up and you're not given affection it affects you even if not in an obvious way. There is something that is missing, or that you might feel is missing. I feel that it's important to experience these things, even if not from society, by ourselves.

NM: I think we'll come back to that idea of affection. But I wanted to hear from everybody else about your background. What's your background as an artist; or what would you consider to be your background as an artist; and what is it about this project that interested you enough to actually get involved?

Awuor Onyango: OK, so if I break this down, the question is 'what's your artistic background; and what drew you to this?' OK, so I'm a writer and a visual artist in many regards. And I was taught to come to art as though I'm the medium so I sometimes feel uncomfortable with being called an artist because that then brings the question 'what kind of art do you make?' and I do a bunch of things depending on what best expresses what it is that I'm trying to express. I came into this project because it gave me an opportunity to create something for the queer canon here. Like a lot of my references, and I think a lot of queer references here are American, and which is why a lot of my references even for this project were like Foucault, and Audre Lourde. and so it was important for me to kind of fill that space. I just felt that there was space, there was an opportunity there that we could come together. There is queer photography that is happening. but it's happening in pockets and it's kind of hard to access and this provided the opportunity to come together for that purpose of coalescing in a certain space.

NM: It's interesting that you bring up the idea of a canon. Is it a mirror kind of thing that is going on? There is the non-LGBTQ canon out there, so are we simply taking that structure and filling it with different content? And is that even something that we want to do? The canon is a political thing as well. so I'm curious what else is going on?

Awuor Onyango: Yeah, and so that's where I think I came from. I think I just reached a point where I realised that a lot of my feminist references aren't from here, a lot of my queer references aren't from here and I didn't have anything to refer to, do I subvert it or do I add to it? And I think that it's an important structure if you're going to revolutionise ... it's an important structure to refer to, at least for me. So, that and the question of representing the complexity of 'Nairobiness', which is like you're African, you're Kenyan, but then there's different parts of Kenya. So there's a lot going on that I didn't think I could find when I'm looking for it. For me that was my approach: this is my chance to create that. Whether we're doing it intentionally or not, this is going to be a reference.

NM: There'll be a record and remnants. What response would other people have about that kind of background moment as an 'artist?' The word artist is, interestingly, a term that people are engaging and disengaging with simultaneously, so I think there's more to dig into that. But also you brought up the idea ... from your Foreword I believe, the project begins with a kind of open-ended description. It's either lived experience or theoretical. So to my question about background and interest, then what decisions did you go through as an individual to be like, 'I'm going to do the lived experience part', or 'I'm going to do the theory part'?. Or maybe there isn't even that binary to begin with?

Kawira Mwirichia: When we were talking about the inspiration for the photography, we were talking about it could be anything, either a lived experience that you want to capture, or your idea of love, or your imagining.

Mal Muga: For me this particular project wasn't really lived experience, but it also wasn't theoretical. I think it was more about my values as an individual, and what I think is important. Whether or not I have accessed it is not really the point. So, for me, I focus on sexual vulnerability. Which, I guess you could say, I struggled with a bit – I thought it was a bit predictable, but for me it's also really important. And so that's where I took my inspiration.

Kawira Mwirichia: And your background?

Mal Muga: All right, you still want to know. What is my background? You know, honestly, I've only recently begun to refer to myself as an artist. I've struggled with it for a very long time. I've always been drawn to aesthetics. And over the years it's manifested in very different ways. But it began with painting, and then went into fashion, and then film – in terms of visual aesthetics. I've always had a very strong connection to music. For me it's all about expression: arts in general. Anything that ever allowed me to express myself I was into. Actually to be honest, even events and just experiences like spaces that allow you to express yourself. For me, it's an art form in itself, just being alive, and being yourself is participating heavily in arts and culture. As far as visual arts, which is what I think I'm into right now, that is the background: there's fashion, then film and photography which kind of happened concurrently after giving up music but then it turned out to be something I'm really into.

NM: So I then wonder, you might not be doing music right now, but all that is flowing into what you're doing presumably?

Mal Muga: Yeah, currently I'm primarily using photography as my main medium. My main avenue is photography, of expression, right now. But then I also keep on telling people that I really don't like hanging out with photographers, because I don't want to be heavily influenced by their work. I don't want my work to become too similar to theirs because there's the whole concept of originality in art. That's debatable whether your art work is original or not, but you're constantly going from everyday life. So I like to expose myself to artists of other genres, so like musicians, painters, filmmakers, writers. So I'm constantly accessing inspiration from these different kinds of artistes. I try to avoid photographers, and exposing myself too much unless their style is significantly different from mine. And I think that is one of the things from this exhibition that I worried about. Because of constantly looking at their work, I started to worry that the exhibition would present work that was very similar. And you know what, to be honest, it did. Kinda did, not very similar, like everyone was very unique but there were aspects that were shared. So for example, the way I presented my models, as far as positioning and interacting with each other was very similar to one of the photographers. And then the visual aesthetic I went with was also very similar to another one of the photographers. So like the colour and everything. So we got a lot of questions; I remember getting questions where they'd look at her work and they were like, 'is that your work?' And I'm like, 'no'. And then they'd ask her the same thing.

NM: And that was not pre-planned?

Mal Muga: OK, well, I will say to be honest, we did work closely together; we constantly are working closely together.

Awuor Onyango: We're close friends, and he helped me with my shoot and I helped him with his. And that kind of shows.

NM: I want to hear about the actual creation. From whether you did rough shoots to the editing, to choosing; I'm guessing if you presented five images you had ten but then you had to cut down. So I'm curious about that process as well. But I do want to go back to the background question from the folks I haven't heard from.

Faith Wanjala: Mine was interesting; I was actually doing a proposal for something else, a New York thing. And there were 15 images. And then I realised I'm too lazy to finish the whole project. so I chose … I started to think to Kawira's … it was actually your expression of queer love. So I decided my year in 2012. It was an interesting year and the whole visual story of my project is what happened the whole year. So, from the 15 images I did, I chose five that can tell a story.

NM: So unlike them who kinda had to create something new for this particular project you already had something to choose from? ... Before Kawira approached you?

Faith Wanjala: No, at the same time ... Yeah, I was working on two different things at the same time.

NM: Background?

Mal Muga: What's your background as an artist?

Wawira Njeru: I was just telling him I have issues referring to myself as an artist. In regards to Kawira's project, I chose an activist I'd seen even before the whole project became an exhibition. So I just chose someone who perhaps has gone through major shit for this whole LGBTI thing; and also I was looking at individual anarchy. Yeah, because I believe everything you do is to progress yourself, including being in love or being in a relationship. It's all about enhancing your survival. And this particular individual he's narcissistic; like I've not met anyone so proudly ... Like I'm happy.

NM: But at the same time an activist?

Wawira Njeru: Yeah, it's a contradiction of sorts! He told me his story. 'They want me to be a role model. You know, like date someone, look like a progressive kid. And stop picking men and boys and going home with them.' But he doesn't want that. I can be an activist and still live my life, regardless of what society expects from me. So that was my main motivation.

Neo Musangi: I think in this project I'm the outlier. I don't consider myself an artist, and my biography changes depending on the project. Majorly, I actually do research. I've been involved with photographic kinds of exhibitions before where I've shown photographic work. But also art performances; I still work on similar subjects regardless of whether it's academic research or it's creative writing, or it's visual work. And I got into this project because Kawira invited me and invited me on very specific terms that I was going to come in as a photographer, and I had to make new work. Whether it's lived experience or whether it's theoretical, I'm very consciously involved in trying to create a transgender archive. That's my commitment. So outside or beyond sexualities I'm interested in creating an archive on gender and ways of visualising gender.

NM: So, through the research, through the performance work, questions about gender come up. It's different media, but the questions, the concerns are fairly similar.

Neo Musangi: Yeah, but all these are research projects, just different methods.

NM: So I love that the archive and the canon are coming up, because it makes me wonder, what is it that we're archiving and canonising in Nairobi, or Kenya, or the continent that's different from what's out there in the global queer community? What is it that we want to archive and canonise; and why? What is it that we're trying to archive, keep track of, conserve, preserve? Is it just the materials – photographs, or is it ideas? Is it different ways of being queer in Nairobi versus New York, etc.? And the background for me about this question is the idea that queer love is not African. It's foreign, from abroad, etc. But obviously it's not. So what are the tensions; what are the differences between what's here and what's out there?

Awuor Onyango: I had to face similar questions when I was creating my work, because the drag scene here is nothing like what people call drag. It's not drag for performance. And when you say drag you have to struggle to contextualise … So, I had to face a lot of those questions and why I was choosing to do it. And it's because I have friends who do drag. I think in comedy here there's a lot of cross-dressing that happens for comic relief.

Mal Muga: Even within drag culture, there are comedy queens, who are there for comedy. So that's an integral part of drag culture, but then what we're doing if it's comedy then it's OK because it's disassociated from any sexual, queer culture. Then it's OK, because it's just a funny guy. The thing I struggle with is associating drag with queer culture because I've come across a lot of people who do drag and partake in drag culture without identifying as queer in any sexual form. For example, it could be a man who identifies as cis-gender straight but then does drag, and does a good drag. And so it is possible, drag culture could stand alone, but then for some reason it is associated with queer culture. So, I've never really understood that.

Kawira Mwirichia: For me, when it comes to this project, our expressions – and when I say 'our' I mean African and specifically

Kenyan – I'm particularly interested in keeping records of our expressions of sexuality, of affection, of how we feel about love whether it's proclaiming it or questioning it, however that comes about. Because I feel like a lot of sexuality that is portrayed in Kenya is from outside. I'd like to see our sexuality as mainstream, because I feel like it's a very integral part of our humanity as people. We have sex; it's our humanity. For it to be always, when it's been discussed, it's discussed on a Western frame or soap operas from Latin America, like where's our expression? And that's why the project has *kangas* with sayings collected from the community and it has photographs documenting their sexual expression whether you're talking about vulnerability or just talking about androgyny or the power dynamics of sex. As in all these discussions but they are ours and we're the ones having them and sharing them amongst ourselves. I think that's very powerful, and I think that's something we need to have.

NM: It's also the moment where in Kenyan public spaces, sex is always relegated as the last topic of discussion.

Kawira Mwirichia: Yeah, it's like we don't have it; we just appeared!

Mal Muga: But then there's also the argument about how everything, almost everything we do as human beings, is about sex. Everything we strive for is about sex. It's about being desired, or in one way or the other it's being dominant. Just because we're not going to be doing a fancy dance with our feathers open or fighting. That's how we as humans express dominance and in the end everyone wants to shack up with the most dominant person. Even in queer culture it's about the most beautiful and that sense of superiority. Basically it's about genetic superiority and so everything is about sex. I honestly do not know how these conversations go on in other African countries, but I'm assuming it's quite similar. First of all, sex is intercourse or it's intercourse-related so it's about foreplay. It's a very religious, very Christian sense of sex. Which, first of all, the most Western thing in our culture is religion. Or the most foreign thing. All the religions we have now are imported.

NM: Yeah, it's that moment where we will argue that queer love is not African because it's not Christian. Mal: And Christianity is not …

Faith Wanjala: But you can't just push it aside and it's usually something that people do. So there are things you just can't push aside; we just deal with it when it's there.

Mal Muga: And that comes back to your question about what it is we were trying to archive or canonise. And I don't think I was trying to do either and it's about what Faith just said, that I'm trying to live in the now. And tackling the issues now, whether these things are remembered or the way I do my thing becomes or is part of the standard is not important. It's about what is happening in my space. It's about my experience; it's about how I experience other people around me and I feel like even my friendships are about how I experience them. So for me it's just what is happening now; what am I doing first and foremost; how am I experiencing it; how do I want others to experience it with me?

Awuor Onyango: The weird thing about that is that those are the perfect ingredients for creating a canon. Because if you're perfectly in the present then you're perfectly capturing something that people in the year 3000 can look at and say that's authentically 2017.

Neo Musangi: I get when Awuor is saying about the ingredients for creating archives. I'm very deliberate, even in the now, to actually – as a colonial subject – to make sure that erasure, that absence, is not the basis of the oppression of another. By creating this is to actually have the physical archival document, the archival record so that with a projection of the future, whatever that future looks like. In my creation of a utopia I do want to be involved in documenting what is happening here and now. I'm not interested in what the U.S. is doing; of course, I'm interested in the black diaspora but I'm not going to document people's lives based on the kinds of limitations from language. When I say transgender I'm just using that because that is the term that has been made available, but I want to understand the vernaculars of those things, because the visual work doesn't do that kind of work for me, at the moment, unless it's in text. Then it's important even to think of the future; it's not going to be a canon, perhaps, and I would love it to be a canon, for me. But I do want to have the physical document, just as projection of what might happen to other people.

Faith Wanjala: You don't want to go researching and seeing things that you can't relate to. You want to do things that you can see, 'Oh this is my colour; this is my … any kind of mind changing. This is what I want to see.' So I'm doing this if someone wants to come and see.

NM: So, it's that moment of kinda pushing back against the erasure of coloured subjects, queer subjects, colonised subjects. OK, tell me a little bit more about the process of creating the work. I'm walking into the gallery and seeing the framed images, but what's the time, resource commitment that brings us to that point of framed print on the wall? – the printing, the framing, the editing?

Awuor Onyango: I was promised almost thrice the amount of funds that then became available. I was also promised twice the amount of time that became available. So, there was a lot of last minute panic for, I would say everyone, apart from Faith. Kawira was like here's the money, and the next day Faith was like here's the project. But for the rest of us, I mean … I cried. I had a crisis. I Skyped my best friend until he came into the country.

Mal Muga: We were running around in town, and carrying heavy bags on the day before we are supposed to submit the thing – and these were bags of props, on the day before we were supposed to submit it. For me, another thing was that we started talking about this project a while ago. And so I had an idea in my head and it was very structured and I was just going to come in and do it. And then I came in and it was like a third. And two weeks before I was just like 'Oh God, I can't even attempt to do this! I have to re- think'. Then I go into panic of re-thinking, re-thinking, and of course when you're trying to do something really quickly you get a lot of distraction and outside influence coming into play. So I was thinking, we're launching IDAHO [International Day Against Homophobia]. What's the theme of IDAHO this year, what am I doing about it? Then there were a lot of calls back and forth, especially with Kawira. And even though we'd discussed everything, I needed to clarify. I think for me it was highly stressful. And then Awuor had to sit me down, you need to take a breather and stay true to your style. Because you have clearly come up with projects faster than this, so why can't you come up with this? But then it's because I was so set on one thing already.

Awuor Onyango: And then there was also the added pressure which, for me, was that I was giving to the queer community. This wasn't something that I was doing and whoever wants to come for it can come. This was like me giving to family. And you don't just give whatever to family. I mean, family has problems, but at the end of the day it's people that I have relations with, that we're together in a struggle of existence in this space and I couldn't just give them nothing. There was that pressure of presenting this thing to people who mean a lot. And then there is also the question of I'm queer and I'm a photographer, so does that make everything I do queer photography? There were just layers that we didn't have the time to go through.

Neo Musangi: To be honest, even as someone making work, I didn't … I do know individual people and I put it there, and it's going to be in the exhibition hall. But I just felt like, I'm making this work, but it's not for these people. I feel like this is a very defined community of people and it's not for them. And, quite honestly, in the room, at least … people from a very small trans community that I'm friends with or know, they didn't even show up because their assumption is like, 'Oh, it's for LGB people!' So, that already is … You know, which puts me in a really weird position as someone, even as part of the community who is making work. Because they'll … 'Oh, so you come take pictures of us, and then we're not even part of the audience'. I mean we know some people that we've worked with who are like the trans community in Nairobi but they don't even show up for these things.

Kawira Mwirichia: You've actually shed light on something that I had noticed when collecting the quotes. Because I sent the callout also to the trans community, but I guess they didn't feel like they were a part of it – part of the audience I was covering. Because I was getting quotes from everyone else, and I really wanted to hear from them, actually.

Awuor Onyango: I think that's an interesting point, because it is something that I had to work my way through to feel some kind of acceptance into the community. Because I'm not in the IDAHO-BIT [International Day Against Homophobia, Biphobia and Transphobia], my letter is not there, if there's a letter that I can be given, either. So, I had to give myself permission. I had to allow myself in, because I don't think there's a way in which these spaces can truly accommodate everyone. Because everything is just too fluid for it have a term that …

Kawira Mwirichia: But can't you accommodate the fluidity?

Mal Muga: I think that's why reason I love this; the reason I love this is because there was no LGBTQI. It was just queer, and that enabled it to encompass all of us. Humans are too fluid to be defined by actual letters. We can't be defined by language as well, the only word that's worked so far is queer, and how long will queer even work? Because queer only works as far as something is not considered normal. So, for example, if you're a cis-gender woman who likes to make out with girls, you're actually not queer, because that's considered quite normal. And you know, it's alright for a cis-gender woman to make out with girls from time to time; the normative society thinks that's hot. Fine, it may be fetishised, but then it's still OK, so it doesn't actually call it a queer space. And so any time something moves from the queer space into the accepted space it stops being queer. So, even queer won't be ... can't be enough to handle this extra version of sexuality. And even the word queer, being at this point it's the widest to capture it, it's not enough.

NM: So, creating spaces, archiving, canonising it's important while kinda resisting that erasure, but at the same time it produces this pressure of 'Is this good enough? Does it fit in the canon? Is it worthy of archiving?' So for you [Mal], your audience wasn't the people you were working with, but Awuor, your audience *was* the family. So, I'm curious about the intended audience.

Neo Musangi: I mean, I ... I don't necessarily mean to say that that wasn't the audience. I think for me particularly with photography as a medium, it's very telling when the people you photograph don't even want to see, or are not interested in finished work. When they don't participate, it worries me. But not to say that everyone who came to that exhibition I knew whether they were trans or not or non-binary. I might not know. But there was that kind of silence that even out of the people I photographed only one showed up for like five minutes and left.

NM: So is it the work that they don't connect with or is it the venue where the work is being presented?

Neo Musangi: I really don't know.

Mal Muga: I think it's ... it might be the community.

Neo Musangi: But it's also part of a larger kind of contextual conversation to be had with – particularly in Nairobi – the trans non-binary community. We only participate in our trans exclusive events.

Mal Muga: You know what, Nairobi is even more segregated than that ...

NM: Really?

Neo Musangi: Yeah, it's very clear. Conversations on gender and conversations on sexualities need to be separated.

Mal Muga: So, even all the letters tend to stand alone in Nairobi.

NM: So, in that case, queer doesn't really seem to work either as a term ...

Neo Musangi: No, queer ... that's why the term itself, of course, is very difficult to define, but then often queer just refers to sexual identities, right? So, and we're aware of that. Theoretically we know what it could do, and what we could make queer do. But a lot of times people say 'queer just means same sex ... whatever'. But it's not; but that's how it's used.

NM: Well, OK. I guess going back to the audience, what have been some remarkable or memorable comments from audiences that have seen the work or interacted with the work? Anything that stands out: good, bad, everything in between?

Kawira Mwirichia: I guess there's been a lot of pride and a lot of love for the exhibition.

NM: Was it something you had foreseen?

Kawira Mwirichia: It's something you hope for, but you can't really plan for it. I'd love to for people to love my work, but I don't know how to do that.

Awuor Onyango: I think we did have conversations about that the venue, at the PAWA rooftop [PAWA 254 Street Festival], like maybe last year August, and I remember saying I don't want it to be like Runda [upscale neighbourhood about 10 miles north of Nairobi's central business district], because there's this thing of you're only allowed to be queer in white spaces. Which is something that I'm uncomfortable with ...

NM: Yeah, because that also goes back to the foreign, non-African thing.

Awuor Onyango: But we settled on Goethe because it is accessible; it's central. Everyone can get a *matatu* [small bus] to town from wherever. So we had discussions about accessibility and even the pricing that we put. We put that pricing for the duration of the exhibition, because we're like, this is something that people can afford ...

Faith Wanjala: It's still expensive ...

Mal Muga: No, it's still expensive, but then it also, it opened it up to a lot more people and you'd be surprised. Because if we'd have done ... if I'd done my standard pricing, it would have been ...

Awuor Onyango: We more than halved our prices for the work because it is important to us that the community be able to own these things.

We're doing it for them. We don't want to be like, 'now you've seen, OK, now it's KSHS 500,000 and if you don't have it it's fine, someone else white, or rich, can have it'. There were things that we put in place and discussions that we had about what's the best place to have this; how can people access it; how can people be safe if they come for this thing? All those things were … accessibility is very important to my work, and I think it's important to all of us. So it's always like, if I'm making the work, I always have my audience in mind and it's always important that my audience can access the work.

Kawira Mwirichia: No, definitely, we did try as much as possible, and we're trying also now going ahead to make it be as affordable as possible. We also recognise that not everyone can afford the prices as they are right now, so we are looking into ways of maybe merchandising and we're actually also selling catalogues so even if you couldn't buy the whole thing you could get something. So, there's that consideration.

NM: So, here's a question emerging from the photographs that I saw. In both your work, Awuor and Faith, there were references to light and visibility, and the idea of mirrors. Tell me more about that. Where's that from? Where's it headed; was that connection pre-determined? I don't think so, right? Because you had your work on a separate track.

Awuor Onyango: We're both Geminis, though. For me, I was looking at the context of Nairobi, and the context of what it is you can get access to. Because there was a time I was talking to a friend from The Nest [Arts Company/Collective], and she was like 'Eh, that guy's hetero-drag is on point!' And when you think of drag, you think of it in the ribald sense; you think about the make-up, and the drama, and all that stuff. And for me, I think Kenyans wear drag a lot. Whether we're performing straightness so we can get into a space, or we're performing normativity. Like there's people … Just two weekends ago, a friend of mine was having a barbecue and he was like, 'this person and this person can't come; they're too flamboyant!' And like the rest of us had to come and say hi to his grandma and act in certain ways. So there's ways in which we play with our own visibility. There's ways in which we let people in and ways we don't. So that's where the mirror, the fractal mirror, came from. Because in many ways, how the entire queer community works is like I don't know a lot of the trans people because the trans people are only out to each other, and they're like that. So, it's a question of permissions and allowance; that I thought was something I wanted to celebrate. That we re-invent ourselves constantly and sometimes it's just a matter of 'are we in public?' or 'are we safe?'

NM: But that doesn't mean that the individual is re-inventing themselves constantly based on the audience; it's more of only projecting or offering certain variants of who they are based on who's receiving, right? Because then it's not about changing myself because of who's viewing me it's about, I'm going to show this side of myself to this person, but this slightly different version to this other person.

Awuor Onyango: Right. And I mean it's that and then there's people that I've seen that do completely re-invent themselves. Like I had a friend who we hang out for a while and then when it was time for him to get married he was like, 'OK!' and he had this entire persona when he was in the queer community – like name and everything. And then he wrote us this letter being like 'It's been real; it's been great. See ya! And you don't know me anymore.' And then now his real name and everything got married and has a child and moved on. I wanted to celebrate that. That you can be like, 'OK, now I have to do my civic duty of forming a family and everything, so like, peace!' I think that because everything is so undefined, it's a very fertile ground to be whoever you want to be. Like there's people who are like a clerk at KRA [Kenya Revenue Authority], and they're wearing the baggy suits and everything, and then they do drag. So you literally can have multiple personalities.

NM: Faith – light ... or visibility? Or anything to add?

Faith Wanjala: The thing about me, it's a weird thing. I never have these preconceived notions of ... now like how she's put hers into this big thing. The previous night before doing this thing, there were no lights. And I used my lantern. And my lantern was sitting on my desk, and I saw, I can use this on my body. And I kept setting the timer to ten seconds and three frames, and I would do like performance and everything. And then after I edited the work, then I think Kawira wants queer something, so I'm like, that is the light. For me, if you want to interpret it into the light, that is the light. I have no this ... I let people put their own views. I never explain. People tell me they were seeing monosexual stuff.

I would like to express my heartfelt gratitude to Kawira, Mal, Neo, Wawira, Awuor and Faith for making this interview possible; and many thanks to Igiza Lounge at the Kenya National Theatre for providing us with a quiet space. Please visit https://torevolutionarytypelove.com for kanga and photography catalogues.

Liminal Spaces & Conflicts of Culture in South African Queer Films

Inxeba (The Wound)

GRANT ANDREWS

South Africa has an ambivalent history with queer representation, being simultaneously one of the largest producers and consumers of queer media on the African continent, as well as often still exhibiting extreme homophobia and backlash when particular kinds of queer media are released in the country. Nowhere is the debate more heated than in the arena of visual media such as television and film, where access is easier, cultural impact is more direct, and the public nature of these media seem to provoke animated reactions. This backlash is often based around culture, a theme which is part of a highly contentious public discourse in a country which remains so racially divided politically, economically and in terms of social spaces. Xavier Livermon explains that particularly black queer visibilities are 'policed' in 'black cultural and political spaces' ('Queer(y)ing Freedom: Black Queer Visibilities in Postapartheid South Africa': 300). Additionally, consumption and production of media like queer South African films are largely still subject to racial and economic divisions. A mostly-white and middle-class market and production apparatus surround these films, even when they represent black subjects, and many black queer visibilities are thus ostensibly produced through white perspectives and subject to the white gaze.

The debates around culture in queer film usually centre on two themes: firstly, the prevalent and confounding assertion by many conservative commenters and groups that homosexuality is 'un-African' and a Western import (Livermon: 301); and secondly, and more logically and convincingly, the films are criticised for the fact that the stories of queer black individuals are not told authentically by black directors, but rather the stories are impositions on 'black culture' by Western or white South African filmmakers. These conflicts of culture are disrupted, and indeed undercut, by the very filmmaking process, mainly through the cross-cultural collaborations which take place in the production of many of these films, as well as the ways that all of the most celebrated queer films in the country directly address questions of culture in ways that challenge heteropatriarchy, racism and cultural exploitation.

In response to the various conflicts of culture and widespread homophobia, it seems that queer films in South Africa have become liminal in nature as well as liminal in approach, playing with and crossing the cultural boundaries which might push against their very existence. Additionally, the films, through their content, create liminalities, spaces outside of space where queer subjects and same-sex intimacies can exist.

Liminality, a concept employed in anthropology, psychology and literary theory, among other fields, refers broadly to in-between moments, spaces, states or peoples. Bjørn Thomassen explores how liminality can be applied to describe minority groups who are, as Victor Turner explains, 'in another place' ('The Uses and Meanings of Liminality': 97) and 'have physical but not social reality, hence they have to be hidden, since it is a paradox, a scandal, to see what ought not to be there' (97). While Thomassen applies the concept to stateless people or illegal immigrants (2009: 19), it applies equally well to queer individuals in oppressive societies like South Africa, who are excluded culturally and invisibilised in many ways. The term liminality, as it is applied in this article, refers to queer people's state of in-between within society, both present and excluded, as well as the abstract spaces outside of space where queer individuals can find a sense of freedom and demonstrate their queer desires which, based on cultural attitudes and mores, ought not to exist.

An overwhelming amount of the major films exploring South African queer realities seem to construct these liminal spaces simultaneously, these films engage with the in-between nature of queer lives in South Africa, pointing to the contradictions of a liberal legislature which, ostensibly, embraces and protects queer identities, and a conservative society that rejects, brutalises and invisibilises queer bodies and realities.

This article discusses a few of the most celebrated recent South African queer films, and examines the complexities of representation, particularly around culture, that apply to them. The discussion looks at how each of these films constructs liminal spaces to represent queer identities. The films under discussion are John Greyson's *Proteus* (2003), Shamim Sarif's *The World Unseen* (2007), Oliver Hermanus' *Skoonheid (Beauty)* (2011), and the John Trengove film *Inxeba (The*

Wound) (2017). The article focuses primarily on Trengove's film, which explores the liminality of South African queer representation in a multitude of ways. The film is currently experiencing massive backlash as it represents the sacred and secretive Xhosa initiation process, where boys transition into manhood. This backlash is interspersed with blatant homophobia and accusations that the white filmmaker is exploiting Xhosa culture and that the black actors are 'traitors' (Jay '*Inxeba*: A Moment of Confrontation'). However, even in the hyper-masculine context of initiation, the film is able to create spaces for queer love, expression, and pleasure where, according to commenters and the way the ritual is performed, these spaces should not exist. These liminal spaces, both within hyper-masculine settings and at the same time deconstructing and challenging them, will be examined in relation to the other queer South African films under discussion, demonstrating how diverse queer identities struggle for recognition and representation within South African film.

It is useful to explore the queer films under discussion in the context of social and political changes, and how these affected the creative spaces within which queer films could be produced. During the oppressive and racially exploitative system of apartheid, a time when homosexuality was criminalised in the country, there was very little representation of queer stories in literature, film or other media. Richard Dyer explains that the media was often seen as 'a carrier, reinforcer and shaper of [the] oppression [of queer people]' ('Gays in Film': 15), and Sheila Croucher notes that 'policing of sexual minorities was consistent with repressive apartheid ideology' ('South Africa's Democratisation and the Politics of Gay Liberation': 317). Even though scholars like Martin Botha have traced moments that could be read as queer in South African films released during apartheid (*South African Cinema 1896-2010*: 56), these representations were usually limited to depictions of men who were gender nonconforming and who cross-dressed for comedic effect, rather than explicitly demonstrating same-sex attraction or affection (Peach *Queer Cinema as a Fifth Cinema*). Moreover, these early queer representations were almost exclusively white, with a few black queer characters appearing in literature but never explicitly in film. Literature seemed to offer slightly more space for queer representation, although the threat of apartheid-era censorship meant that queer texts were stringently policed.

A puzzling example is the case of J.M. Coetzee's novel *In the Heart of the Country* (1977), where an ostensibly queer female character is effectively stripped of her queerness in the public reaction to the novel both nationally and internationally. The novel itself, provocative and affecting, and arguably on equal creative footing among Coetzee's early oeuvre, was almost entirely ignored by critics and even escaped initial censorship (Attwell *J.M. Coetzee and the Life of Writing*). Some feminist critics have argued that since the protagonist, Magda, was female, her voice was drowned out both within the novel and culturally (Briganti 'A Bored Spinster with a Locked Diary': 34), but there is also the sense that her queerness is invisibilised even when the novel is discussed, as almost none of the reviews of the novel at the time openly acknowledged Magda's queer desires. Liminality is present in the text since Magda's yearning is confined to the family farm, her fantasies seeming to be the only space she can express her queer (and, notably, cross-racial) desires. Additionally, the novel itself becomes liminal, written by one of South Africa's most celebrated authors, and yet largely ignored, even when it speaks to such complex themes and is a riveting read.

A similarly perplexing example in the realm of film is Helen Nogueira's *Quest for Love* (1988), which depicts lesbian women who visit a fictional African nation called Mozania, an amalgam of Mozambique and Azania (South Africa), which had managed to overthrow the oppressive government and achieve liberation. The film starred two of the most celebrated white Afrikaans actresses at the time, Jana Cilliers and Sandra Prinsloo and, despite its extremely controversial material, it still managed to receive limited distribution within South Africa at an extremely volatile period in the country. The fictional nation seemed to represent a type of liminal space in the film where both racially oppressive systems and the effects of widespread African homophobia could be overcome; the film was released during the dying days of apartheid, amidst a second state of emergency in the span of three years that saw the desperate apartheid government clamp down on news media as the propaganda machine attempted to work full force and allow the state to cling to power. The film's production and release are anomalous, and even though the film enjoyed almost no cultural impact, I argue that it was a precursor for the post-apartheid queer cinematic focus. Its subject matter was so far outside of the conservative milieu that it effectively passed under the radar, creating something that was not meant to exist, functioning within the liminal space that much queer media in the country inhabits. These early queer representations were able to exist as marginal to public scrutiny or debates, and I argue that this is, at least partially, because of their queer subject matter. These texts seem to inhabit an alternate reality in the same way that their protagonists do within the texts.

South Africa emerged from apartheid with one of the most progressive constitutions in the world, containing protections for sexual and gender minorities at a time when these issues were far more contentious even in the Western world. This constitution paved the way for South Africa to be the fifth country worldwide to legalise same-sex marriage in 2006, and it is still the only African country to do so after more than a decade. Nevertheless, the cultural changes in South Africa have been extremely slow, and progressive changes were met with much political and social resistance. For example, many in the ruling African National Congress, along with traditional leaders, were reluctant to support the passage of the Civil Union Act of 2006, which paved the way for same-sex marriage (Livermon: 301). The passage of the Act was described by African Christian Democratic Party leader Kenneth Meshue as 'the saddest day in our 12 years of democracy' (Burchardt 'Equals Before the Law?': 250). Islamic leader Sheikh Sharif Ahmed called the Act a 'foreign action imposed on Africa' (Ireland 'A Macro-Level Analysis of the Scope, Causes, and Consequences of Homophobia in Africa': 54). This 'separate but equal' Civil Union Act, passed instead of amending the Marriage Act, was seen by many as a conciliatory measure to try to appease these conservative voices. These perspectives seem to again point to a conflict of culture in relation to queer identities, where many feel that same-sex relationships are counter to what it means to be African (Roehr 'How Homophobia is Fuelling Africa's HIV Epidemic'). This framing might serve to invisibilise queer black subjects in South Africa (Cock 'Engendering Gay and Lesbian Rights': 35), and might account for some of the disparity between the numbers of white and black queer characters, and public reactions to them, in post-apartheid South African queer cinema.

The post-apartheid period has seen much greater numbers of representations of queer identities within the country, and the representations have become more varied and nuanced. A large number of authors have begun to write the stories of queer characters, including Mark Behr, K. Sello Duiker, Damon Galgut, Zukiswa Wanner, Fred Khumalo, Lauren Beukes and others; they begin to provide a 'retrospective cartography of the previously occluded queer nation' (Stobie 'Postcolonial Pomosexuality': 320-1). On television, as early as the 1990s, flamboyant queer men were featured in shows like *Streaks* and *Generations*, again filling the comedic and stereotypical roles. By the early 2000s, shows like *Isidingo* introduced more nuanced gay male characters and featured the first gay kiss on South African television between the characters Steve and Len.

One of the clear trends in queer representation, especially in the transition from apartheid, is that most queer representations focused on white characters, with very few black queer characters present in literature, television or film. The majority of the backlash to queer representation is due to black queer characters. As an example, two traditionally conservative South African soap operas, one featuring mostly white Afrikaans characters, *7de Laan,* and one featuring mostly black characters, *Generations,* had storylines with gay characters and on-screen male-male kisses over the past few years. The overwhelming response to the same-sex kiss on *7de Laan* between two white, Afrikaans characters in 2017, was positive and supportive, with the show's Facebook group seeing many messages of support (*MambaOnline* '7de Laan Surprises Viewers'). However, for the first on-screen kiss between the black characters Senzo and Jason in *Generations*, the response was very different. Massive public backlash greeted the kiss in 2009, and Facebook groups calling for the show to discontinue the gay storyline became some of the fastest-growing groups on the social network that the country had seen (*news24* 'Storm Over Gay Kiss').

Even though seven years separate the two television kisses, which might account for a more tolerant society, the cultural differences should not be discounted, and have repeated themselves in the reactions to the Afrikaans film *Skoonheid*, released in 2011, and *Inxeba (The Wound)*, released in 2017. While *Skoonheid* was met with no tangible public backlash outside of small pockets, *Inxeba* is currently facing a broad, heated public campaign surrounding its release, with public demonstrations and Xhosa groups calling for the film to be banned. The objections seem to focus on culture, much in the same way that queer dialogues in the country often have. Xhosa groups are claiming that the film is a disrespect to their cultural tradition of initiation and circumcision, and that it might reveal secrets of the sacred initiation practice, even though the filmmakers have asserted that the film does not reveal any of these secrets (Gqirana 'No Secrets Revealed'). Many other commenters are outraged at the fact that the film is directed by a white man, commenting that it is an imposition on the Xhosa culture (Bongela 'Exposing a Culture's Wounds'). The film, however, is a cross-cultural and multiracial collaboration, with two acclaimed black screenwriters in Melusi Bhengu and Thando Mgqolozana, as well as many black actors collaborating with the white director on the project. The debates seem to evince a type of protectionism of culture in the face of queer media.

In the context of the liminality constituted by these queer media, how they skirt the boundaries of culture, and how they seem to represent conflicts with particular emphasis on the imagined incompatibility of queerness and blackness, it is illuminating to explore how queer films themselves represent liminality and liminal spaces. The films all tackle culture and represent the outsider status of queer individuals within South Africa. Since these characters are both outsiders and so intimately situated within culture, both invisibilised and yet existing and interacting with their worlds in disruptive ways, these subjects demand spaces where they can exist, find pleasure and love. These spaces present themselves in the films as distinctly liminal, and particularly in *Inxeba (The Wound)*, when these spaces become visible or spoken about, and when the queer characters assert themselves, they are met with hostility and violence, both culturally through backlash, as well as within the film itself.

One of the first major post-apartheid queer films, *Proteus,* was released in 2003 and directed by Canadian director John Greyson. The film represents the same-sex, cross-racial relationship between two prisoners on Robben Island. It is based on the true story of two eighteenth-century prisoners, Khoi man Claas Blank (portrayed by actor Rouxnet Brown) and Dutch sailor Rijkhaart Jacobsz (Neil Sandilands), who were in a relationship on the island for over a decade before finally being executed for contravening sodomy laws in 1735. Robben Island, off the coast of Cape Town, was also used as a political prison during apartheid, where activists like Nelson Mandela, Govan Mbeki and Ahmed Kathrada were detained. The island itself is a liminal space, a space where the political prisoners could somehow capture the imagination of South Africans precisely because of their absence. They are at the threshold of absence and presence, barely out of sight and yet taking on the role of almost mythical leaders.

A similar function is served by the island in the film *Proteus,* as the island gives the lovers a space outside of place to find the possibility for love and companionship across the boundaries imposed on gender and race. The setting also seems to exist outside of time, as is indicated in the film by the anachronous clothing and technology, like modern cars and radios, which appear at times. The island prison in *Proteus* thus becomes a setting where queerness can exist precisely because there is the character of something unreal about the island and prison setting. The interracial, queer relationship is allowed to flourish where queerness can both be openly acknowledged and simultaneously hidden at the far-off, otherworldly island setting. The lovers are often reprimanded and charged for their physical relationship, but the law requires that, to be convicted, there must be a confession. Their silence keeps them in limbo, never confessing to their sexual relationship even though they are seen by others on the island repeatedly engaging in sex. In one scene, Rijkhaart begs Claas, in private, to once just say what they have between them, but Claas cannot say the words; there is something unspeakable about what the men have between them, precisely because it was never meant to exist. On the liminal island setting, never confessed to by the two men, there is the sense that the relationship never truly exists. The relationship lasts for ten years until a confession by Rijkhaart, under torture, finally leads to both men being executed by drowning. The water that surrounds the island finally consumes them, and they are taken from their liminal space with the effect that they can no longer exist. Furthermore, just like the political prisoners on Robben Island, the liminality gives their story greater resonance; Jesse Arsenault notes that the fact that the characters die off-screen has the effect of highlighting the lingering political relevance of their struggle ('Queer Desire and the Men of the Nation': 52-3).

In Shamim Sarif's *The World Unseen*, based on her novel of the same name, the idea of liminality is created within the very title of the text. The film is set in Cape Town in 1952, where two women of Indian descent, the rebellious Amina (Sheetal Sheth) and the reserved, demure housewife Miriam (Lisa Ray), fall in love in a country strictly enforcing the recently-adopted apartheid laws. The film explores the liminality of gender of the queer character Amina, who works in trousers in the café she owns and is met with scorn by Miriam's sister-in-law for looking 'like a man'. Additionally, the aspect of racial in-between is represented in the film through various interracial romances and sexual experiences, and through the in-between status of Indian people in apartheid as neither black nor white. Amina's grandmother was raped by a black man, also adding to Amina's status as an outsider to her Indian community and making her the subject of gossip. Both Amina and Miriam are oppressed by their surroundings, Miriam's abusive husband limiting her freedom in the same way that Amina is forced to keep her same-sex relationships secret. The relationship between them becomes possible in the Liminal Location Café, which Amina owns, where many racial groups eat together and where Amina can express her genderqueer identity with some level of freedom. Additionally, the two find hidden spaces to demonstrate affection, such as the pickup truck in which Amina gives Miriam driving lessons, and Miriam's room when her husband is away. The liminality is encapsulated by Amina when she says to Miriam, as they lie on Miriam's bed about to kiss: 'Will you just imagine, just for now, just for these moments, that nothing exists except for you and me'. Of course, the outside world encroaches on them again, and the two women are forced to hide their relationship as Miriam takes a job at the Location Café, in a falsely upbeat ending where they can continue their romance in secret.

A notable contrast to the type of freeing liminality presented in *Proteus* and *The World Unseen* is the case of Oliver Hermanus' film *Skoonheid*. The film presents queer white Afrikaans characters who enjoy sex away from the disapproving eyes of society, in the secrecy of darkened rooms. These men still identify as 'straight' and are still in heterosexual relationships, only ever practising same-sex sexual behaviour in secrecy. However, in this case, the liminality does not provide the freedom of cross-cultural relationships or the disruption of patriarchal constructions as it does in the two other films. In fact, the heteropatriarchal constructions of the liminal space seem to resist 'queerness' altogether. The men reject those who fall under the label '*moffie*' (queer or faggot in Afrikaans), and they are sexually active only with other white men. In fact, they seem to reinforce their whiteness, masculinity and even their 'straightness' within the space of the liminal darkened room, where the boundaries of masculinity can be skirted while still being maintained. When the protagonist, François, eventually leaves the liminal space and begins to explore the possibility of fulfilling his desire in a more open way, the conflicts of queer desire and conservative ideologies rise to the surface, and the result is another case of violence, just as the violence suffered in *Proteus* and as is constantly threatened in *The World Unseen*.

These queer representations in South African films represent multiple facets of liminality which inform a reading of Trengove's *Inxeba (The Wound)*. However, this recent film is further complicated by the fact that it confronts tensions of queer desires and black cultures in South Africa in the most direct way seen in film to date.

Inxeba tells the story of a young, working class man, Xolani, who is hired as a caregiver for the initiation of a wealthy, city-dwelling teenager named Kwanda, whose father acknowledges that his son is 'soft', and blames his mother for spoiling him. Xolani has been returning to the site of the initiation every year to be a caregiver, chiefly so that he can resume his sexual relationship with another one of the caregivers, the hyper-masculine Vija. Both men are closeted, and Vija has a wife and child, fulfilling the cultural expectations on his masculinity. Xolani wants more from their relationship than simply the yearly escape for sex, but Vija is highly uncomfortable whenever Xolani tries to express his true feelings, and seems conflicted about his same-sex desires.

It is a part of the complexity of the film that initiation itself is a type of liminality for the young men, where the initiates are transitioning from boyhood and becoming men. Arnold van Gennep, the anthropologist who originally coined the term 'liminality' in 1909, used it to describe the status of being 'transitional' through undergoing rites of passage (*The Rites of Passage*: 11). The initiates in *Inxeba* are straddling boyhood and manhood, partaking in something sacred which needs to exist in secrecy, a state of limbo which acts as a perfect parallel for the constructions of queerness in many other South African films. Kwanda even becomes frustrated with the idea that the initiation is a prolonged process, and questions why they have to stay in the mountain for two weeks when they had already been circumcised; there is a feeling of frustration with the period of limbo, especially for a young man like Kwanda who is outspoken and open about being gay, and who never wanted to be initiated. Kwanda seems to resist the liminality imposed on him, something which seems possible due to his acceptance of his sexuality, but which is subject to pushback by the other men in the film.

Furthermore, the mountain initiation setting is a remarkably queer space in terms of the types of expressions afforded to the young men. There is heightened male-male intimacy within the setting. A brotherhood is formed between the young men as they go through the initiation together. Through this, they are able to perform in ways that might have been viewed as 'queer' in other settings. For example, the boys expose their newly-circumcised penises to one another, demonstrating the scars and commenting on how desirable the penises will be to women. The young men are able to admire the penises of others in this sexually performative setting. However, there still are boundaries set here; Kwanda sits at a distance as the other young men admire one another's penises. When he is invited by one of the initiates to join the group, and to show his scar, which they had been told was 'one of the best looking', the boys begin to cover up their bodies and Kwanda is told that because he 'sleeps with men' and is a 'faggot', he should not be looking at the penises of the other young men. Despite the queerness inherent in the scene, the performance is still masculine and heteronormative in nature, and the acknowledged queer figure represented by Kwanda would unsettle the meaning of the scene for the initiates; he would make it overtly queer.

There is also the element of the older men who act as 'caregivers' to the young initiates, sleeping in the huts with them, feeding them and caring for the wounds on their penises while also instructing them about what it means to be men. This seemingly feminised role taken by Xolani towards Kwanda already invites a queer reading of the film, and heightens the intimacy between the men in the mountain setting. Many scenes show Xolani inspecting and caring for Kwanda's penis, and Kwanda is led to a river where he is submerged naked as Xolani watches him. With the knowledge that both Xolani and Kwanda are same-sex attracted, there seems to be another unspoken level to the initiation process; the men are clearly aware of each other's sexuality, and this creates tension between them. When Vija finds out that Xolani is the caregiver for Kwanda, he says, 'they trust you with the softies', and later asks if Kwanda is a 'faggot'. There is additionally the persistent sense that Kwanda is attracted to Xolani and is frustrated that Xolani seems to be smitten with Vija.

Another queer moment that seems to be openly allowed is when the initiates and the caregivers are dancing around a fire at their campground after the young men are circumcised. The dance seems to possess the men, and Vija and Xolani are dancing close to the fire when Vija embraces him and even kisses Xolani on his cheek in front of the other men. For some reason, the moment allows an expression of affection between the two men which Vija had tried so desperately to hide before. The liminal space allows for heterosocial bonding in ways that demonstrate intimacy that would be viewed as unacceptably queer in other settings. In another night-time fire scene, Kwanda is drinking excessively and embraces another initiate intimately, with commenters calling out: 'They are falling in love!' Whereas Kwanda is often seen as an outsider, at these moments he can find intimacy with the other initiates, which would otherwise have been forcefully restricted.

In addition to these queer moments, the conflicts around culture, referred to variously in this article, find expression within the initiation setting in three interesting ways where 'whiteness' enters the liminal space. The first is when Kwanda's difference from the other young men is reflected through whiteness. He is seen as a 'soft' city boy whose wealth has made him lose touch with his traditions. At the same time, the others can tell that he is queer, and associate his difference with whiteness. Some of the other young men ask Kwanda about whether white woman have pubic hair, and after Kwanda stays silent, another initiate says that Kwanda 'thinks that he is white'. This association with whiteness is highly evocative in this setting. Queerness is already often constructed as something 'white' or 'un-African' in South Africa, and placing Kwanda within that discourse accounts for not only his distance from the other initiates but also for his queerness. This construction could also account for why Xolani and Vija cannot accept themselves as queer; they do not have the wealth or the proximity to the cosmopolitan city, and thus lack the links to 'whiteness' and cannot find the distance from 'traditional' Xhosa culture that might somehow allow their attraction to exist beyond the liminal setting. When Kwanda later suggests that Xolani should go to Johannesburg to be near him, Xolani demands: 'What would I do in Johannesburg?' He does not fit into the same spaces that Kwanda inhabits, and consequently, his queerness has no space for open expression other than the liminal space of the mountain setting.

The second reference to whiteness is when the group of caregivers and initiates come across a white farmer on the mountain, and need to ask him for permission to cross the land towards a waterfall. The encounter with the white farmer is filled with a sense of dread as some of the men warn that they should turn back rather than 'start trouble'. The encounter seems to disrupt the liminality of the initiation setting, bringing the men back to the conflicts that exist in the outside world. For the viewer, it is a jarring moment in the film because it contrasts so strongly with the otherworldly limbo and isolation which the men had inhabited on the mountain. Furthermore, it undercuts the performative masculinity which is inherent in the initiation setting. The white man is shown to have ultimate power in the setting, and Xolani takes off his hat, trying to explain to the white man in Afrikaans why the group would like to cross. Vija, because of his aggressive hyper-masculinity, is visibly frustrated with the situation, and steals one of the farmer's goats from his pickup truck, desperate to re-establish the patriarchal, sacred and trance-like state constituted in the initiation. He commands the initiates to slaughter the goat, and they seem uncertain of what to do. Interestingly, Kwanda is the one to follow the instruction and slaughter the goat, in a violent, unsettling scene where he covers himself in the goat's blood. The scene acts as foreshadowing for the violence that forms the undercurrent of the film, and at the same time shows the reactions when these liminal spaces are disrupted by influences like whiteness, challenges to masculinity, and, by extension and in the context of this discussion, by acknowledged and open 'queerness'. The scene thus sets up what the consequences will be once the relationship between Vija and Xolani is exposed.

The final reference to whiteness is in a scene near the end of the initiation process when one of the elders in the group invokes the ancestors to protect them from the 'white devils' and the danger of them 'impregnating' the 'womb' of the Xhosa people. It is an evocative image and speaks to the many attempts at warding off the influence of whiteness in the film and more broadly in South African society. There is a sense that there is something vulnerable about the Xhosa culture, feminising it in relation to the predatory 'white devils'. The image speaks of the influence of white cultural hegemony, something which Kwanda has indirectly represented throughout the film. It also reinforces the idea of an imposition, a penetration of tradition by social changes. Indirectly, the image speaks to the openly queer character who might be seen as the product of this 'white devil', something infecting a vulnerable Xhosa tradition. While the liminality of the mountain initiation setting might allow for discreet, unacknowledged queer moments, like Xolani and Vaji's sexual trysts, these moments cannot extend to the outside world, and cannot be spoken of or acknowledged.

When Xolani and Vaji are discovered by Kwanda, naked after sex, and he threatens to expose Vaji, all of these conflicts are brought to the fore, and the film, as with many of the other films discussed in this article, leads to violence. This acknowledged queerness is the same reason why Claas and Rijkhaart are put to death in *Proteus*. It is the reason why Amina and Miriam suffer scorn and decide to keep their relationship secret in *The World Unseen*. It is a part of the reason why François attacks the object of his desire, Christian, in *Skoonheid*, that moment of finally escaping his liminal queer space requiring patriarchal violence in order to reassert his position of power.

Inxeba challenges the liminality of queer representations and simultaneously disrupts the invisibility of black queer subjects, and the heated debate and even threats of violence on the actors with the film's release evince the pushback when these liminal subjects are finally acknowledged, made visible, and situated within culture. These stories are vital within South Africa, and more of them are needed in order to disrupt the marginalisation of queer people, especially black queer people. The important work of *Inxeba* can allow for queer stories to move out of the liminal space, to be acknowledged, and for queer people to be seen as a part of South African cultures instead of somehow conflicting with them. There is the suggestion that with a more tolerant society, representations can become less liminal, more mainstream, and represent black queer sexualities in ways that are open and acknowledged. There are already signs of this shift in films like Catherine Stewart's *While You Weren't Looking* (2015), set in Cape Town, where queer relationships are much more mainstream and where there exists a mix of closeted and out queer characters who live very diverse lives. With the debates around masculinity, culture and queerness sparked by *Inxeba*, perhaps the space can be created where diverse queer stories can finally be told openly, and not be met with homophobic resistance or violence.

WORKS CITED

Arsenault, Jesse. 'Queer Desire and the Men of the Nation: Reading Race, Masculinity, and South African National Identity in John Greyson's *Proteus*'. *Safundi* Vol. 14, No. 1 (2013): 37-58.

Attwell, David. *J.M. Coetzee and the Life of Writing: Face to Face with Time*, Oxford: Oxford University Press, 2015.

Bongela, Milisuthando. 'Exposing a Culture's Wounds'. *Mail & Guardian*, 21 July 2017, https://mg.co.za/article/2017-07-21-00-exposing-a-cultures-wounds (accessed 14 September 2017).

Botha, Martin. *South African Cinema 1896-2010*. Chicago, IL: University of Chicago Press, 2012

Briganti, Chiara. 'A Bored Spinster with a Locked Diary: The Politics of Hysteria in In the Heart of the Country'. *Research in African Literatures* Vol. 25, No. 4 (1994): 33-49

Burchardt, Marian. 'Equals Before the Law? Public Religion and Queer Activism in the Age of Judicial Politics in South Africa'. *Journal of Religion in Africa* Vol. 43, No. 2 (2013): 237-60.

Cock, Jacklyn. 'Engendering Gay and Lesbian Rights: The Equality Clause in the South African Constitution'. *Women's Studies International Forum* Vol. 26, No. 1 (2003): 35-45

Coetzee, J. M. *In the Heart of the Country*. London: Martin Secker & Warburg, 1977.

Croucher, Sheila. 'South Africa's Democratisation and the Politics of Gay Liberation'. *Journal of Southern African Studies* Vol. 28, No. 2 (2002): 315-30.

Dyer, Richard. 'Gays in Film'. *Jump Cut: A Review of Contemporary Media* 18 (1978): 15-16.

Gqirana, Thulani. 'No Secrets Revealed in *Inxeba* Movie – Producer'. *Channel24*, 22 August 2017. www.channel24.co.za/Movies/News/no-secrets-revealed-on-inxeba-movie-producer-20170822 (accessed 14 September 2017).

Greyson, John (dir.). *Proteus* Pluck Productions, 2003.

Hermanus. Oliver (dir.), *Skoonheid (Beauty)*. Swift Productions, 2011.
Ireland, Patrick R. 'A Macro-Level Analysis of the Scope, Causes, and Consequences of Homophobia in Africa'. *African Studies Review* Vol. 56, No. 2 (2013): 47-66.
Jay, Niza. '*Inxeba*: A Moment of Confrontation'. *Mail & Guardian* 19 July 2017 https://mg.co.za/article/2017-07-18-inxeba-a-moment-of-confrontation (accessed 13 September 2017).
Livermon, Xavier. 'Queer(y)ing Freedom: Black Queer Visibilities in Post-apartheid South Africa'. *GLQ* Vol. 18, Nos 2-3 (2012): 297-323.
MambaOnline. '7de Laan Surprises Viewers with its First Gay Kiss'. *MambaOnline* 3 March 2017. www.mambaonline.com/2017/03/03/7de-laan-surprises-viewers-first-gay-kiss-watch (accessed 14 September 2017).
news24. 'Storm Over TV Gay Kiss'. *news24*, 8 September 2009. www.news24.com/Archives/City-Press/Storm-over-TV-gay-kiss-20150430 (accessed 14 September 2017).
Odendaal, Danie (creator). *7de Laan*. Danie Odendaal Productions, 2000 to present.
Peach, Ricardo. *Queer Cinema as a Fifth Cinema in South Africa and Australia* (diss.), University of Technology, Sydney, 2005. https://opus.lib.uts.edu.au/bitstream/10453/20344/4/01front.pdf (accessed 25 January 2018).
Roehr, Bob. 'How Homophobia is Fuelling Africa's HIV Epidemic'. *British Medical Journal* (online), 11 May 2010. www.bmj.com/content/340/bmj.c2245 (accessed 11 February 2018).
Sarif, Shamim (dir.). *The World Unseen*. Enlightenment Productions, 2007.
Stewart, Catherine (dir.). *While You Weren't Looking*. Phat Free Films, 2015.
Stobie, Cheryl. 'Postcolonial Pomosexuality: Queer/Alternative Fiction after *Disgrace*'. *Current Writing: Text and Reception in Southern Africa* Vol. 21, Nos 1-2 (2009): 320-41. Thomassen, Bjørn. 'The Uses and Meanings of Liminality'. *International Political Anthropology* Vol. 2, No. 1 (2009): 5-27.
Trengove, John (dir.). *Inxeba (The Wound)*. Riva Filmproduktion, 2017.
Turner, Victor. 'Betwixt and Between: The Liminal Period in Rites de Passage'. In *The Forest of Symbols*, Victor Turner. New York: Cornell University Press, 1967.
van Gennep, Arnold. *The Rites of Passage*. Trans. Monika Vizedom and Gabrielle L. Caffee. Chicago, IL: University of Chicago Press, 1960.
Vundla, Mfundi (creator). *Generations*. Morula Pictures, 1993 to present.

Gay, African, Middle-Class & Fabulous

Writing Queerness in New Writing from Nigeria & South Africa

SHOLA ADENEKAN

In my earlier research (Adenekan 2012), I constructed a historical footprint of the agenda of same-sex desire in African literature and how this may be changing in the age of the internet. I argued that some members of the older generation of contemporary African writers used fictional homosexual characters as part of a larger project of decolonising the African body, but despite this agenda, their writing, such as that of Wole Soyinka's *The Interpreters*, also gave us a good insight into the figure of the homosexual. For some of the emerging voices, these earlier nationalistic projects contributed to the marginalisation of the figure of the African homosexual. In addition, their position seems to indicate that this figure is central to our understanding of the history of spectrality surrounding all marginalised bodies. In this article, I will be examining how some of the online fictional narratives are suggesting that the queer African body is also surrounded by the agenda of global capital.

It is obvious that, for a growing number of young Africans, straight or gay – as well as for many across the continent – the internet is ensuring that knowledge once privileged and situated within the confines of higher education has never been more free, more plentiful nor more available. For the sexually marginalised, digital technologies make romantic and sexual connections possible. They also reduce isolation from human contacts and even enable offline social interaction. Eve Sedgwick ('Paranoid Reading and Reparative Reading') surmises that capitalism relies on stimulating or creating consumer interest and participation and, through some of these emerging narratives in the online writing space, we are seeing how the internet, as a product of capitalism, has become a tool for generating contemporary queer identity, particularly in Nigeria and Kenya. Most importantly, much of the queer writing focuses mainly on the everyday middle-class African experience. Keguro Macharia, in an examination of queer Kenyan writing, recognises the shift in literary representation, 'from the allegorical mode' of the Ngugi and Soyinka generation, to a pre-occupation that is 'now focused on quotidian details, without taking on the burden of representing revolutionary peasants, the urban working class, or betrayed freedom fighters' ('Blogging Queer Kenya': 3). While Macharia points out that while these tropes are still present in fictional narratives, 'they are no longer the privileged subjects of representation'. What Macharia signposts us to is the way in which materialism and the pursuit of the quotidian are intricately linked with regards to literary depiction of queer Africa. And given the representations in many of these online queer writings, we may indeed assume that material culture has become implicated in the construction of queer identity. Queer performances in some of the online fiction often leave little space for the expression of lower and underclass queer experience, since these groups have already been excluded by the barrier of language (the inability to read and write in the European languages on which the internet is mostly based), and many may not be able to afford regular internet access due to subscription cost and bandwidth limitation.

The protagonist in 'Shades of the New South Africa', an online short story by the Oxford-University-educated South African writer Eusebius McKaiser, recognises the omission of destitute gay Africans from the continent's mainstream gay culture, as he depicts a would-be lover's unconcern about the plight of young, poor, gay, black men in Cape Town:

> Sifiso seems totally oblivious. These street kids are just part of the familiar landscape of Seapoint; to be negotiated but never to be acknowledged ... such honesty may ruin your appetite while sitting at Newscafe enjoying the morning's paper and overlooking the gorgeously blue ocean but for the aesthetic blotch of stray dogs and streetkids. (McKaiser 'Shades of the New South Africa')

McKaiser's depiction of Sofiso points us towards an intersectionality of class and sexuality. Sofiso is marginalised because of his sexuality but he is privileged because he is a middle-class South African, and therefore, his experience of marginality differs from those who are marginalised by poverty. Additionally, the material capital that Sofiso possesses insulates him from the experience of those who are simultaneously gay and poor. The queer African project, argues Massaquoi is, after all, 'a utopian story' of courage, power, and resistance ('The Continent as a Closet': 52), but it hardly accounts for the mirror function.

While state control of the media across the African continent has been widely discussed and studied by scholars (e.g. Ebenezer Obadare 'Playing Politics with the Mobile Phone in Nigeria'; George Ogola 'The Political Economy of the Media in Kenya'). Digital African literature is showing us that we also need to focus our attention on the potential level of control that access to the new media space gives to the educated class, and how members of the digital network may unconsciously use the medium to their sole advantage – so much so that the unconnected may not be heard at all. Cultural and economic power thus matters in our articulation of the way in which same-sex and queer desire are being represented. Our attention should not just be on the state and on business corporations: we should also focus on powerful stakeholders beyond these two entities.

Furthermore, some of the emerging African queer texts are showing us how the lower classes can easily be excluded and displaced from global cultural consciousness, and how this invisibility has been carried over into the digital space: This is because the lifestyle of transnational young African writers who are easily at home in Lagos, London and Los Angeles is now being transplanted into fictional gay characters. The gay protagonist in 'Shades of the New South Africa' attests to this phenomenon:

> So there I am in Joburg [bar] in Cape Town. Celebrating thirty years of survival. The crazy world refuses to stop and acknowledge my tenacity. I am invisible in a space littered with twig-figured girls and boys with bulging muscle, as sexy as Popeye after a can of spinach, about to rescue his beloved twig-figurine, Olive. They are all draped in Diesel, Levi's, CK and other funk-indicating labels I cannot pronounce, let alone spell. They dance and giggle and strut around the dance floor, moving skilfully to local house beats, the imported cosmopolitan sounds of London mixed with a hint of Gugulethu [township 15 km from Cape Town], to mask the victory of cultural imperialism. This is the new resistance politics. I inhale the sweet, horny smells of booze and cigarettes and sweat and hormones and youth and promise and life … the intoxicating aroma of the new south africa [sic]. I sit in a corner, making love to a bottle of Castle while scanning the room. For sex. For escapism. I choose my strategy. I try hard to look 'upwardly mobile' … yet chilled. The popular look seems to say 'I'm-an-assistant-MD-but-have-loxion-kulca-flowing-through-my-soul'. I realise I am screwed. (Or rather I won't be.) I'm not darkie enough to ooze even an ounce of loxion kulca through my coloured veins. I'm not rich enough to ooze assistant-MD. I m not scrawny enough to masquerade the lie of 'youthful innocence'. How did I sneak past the doorman? It must have been my coconut twang, I guess – but that brand seems so last year, as stale as the 'I-spent-a-gap-year-in-London' gag. (McKaiser 'Shades of the New South Africa')

The protagonist depicts the pretension of affluence with 'funk-indicating labels', gay men and women who affect foreign 'twang' and like to display their collection of foreign clothes and other luxuries so as to be accepted into the gay scene. The London-Gugulethu space is marked by class division because it is a world that is far removed from the South African townships and a million miles away from most villages in Nigeria and Kenya. But this world is real to many middle-class writers.

In this new century, as in the last, class remains a very important factor in literature's representation of queer African life, because what literature is imitating is the fact that class embodies the experience of most African writers, with a middle-class queer experience that is manifesting itself overwhelmingly in much of emerging queer African literature. As market forces – modern education and the affordability of the internet – have bestowed on middle-class writers the role of cultural ambassador, the social relationships that fictional queer characters form online mirrors the communities that writers themselves form in cyberspace (in literary networks and social media communities). A global middle-class identity is thus projected as the norm for non-straight Africans, in a continent in which many are still poor. Digital capital is therefore becoming the cultural capital.

Rarely do we see fictional narratives or poems that capture the experience of African homosexuals who live in rural areas, or who are struggling to make ends meet in urban areas. Instead, fictional gay characters like real-life writers are often affluent, educated and socially mobile. The protagonist in 'Shades of the New South Africa' expresses frustration at the limited pool of lovers, and tells us that he is used to 'being spoiled by choice gay hangouts on Christopher Street in New York and Old Compton Street in London'. We hear his complaint because he has the financial capability to enter the gay metropolis, as both the character and the writer who created him come from the same world – that of the professional African middle class. Furthermore, these short stories in the new media space confirm Rob Cover's assertion that capital labour is linked to both same-sex desire and homophobia ('Queer with Class: Absence of the Third World Sweatshop'). Through these fictions, we are seeing the way that capital labour leads to social exclusion for many Africans, in this case, lower-class queers – people who cannot afford to pay for internet dating, who are excluded from many queer activities for instance in Nigeria and South Africa. The media space functions as a Foucauldian mirror between a utopia and the heterotopia that thrives on its distance from, and its marginalising energy against, queer existence among the lower classes.

Cyberspace is a construct of both reality and fiction, because art continuously imitates lived experience. As Michelle Kendrick argues, cyberspace 'foregrounds the ways in which technology intervenes in our subjectivity' ('Cyberspace and the Technological Real': 143). The urban gay lifestyle is no different from the lifestyle that middle-class straight characters lead in the fictional narratives being produced by some of Africa's notable transnational literary figures such as Chimamanda Adichie and Teju Cole – they are immersed in Blackberry phones, bling, popular music and digital connectivity. Just as these writers spend much of their time in the metropolitan spaces of Lagos and New York, so do the fictional characters they give us. Nkem, the closeted lesbian lover in Okonkwo's 'Prisoners of the Sky', arrives in America from Nigeria, sporting 'sparkling gold bracelets dangled around her neck and wrists' (20). As he enters a gay club in downtown Cape Town, the protagonist in 'Shades of the New South Africa' takes in the bar staff and surmises straight away: 'I can just imagine the job ads: "Fat and ugly men need not apply". The gay market is tough. Certainly no place for oldies or fatties.'

The world of most fictional African queer characters appears to be that of CNN, the music of the American R&B singer R. Kelly, physically-fit gay lovers, and luxurious hotel rooms in Abuja and Cape Town – two of the most expensive cities in the world. And since affordability equals accessibility, a subscription to Gaydar.com and a bottle of wine in a trendy Cape Town gay bar may well be beyond the reach of many less affluent gays and lesbians. The affluent lifestyle depicted in these online fictional narratives shows the way in which this growing quest for a connection with the outside world by Africans with disposable incomes may lead to exploitation. Organisations like Gaydar (www.gaydar.com) appear to be a place where middle-class gay Africans congregate, and since the narrator is emotionally and geographically separated from his family and community, he is prone to capitalist exploitation since he has no choice but to buy companionship on the internet and can be induced to lead an ostentatious gay lifestyle. Music by U.S. artists Fat Joe and then Angie Stone is shown to be subtly relevant to a desperate, possibly homicidal effort to 'two-step skip' and thus escape a sexual predator – only to grow aware that there are more waiting (Abasi 2008: 16). Cover suggests that, when global online companies sell to the middle class from the non-West, they hope to get some level of brand loyalty in return ('Queer with Class'). This is how some of the world's most dynamic, far-sighted cultural organisations are enhancing their income and securing their future – by linking with young African professionals, that most affluent, influential, sought-after demographic. In cyberspace, the queer African body thus simultaneously reveals and signifies the obscenity of materialism and exploitation.

The inter-connectedness between different literary spaces, especially between the metropolitan centres of Africa and the West, has helped advance the cause of gay rights movements in postcolonial Africa. Yet literature depicting transnational figures also shows the challenges faced by people whom many would deem privileged due to the economic and cultural power they possess. Given the fact that many African national leaders and their followers wrongly perceive homosexuality as being un-African, literature helps to undermine this notion by bringing to the fore nuanced representations of queerness and same-sex desire in an African context. Transnational characters who criss-cross these fictional spaces, moreover, reveal the experience that homophobia is not just an African dilemma but is very active in North America, especially for black queers. For these characters, the experience of being different or queer is not fully mitigated by their being members of the global middle classes, as they are not fully accepted either in Africa or in North America.

Furthermore, some of these online short stories are revealing to us that capital labour is connected to queer identity and also to the rising level of homophobia. In addition, what some of these young writers who are bold enough to write about fictional homosexual characters are showing is that African literature is now at the genesis of the localisation of queerness.

The idea of 'coming out' in the twenty-first century in an African context can arguably best be understood if we look into, read and theorise the digital age. A key significant factor in this regard is the fact that online writings are suggesting that many young gay Africans may be choosing to 'come out' – through the internet, because it is safe and probably because it allows for anonymity. In the online short story 'Two-Step Skip' (2008), written for *Outliers* by the Nigerian author Crispin Oduobuk-Mfon Abasi, sexual violence becomes the only means of correcting that which is un-African. In the physical space, 'corrective rape' has reportedly been used by some men on some African lesbians (Fihlani 'South Africa's Lesbians Fear "Corrective Rape"'). Moreover, some of the online literary texts also suggest that the theme of 'rape' is a very complex and highly problematic one for African queer study and literature.

The gay protagonist in 'Two-Step Skip' is a young up-and-coming Nigerian journalist. Trying to avoid the danger and the social stigma of looking for a male lover in the physical space of Abuja, Nigeria, he decides to try internet dating. And through the popular gay dating website, Gaydar.com, he meets a man, who he secretly visits for the first time in a hotel suite. Through this story we see another way in which the online space can pose a danger for a gay person. That danger is manifested in the fact that the protagonist is lured from the safe environment of cyberspace into the physical space by a man who is using a fake name – 'Dave' – and who ends up raping the narrator. As will be subsequently discussed, the rape of the narrator shows us how otherness is lived, embodied, represented, experienced and transgressed in contemporary Africa. Relishing the prospect that internet dating will be more liberating and safer than meeting men in the physical space, the protagonist enthuses: 'why should I bring the mysterious too close? There's a degree of safety in arms-length. So when I'm done, I do a little happy two-step skip; once again a child out to buy sweets and chewing gum and looking forward to savouring their sugary sweetness' (Abasi: 11).

The protagonist's experience symbolises the loneliness of being gay or lesbian in Nigeria. It also echoes the lamentation of 'Sometimes I feel like a motherless child', which Joe Golder utters in Wole Soyinka's *The Interpreters* – just as, more than four decades ago when *The Interpreters* was written, the world inhabited by gay and lesbian characters in many of these new online fictions is one of alienation. Alienation is derived from the Latin *alius* meaning 'another' and *dienatus* meaning 'estranged'. Hegel sees alienations as 'a characteristic feature of the modern man, his sense of inward estrangements, of more or less conscious awareness that the inner being, the real "I", is alienated from the "me," the person as an object in society' (Ogungbesan 'The Cape Gooseberry Also Grows in Botswana': 206).

We see in these characters the constant notion of being described as un-African because of their sexuality, so in the process we see estrangement, uneasiness and friction in the physical space, which may have driven them to cyberspace in the first place. The protagonist chats up men online, but he is forced to meet them secretly in the physical space. He tries to not incur the wrath of the contemporary society's homophobia and informs us 'That way, I two-step skip the security system' (Abasi: 12). So desire is expressed openly in the online space, and experienced secretly – as a shadow – in the offline space.

Both the protagonist and his rapist use Gaydar.com because of the promise that online dating holds for those gays and lesbians who can afford online dating subscriptions. Like his rapist, the protagonist is also a closeted gay man, and he tells us that:

> Several people I know, including my girl and co-workers, question my sexuality sometimes because, braided hair and ladylike clothes apart, I'm one of those men born with very noticeable feminine traits. My colleagues often tease me about my voice and gestures. I've even overheard some call me Dan Daudu, the northern derogatory term for a gay sex worker. Okay, so I too have sometimes wondered about myself. It's why I registered with Gaydar. In meeting Dave, I've come for an evening of intelligent conversation on art, politics, and, well, okay, gay issues as well. I guess at some level it can be said that I'm exploring. Perhaps even experimenting, though this truly is a mysterious world to me. (Abasi: 13)

This is a 'coming-out' narrative that speaks to the role which the internet may be playing in the discovery of the 'real' self for many young Africans who have access to the internet, and perhaps, those who also have mobile phones. On the other hand, the people in the narrator's life suspect his homosexuality but have chosen not to take this possibility seriously; instead they jokingly tag him a 'Dan Daudu'. So, the Nigerian society is also in the closet. Also, maintaining a front in having a girlfriend in the offline space while seeking a boyfriend in the digital space not only speaks to a crossing of boundaries, but to the 'down low' phenomenon, which Keith Boykin (*Beyond The Down Low*) suggests is common in African-American gay men, who are sleeping with men (who they often meet online) while maintaining a female partner because of their community's homophobia. So, this is a Nigerian version of this 'down low'. The digital space is therefore arguably becoming the space for gay and lesbian Africans to meet fellow Africans for either sex or a secret relationship. The protagonist's view of online dating as a site of queer enlightenment and experimentation confirms Mary Bryson's argument that cyberspace can be 'a powerful tool for learning to be, or perhaps more specifically, to do, queer' ('Conjuring the Quotidian': 85).

The chat-room of Gaydar.com is a site for the outing of the queer self and this corroborates the argument that gender is an act of performance (Chang 'The Dynamics of Motherhood Performance'). The social interaction between the protagonist and Dave alludes to the fact that internet chat is a prelude to dating, which is an essential element of the twenty-first century narrative discourse. It depicts how the 'self' connects with like-minded people in this new media age. Gazi Islam points out that internet chat-rooms make 'metasocial commentary ... a story they tell themselves about themselves, which can be seen as a reproduction of the collective life of the group, a self-enacted story with its users as narrators' ('Virtual Speakers, Virtual Audiences': 82).

As Dave notices that the narrator speaks and looks like a girl, the narrator on his part confirms the desire to be a girl. He tells us that 'I'd shown him my pictures on the net and had explained that I wished more than anything else that I'd been born a girl ... I thought he understood all that well enough' (13). He tells us about the look people give him when he acts like a woman as 'That look I get every day. The one which says. He must be gay!' (Abasi: 11). Here we see that the internet can also serve as a site for gender desire. At the root of the desire of the narrator (who is also the protagonist) to acquire gender through his online dating profile is the offline heteronormativity brought about by colonial modernity, which demands that a man must sound and act like a man, otherwise he could be considered neither a man nor a woman. This is where we see the way in which people who do not fit into this man-woman binary can become spectres, invisible beings that history refuses to place or acknowledge.

Dave (the rapist) has not experienced gay sex before and he is also a self-loathing gay character; the twin brother who, in online chats with the protagonist, he has earlier suggested on Gaydar.com as 'the most enviable man alive for being successful with women' (13), turns out to be gay and the object of Dave's homophobic rage. Dave's self-loathing is also born out of his cowardice – the lack of courage to proclaim his sexuality in the physical space and instead restricted to avowing this queer desire only in cyberspace because of the heteronormative patriarchy of the 'real' world. Dave thus represents the authoritative and hypocritical figure in the 'real' world, who, while publicly condemning homosexuality as corrupting social mores, is secretly a closeted homosexual. His anger, which resulted in sexual violence, is perhaps the consequence of pent-up shame and sorrow.

An analysis of the pivotal figure of Dave, the man who raped the protagonist, is important to the way in which the queer African body has been consistently violated in silence, with no one to offer support and no possibility to legal recourse for justice. Monica Whitty ('Cyber-Flirting') asks researchers interested in cyber-flirting to look at how online daters choose to reconstruct the body in cyberspace. In the online space, the narrator tells us that Dave 'is usually chatty and funny, eager to share anecdotes about his work and family,' but in the physical space he is 'bland,' 'inane,' and 'unsophisticated' (Abasi: 13). The screen name or alias of Dave therefore represents a certain image of homosexual self in the virtual world. Monica Whitty and Tom Buchanan argue in 'What's in a Screen Name?' that the name that online daters choose is an important factor in drawing people to their profiles as screen names are assumed by other punters as the initial window into one's online and offline personality. Moreover, 'Two-Step Skip' reflects a true life story told by Sokari Ekine, the publisher of the queer blog *Black Looks*, about gay-baiting in Kenya and Ghana. She reveals that emerging gay websites in Kenya and Ghana 'are being used to trap' gays by men posting fake dating profiles, in the process luring the 'real' gay men from online chat-rooms into isolated offline spaces with promises of sex. The article then says that these gay men 'are then either blackmailed or assaulted by the "fake gays"' (Ekine 'Scammers Targeting Gay Men in Ghana'). In the online fiction 'Two-Step Skip', the charming Dave who initially chatted with the protagonist on Gaydar.com is arguable the 'real' Dave while Dave (the rapist) in the offline space of Abuja, is a by-product of an imposition from the larger society, the community that demands wife, children and toughness from a man. The sexual violence visited on the protagonist symbolises the fight-back by the heteronormative society against the coming out of queerness. Mary Bryson ('Conjuring the Quotidian') argues that the increasing use of the internet and the adoption of digital technologies such as mobile phones may not bring an end to rabid homophobia and social alienation.

While the rape of women (lesbians and straight) in wars and in domestic environments have been well documented around the world, the rape of gay men such as the protagonist in 'Two-Step Skip' reveals the unreported sexual violence visited on gay men every day; not just on the continent of Africa, but in every continent across the globe. These are people who could have met their rapists and may have forged a relationship with them through internet dating, as Sokari Ekine reveals in *Black Looks*. As he rapes the protagonist, Dave loudly mocks the protagonist's effeminate build and clothing: 'You're just like a woman! Look at your face! See your red lips. Did you use lipstick?' (Abasi: 14). By mocking the protagonist this way as he rapes him, Dave is trying to prove to the 'real' world that he is the opposite version of weak 'un-African' gay men who inhabit the digital space. Dave's mocking testifies to a postcolonial Africa's physical, affective and ideological concept of manhood.

QUEER AFRICAN BODIES AND MULTINATIONALS

African literature in the online writing space gives us an insight into the way the global market forces operate within the continent. I am thinking here about Fredric Jameson's notion of 'late capitalism'. What these short stories and poems on African homosexuality have shown us is that there is a connection between the capitalist metropolis, national capitalism and African homosexual culture in the twenty-first century, notably enhanced by the new tools of globalisation of which the internet is an important part.

Some of the fictional queer African characters have become a representation of exploitation by small and big businesses from within and outside of the continent. In addition, these new literary works highlight the history of sexual repression that trade and business foster in many societies. We need to be careful not solely to blame Western capitalism for sexual repression, as oral history and written records have shown that the agenda of the merchant trade on the continent also supports sexual repression, of which the Trans-Atlantic slave trade is a good example. There is a history of sexual repression in many societies across the globe due to the agenda of the local market and heteronormative traditions. As Peter A. Jackson argues:

> The multiple modernities of today's world cannot be explained as the bastard children of a single, foreign Western capitalism that has overpowered and raped local traditions. These modernities have equally emerged from local capitalisms that have revolutionized local pre-modern cultures. ('Capitalism and Global Queering': 364)

On the one hand, what we can be certain of is that the market via the new media technology, has allowed a free space for the expression of queer desire and for us to witness the role that capitalism (both global and national) is playing in the repression of queer identity. Like Abasi's 'Two-Step Skip', Eusebius McKaiser's 'Shades of the New South Africa' highlights the ease with which luxurious goods, foreign images and ideas, as well as people, enter the continent from foreign countries. Likewise 'Shades of the New Africa' reveals the ease with which increasing number of middle-class Africans travel to the West and relate to Western culture through satellite television and the digital space, and shows that the agenda of capitalism within the continent now possesses many similarities to the agenda of global capitalism. Emerging gay culture in African urban areas as depicted in these online short stories therefore epitomises what Jackson (386) refers to as 'the contemporary world of globally interconnected societies and cultures'. The protagonist in 'Shades of the New South Africa' informs us that his 'faghag' (that is a female friend of a gay man) is an African-American Letisha. He also tells us that some of the people in some of Cape Town's gay scene are people of different nationalities. These online short stories show us that the embrace of Western consumerism by the African middle class alongside the rise of local gay culture may be leading to a new hybridisation of the homosexual identity, something which may be completely different from the spectral history of same-sex relationships across many of Africa's pre-colonial societies.

On the other hand, the protagonist in 'Two-Step Skip' represents the unspoken and the unseen tragedy being inflicted by homophobia and the silence surrounding homosexuality. In addition, we rarely hear about the trauma of rape that some African men may have experienced because culturally, African men are supposed to be strong and able to cope with pain. The sexually-violated protagonist reveals the pain which for long has remained hidden in the 'real' world, and which we are now just starting to see in the online space. The traumatic experience of rape also speaks to the aggression that is being visited on the weak (of all sexual persuasions and ethnic origins) by some of Africa's 'big men'.

Rape as it is being revealed in the online writing space has also become a tool which many religious leaders are now using to keep societal order, because some of them have voiced support for violence against homosexuals in Africa (see Hoad *African Intimacies*). The queer African's body, in both the online and offline spaces, as represented by the protagonist in 'Two-Step Skip', is thus a site for experiencing religious and neo-colonial violence. Dave as the rapist likewise embodies the heterosexual middle class and educated African male's determination to remain in control of Africa's destiny, and he carries out this agenda by forcing himself on the protagonist.

After he fought his rapist into a comatose state, the protagonist walks back into the real world as a queer Nigerian with spectral status, as an unreal man. Traumatised but still forced into silence by the hetero masculinity of the outside world, he will only be able to tell his story in cyberspace. Again, we see the queer person as the 'loner' – the person who perhaps has no shoulder to cry on in the physical space and who remains a spectre haunting postcolonial history. The protagonist's experience in that hotel room symbolises a re-enforcement of the culture of silence that currently surrounds queer bodies and identities in the physical space. The internet and the digital space provide this queer figure the chance to emerge from the shadow of African history. Yvette Abrahams argues that this 'new visibility may have led to an escalation of this violence' ('Your Silence Will Not Protect You': 40). Abrahams also points out that such silence does not benefit the queer community, since people are getting raped whether they remain silent or speak out. The online writing space is not only becoming a space for affirming African queer identity but also the space for the outing of repressed memories for marginalised bodies. Therefore, we are seeing why queer activists along with writers and theorists of different sexual persuasions, need to tell the queer story in both the virtual and physical spaces of Africa. From these emerging African cybertexts, we are also seeing the way in which many young African writers are using the online experience of queer characters to portray the society's collective danger, often stemming from those in positions of authority.

In addition, the rape of the narrator reveals the continuous exploitation of Africans by global capital. Rob Cover ('Queer with Class') argues that queerness is often affected by the agenda of 'late capitalism.' Through Dave, we see how emerging queer texts are suggesting that, by supporting violence against the homosexual person, those in positions of power in Africa are carrying out a capitalist agenda, one that sees orderliness and the rule of law as being conducive to national growth and development. Homosexual bodies signify the unpredictability of the African market to foreign investors. As many of these new cybertexts reveal, capitalism weakens the communal spirit of Africa, as the twenty-first century African middle classes have to spread across the globe in order to attain material wealth, but simultaneously, the nuclear heterosexual family setting is seen as the ideal space for business and national development.

Some of these new online writings suggest that there might not be a space for queer expression within this capitalist desire. The protagonist in Uche Peter Umez's online short story 'A Night So Damp', and the lesbian lover in Okonkwo's, 'Prisoners of the Sky', are forced to forgo substantial material benefits from their wealthy families in order to assert their queer identity. The protagonist in 'Two-Step Skip' tells us that he risks becoming persona non grata within his capital-rich circle of friends and clientele, if it is confirmed that he is gay.

So, to violently abuse these queer Africans, as highlighted in these cybertexts, is to make a statement against crisis and chaos, thus telling the outside world that Africa is open and ready for business. Dave, the businessman from Lagos, arguably then represents capitalism's rape of

Africa's human resources, as the violated narrator is a talented young journalist with great potential, who has now been scarred for life by the sexual violence that he experienced in that hotel suite.

WORKS CITED

Abasi, Crispin Oduobuk-Mfon. 'Two-Step Skip'. In *Theorizing (Homo)Eroticism in Africa: A Collection of Essays and Creative Work on Sexuality in Africa*. IRN-Africa, *Outliers*. Nairobi: International Resource Network in Africa, 2008.

Abrahams, Yvette (aka Khib Omsis). 'Your Silence Will Not Protect You'. In *Theorizing (Homo)Eroticism in Africa: A Collection of Essays and Creative Work on Sexuality in Africa*. IRN-Africa, *Outliers*. Nairobi: International Resource Network in Africa, 2008.

Adenekan, Shola. 'African Literature in the Digital Age: Class and Sexual Politics in New Writing From Nigeria and Kenya'. Diss. University of Birmingham, 2012.

Boykin, Keith. *Beyond The Down Low: Sex, Lies, and Denial in Black America*. New York: Carroll & Graff, 2005.

Bryson, Mary. 'Conjuring the Quotidian'. *Journal of Gay and Lesbian Issues in Education*, Vol. 2, No. 4 (2005): 83-92.

Chang, Annie Hau-nung. 'The Dynamics of Motherhood Performance: Hong Kong's Middle Class Working Mothers On- and Off-Line'. *Sociological Research Online* Vol. 13, No. 4 (2008). www.socresonline.org.uk/13/4/4.html (accessed 14 February 2018).

Cover, Rob. 'Queer with Class: Absence of the Third World Sweatshop in Lesbian/Gay Discourse and a Rearticulation of Materialist Queer Theory'. *Ariel: A Review of International English Literature* Vol. 30, No. 2 (2003): 29-48.

Ekine, Sokari. 'Scammers Targeting Gay Men in Ghana'. *Black Looks*, 14 September 2009. www.blacklooks.org/2009/09/scammers_targeting_gay_men_in_ghana_kenya (accessed 14 February 2018).

Fihlani, Pumza. 'South Africa's Lesbians Fear "Corrective Rape"'. *BBC News Online* 30 June 2011. www.bbc.co.uk/news/world-africa-13908662 (accessed 14 February 2018).

Hoad, Neville. *African Intimacies: Race, Homosexuality and Globalization*. Minneapolis, MN: University of Minnesota Press, 2007.

Islam, Gazi. 'Virtual Speakers, Virtual Audiences: Agency, Audience and Constraint in an Online Chat Community'. *Dialectical Anthropology* Vol. 30, Nos1-2 (2006): 71-89.

Jackson, Peter, A. 'Capitalism and Global Queering: National Markets, Parallels Among Sexual Cultures, and Multiple Queer Modernities'. *GLQ: A Journal of Lesbian and Gay Studies* Vol. 15, No. 3 (2009): 357-95.

Kendrick, Michelle. 'Cyberspace and the Technological Real'. In *Virtual*

Realities and Their Discontents, ed. Robert Markley. Baltimore and London: John Hopkins University Press, 1996: 143-60.

Macharia, Keguro. 'Blogging Queer Kenya'. *The African Writer*, University of Maryland, c. 2013. www.theafricanwriter.files.wordpress.com/2012/08/jcps-macharia-1-final.docx (accessed 14 February 2018).

Massaquoi, Notisha. 'The Continent as a Closet: The Making of an African Queer Theory'. In *Theorizing (Homo) Eroticism in Africa: A Collection of Essays and Creative Work on Sexuality in Africa*. IRN-Africa, Outliers. Nairobi: International Resource Network in Africa, 2008.

McKaiser, Eusebius. 'Shades of the New South Africa'. *African Writing*, October/November 2007, www.african-writing.com/mckaiser.htm (accessed 14 February 2018).

Obadare, Ebenezer. 'Playing Politics with the Mobile Phone in Nigeria: Civil Society, Big Business & the State'. *Review of African Political Economy* Vol. 33, No. 107 (2006): 93-111.

Ogola, George. 'The Political Economy of the Media in Kenya: From Kenyatta's Nation-building Press to Kibaki's Local-language FM Radio'. *Africa Today* Vol. 57, No. 3 (2011): 77–95.

Ogungbesan, Kolawole. 'The Cape Gooseberry Also Grows in Botswana'. *Journal of African Studies* Vol. 6, No. 4 (1979): 206-12.

Okonkwo, Rudolph Ogoo. 'Prisoners of the Sky'. In *Theorizing (Homo)Eroticism in Africa: A Collection of Essays and Creative Work on Sexuality in Africa*. IRN-Africa, Outliers. Nairobi: International Resource Network in Africa, 2008.

Sedgwick, Eve K. 'Paranoid Reading and Reparative Reading; or You're So Paranoid, You Probably Think This Introduction is About You'. In *Novel Gazing: Queer Readings in Fiction*, ed. Eve K. Sedgwick. Durham, NC and London: Duke University Press, 1997.

Soyinka, Wole. *The Interpreters*. London, Ibadan and Nairobi: Heinemann Educational Books, 1965.

Umez, Uche Peter. 'A Night So Damp'. *Author-me.com*, n.d. www.author-me.com/fict06/nightsodamp.htm (accessed 14 February 2018).

Whitty, Monica T. 'Cyber-Flirting: Playing at Love on the Internet'. *Theory and Psychology* Vol. 13, no. 3 (2003): 339-57.

Whitty, Monica T. and Tom Buchanan. 'What's in a Screen Name? Attractiveness of Different Types of Screen Names Used by Online Daters'. *International Journal of Internet Science* Vol. 5, No. 1 (2010): 5-19.

The City as a Metaphor of Safe Queer Experimentation
Monica Arac de Nyeko's 'Jambula Tree'
& Beatrice Lamwaka's 'Pillar of Love'

EDGAR NABUTANYI

INTRODUCTION

In the last 15 years, there has emerged in the Ugandan public sphere what can be called a tradition of queer writing, delineating three trajectories. First, there is a furiously homophobic tabloid press, represented by the *Red Pepper* tabloid, whose writing about same-sex activity frames this sexuality as an existential threat to the Ugandan society. Second, there is the Ugandan academia, represented by Sylvia Tamale and Stella Nyanzi, who write proffering universalist human rights statutes in support of Ugandans who engage in same-sex sexuality. Third, there are fictional writers such as Monica Arac de Nyeko, Beatrice Lamwaka, Jennifer Nansubuga Makumbi and Nakisanze Segawa who use fiction to debate this phenomenon. It is important to note that the thread that links the tabloid press, scholarly research and fictional writing in Ugandan homosexuality writing is the fact that often the Ugandan homosexual is a resident of the city. In fact, it can be argued that since the writers are themselves city residents, it is perhaps inevitable that they should locate their subjects in the metropolis.

If the intersection between Ugandan journalistic, academic and fictional writing lies in the fact that these nodes of knowledge production construct the metropolis as a space for possible performance of queerness, then it is useful to interrogate the forms of knowledge production about queerness that are made possible by an urban setting. This question reminds us of Wale Adebanwi's observation that African writers are social thinkers postulating an insightful overview of the African essence. He argues that African writers are 'not merely intellectuals whose works mirror or can be used to mirror social thought, but [are] social thinkers themselves who engage with the nature of existence and questions of knowledge' ('The Writer as

Social Thinker': 406). Adebanwi's point in the above passage is that African writers use fiction to distil the essence, agency and worldview of African subjects. Given that homosexuality is contemporary Africa's most polarising subject, it is plausible to argue that writers like Makumbi, Arac de Nyeko Lamwaka and Nakisanze are using fiction to enact platforms and congregate publics to debate this phenomenon. While this argument opens the outlined writers and their texts to multiple and interesting readings, in this article I focus on the point that the existence of lesbians in Arac de Nyeko and Lamwaka's texts that are set in urban areas allows the selected writers to gesture for the possibility of a queer safe space in some African cities.

I argue that it is plausible to read Lamwaka's 'Pillar of Love' and Arac de Nyeko's 'Jambula Tree' as African creative texts that theorise African gay subjectivity and existence. While these short stories share several characteristics such as the fact that they are all women authored, are set in urban areas and star protagonists who are lesbian, it is their publication date – both are published between 2006 and 2014 – that supports the argument that they distil significant insights about Ugandan queer subjectivity. This is because of the significantly polarised sexuality debates in the country at the time. Here, we recall Amma Darko's argument in an interview with MaryEllen Higgins that if 'a country is going through a crisis, and people are writing around the time, they will be drawn to writing stories that would deal with those crises' ('Creating an Alternative Library': 115). In the above quotation, Darko is echoing Adebanwi's point that African writers are philosophers elucidating African issues. It can be argued that both Darko and Adebanwi underscore the writers' social responsibility, namely, the fact that they have to write about the crises affecting society. It could be argued that writing at this point of crisis regarding sexuality in the country, it is unsurprising that Arac de Nyeko and Lamwaka reflect on the essence and agency of gays in the country.

On the one hand, I argue that the two writers use fiction to engage in the debate around sexuality in their country at the given time. On the other hand, I argue that they use an urban setting – the city as a metaphor of cosmopolitanism, exposure and enlightenment – to unveil the city as a haven for queer sexual experimentation. This argument is aware of anecdotal response to the selected short stories and the work of these writers. It is claimed that these writers pander to Western (European and North American) prize-awarding institutions in choosing to write about homosexuality, in order to win prizes. This is because it is claimed that sexuality is not an existential problem facing the country or the continent such as HIV/AIDS, terrorism, poverty and war are. This criticism is given credence by the fact that Monica Arac de Nyeko won the Caine Prize for African Writing in 2007 and Beatrice Lamwaka was short listed for the same prize in 2010. In fact, this anecdotal argument is provided scholarly justification by Nwaubani's 'African Books for Western Eyes' and Okri's 'A Mental Tyranny is Keeping Black Writers from Greatness'. These scholars argue that internationally acclaimed African writers write either 'a literature of suffering or heaviness' (Okri: 1) or a literature that tells 'only the stories that foreigners allow [them] to tell' (Nwaubani: 1). Following Nwaubani's and Okri's criticism, it could be argued that this form of African writing – including Arac de Nyeko's and Lamwaka's – is mercenary. Granted, it might be true that writers like Arac de Nyeko and Lamwaka write to win literary prizes and/or for validation by Western critics. Unless writing about a topical issue like homosexuality amounts to being a sell-out or a prize-chasing writer, I argue that the selected writers also use their fiction to intervene in national debates about topical issues in a timely manner.

The view that Arac de Nyeko and Lamwaka intervene into sexuality debates for mercenary reasons is rejected by reviews of these texts. Admittedly, these important Ugandan artefacts have not attracted a lot of critical attention. Besides reviews, especially in American and British newspapers, Pumla Dineo Gqola's introduction in *Queer Africa: New and Collected Fiction* and B. Tonkin's comments during the 8th Caine Prize for African Writing, constitute a meagre critical archive on these important texts. Tonkin argues that 'Jambula Tree' is 'an earthquake, which shakes the moral foundations, because the shocking couple are two girls who love without shame' (Tonkin: 1-2). While Tonkin as a member of the panel that awarded Arac de Nyeko the 2007 Caine Prize for African Writing for 'Jambula Tree' is expected and is justified to describe the winning short story in such glowing terms, his praises are also appropriate, and equally applicable to Beatrice Lamwaka's 'Pillar of Love'. These are texts that tackle an important Ugandan socio-sexual issue. The texts' engagement with same-sex sexuality does not typify writing that seeks to satisfy a Western appetite for African horror stories, but rather interventions that seek to broaden the debates on such topics. I argue that in a country where there are efforts to criminalise this form of sexuality, these texts provide important understandings into the lifestyle.

Similarly, Pumla Dineo Gqola glowingly describes the work of the two writers in her introduction in *Queer Africa: New and Collected*

Fiction. About 'Jambula Tree', Gqola argues that the short story 'uses the gentlest, sexy and exquisite prose to speak about desire and growth' (6). She concludes that Arac de Nyeko's and Lamwaka's writings are a 'gift to all of us, whether we ever, always or sometimes call ourselves queer' (7). Gqola underlines two things about their writing. First, is the exquisite craftsmanship of the writing in both 'Jambula Tree' and 'Pillar of Love'. There are numerous textual markers in the two texts that attest to Gqola's characterisation of the short stories particularly, and the work of the two writers generally as wonderfully well written to articulate the subject of queer sexuality. Second, Gqola shows that the message of the short stories resonates with the reading public. I agree with her that, to a certain extent, the writing of the two writers is a gift to readers because of their sensitive and empathetic depiction of same-sex characters in the texts. Their writing resonates because they subtly reveal to the readers what it means to be lesbian in a homophobic country like Uganda.

This is possible because Arac de Nyeko and Lamwaka deploy setting as a subtly affective and nuanced register to distil their insights of homosexuality in the Ugandan public sphere. Here, I am reminded of Nussbaum's and Kruger's arguments about the role of literature in creating awareness about peripheral subjects (*Poetic Justice* and *Women's Literature in Kenya and Uganda* respectively). While Nussbaum asserts that 'the central role of the arts in human self-understanding [is to] give us information about those emotion-histories that we could not easily get otherwise', (236) Kruger claims that fiction functions as 'a medium of social change' (2). Both Nussbaum and Kruger underscore the importance of fiction in not only creating awareness about an issue or subject, but also its role in enacting platforms and congregating publics to interrogate topical issues in a society. I apply Nussbaum's and Kruger's notion that literature creates a space to debate important issues to the selected short stories to ask: how does the urban setting that these short stories share create a realistic portrait of a Ugandan homosexual? A version of an answer to this question recalls Nussbaum's argument that the role of fiction in public judgement involves helping the public to imagine 'the situation of someone different from [themselves]' (xiv). The core point in Nussbaum's quotation above is the idea that fiction helps the public to appreciate what it means, for example, to be a lesbian in Uganda. This is largely because of fiction's ability to provide an aptly empathetic snapshot of this subjectivity.

Arguing that fiction offers vivid snapshots into topical issues of society at a given moment, I examine how Beatrice Lamwaka's 'Pillar of Love' and Monica Arac de Nyeko's 'Jambula Tree' use an urban setting as a site of safe sexual experimentation. This reading gestures to the work of Achille Mbembe and Sarah Nuttall, Diane Janis Stout, Niall McNulty, Richard Lehan, and Yoshinobu Hakutani and Robert Butler on the importance of the city in distilling important societal issues. These scholars variously argue that the city is a metaphor of 'deliverance', (Hakutani and Butler *The City in African-American Literature*: 9) 'a source of intellectual excitement' (Lehan *The City in Literature*: 3) or 'disease of the social body … a cesspool of vice' (Mbembe and Nuttall 'Writing the World from an African Metropolis': 353-4). The collocation of the views of diverse scholars about the image of the city in fiction underlines two perceptions. First, the pessimistic vision of the city as articulated in the works of Mbembe, Nuttall and Lehan. These authors perceive the city as a source of evil and its impact on the characters as negative. Second, are those authors who read the city optimistically. For example, Stout, and Hakutani and Butler argue that the city is a site of modernity, enlightenment and transformation.

It should be noted that both visions of the city – the pessimistic and the optimistic – can be mobilised in the reading of 'Jambula Tree' and 'Pillar of Love' in the Ugandan contemporary discourses on sexuality. On the one hand, a group of Ugandans who passionately believe that homosexuality is a sin and a foreign cultural practice posing an existential threat to Ugandan children and society will read the city as a space where gays can exist as a diseased space or a 'cesspool of vice', to quote Mbembe and Nuttall. The city for them is a place where deviant sexual practices can exist to disrupt or destroy the African traditional way of life. On the other hand, campaigners for the equal rights for gays to engage in the sexual preference of their choice might read the city optimistically, namely, as a place of change, or in the words of Stout 'as an arena of opportunity … material change and cultural advantage' (*Sodomy in Eden*: 1).

In what follows, I argue that in Ugandan sexuality debates generally and in the setting of the selected short stories that feature homosexual characters particularly, the city is a site of progressive representation of queer sexuality or in the words of James Weldon, 'a tempting world of greatly lessened restraints, a world of fascinating perils, but above all, a world of tremendous artistic potentialities' (quoted in Lehan: 10). I take Weldon's concepts of 'lessened restraints' and 'tremendous artistic potentialities' to argue that an urban setting provides the writers with artistic potential to ingeniously talk about a taboo topic and depict their protagonists with lenses of 'lessened restraints' in order to explore their sexuality as depicted in 'Jambula Tree' and a 'Pillar of Love'. The urban setting of these two Ugandan short stories construct the city as haven for lesbian sexual experimentation.

THE CITY AND ADOLESCENT SEXUAL EXPERIMENTATIONS

Monica Arac de Nyeko's 'Jambula Tree' (henceforth JT) has a recognisably urban setting and traces the sexual exploration of two adolescent girls from poor urban families. The short story is structured around Anyango's letter to Sanyu on the eve of the latter's return, years after their sexuality was discovered by Mama Atim, and the two girls were forcibly exiled from the estate. The letter oscillates between first person recollections and an omniscient commentary on the discovery of the protagonists' sexual exploration, cryptically named by Anyango as their 'shame' (JT: 9). The layered nature of Arac's narrative, signalled by her invocation of the Adam/Eve and the Garden of Eden motif complicates the simple polarities associated with this subject in the Ugandan public sphere. This is because the 'exquisitely written' text (Karen and Makhosazana (*Queer Africa*: vi) mirrors a pristinely idyllic attraction between two adolescent girls that is portrayed as an innocent exploration of sexuality. Arac de Nyeko uses an urban setting – Nakawa Housing Estates in a Kampala suburb – to depict how the city is a safe site for sexual experimentation.

It should be noted that the housing estate in which the short story is set, before its demolition to pave way for a satellite city, was a melting pot of Ugandan tribes/cultures. This character of the estate perhaps explains why it exhibited a sense of cosmopolitan freedom and creativity. This is attested to by the fact that many of Uganda's best footballers, musicians and boxers have their roots in this estate. The artists' and sportsmen's success speaks to the estate as a site imbued with the spirit and courage to try the impossible I argue that Arac de Nyeko underlines the same spirit in her depiction of protagonists who are emboldened to experiment with a forbidden sexuality. I read the text as gesturing to a spatial license to dream and break barriers regarding sexual orientation, and I argue that the urban setting of the short story explains why the protagonists explore an alternative sexual orientation to heterosexuality.

Relatedly, it can also be argued that Arac de Nyeko's setting foregrounds the depressing conditions that patriarchy and heterosexuality subject women to in the Nakawa Housing Estates perhaps to explain the protagonists' experimentation with same-sex sexuality. Arac de Nyeko deploys the Judeo-Christian trope of the Garden of Eden to provide a convincing rendition of adolescent sexual exploration. Like Eve who discovers her free will in the Garden of Eden, the girls discover their true sexual orientation in the city and under the jambula tree. The connection between an urban setting and sexual experimentation is gestured by several passages. First is Anyango's recollection that 'Nakawa Estates has never changed. Mr Wangolo our SST teacher once said those houses were just planned slums, with people with broken dreams and unplanned families' (JT: 164). Second, Anyango's paraphrase of Maama Atim's gossip about Sanyu's pending return: 'She says you refuse to live in those areas on the bigger hills and terraced roads in Kololo. You are coming to us and to Nakawa Housing Estate' (JT167). The above passages underline the depressingly deplorable conditions of the estate. First, is Mr Wangolo's declaration that the estate was a planned slum housing people with broken dreams. Second, is Maama Atim's comparison of Nakawa Housing Estate to more affluent suburbs of Kampala such as Kololo and Muyenga. The incredulous tone of the passages seems to suggest that, by the standards of the estate, Sanyu, who has been to London and is a daughter of a rich man, should not return to Nakawa Housing Estate.

The depressing and deplorable conditions of the estate, especially for women hinted at above reminds us of the Anyango-Sanyu vow – that they 'could be anything' (JT: 165) – a rejection of not only what they are at the time, but also what they are likely to be, given their environment. If one were to argue that the pact is a rejection of the status quo and the trajectory of a future it portends, then, it can be argued that the protagonists' observation of the conditions of the female folk of the estate perhaps explains their rejection of such a lifestyle. Here, we are reminded of the passage, 'those women know every love charm by heart and every juju man's shrines because they need to conjure up their husband's love and penises from drinking places with smoking pipes' (JT: 165). It is this pitiable image of women reduced to zombies by poverty and patriarchy that leads to the girls' resolve: 'that's what we fought against when we walked to school each day ... running away from Nakawa Housing Estate's drifting tide which threatened to engulf us and turn us into noisy gossiping and frightening housewives' (165). The sense of rejection and abandonment that the image of running away from Nakawa Estate implies can be read to suggest and/or imply their rejection of heterosexuality.

While the deplorable conditions of women in Nakawa Housing Estate can be read as a critique of patriarchy's oppression and exploitation of women, I argue that the passages offer themselves to alternative interpretations. One such reading of the pathetic dependence of women on men, is the girls' desire to regain their agency and personhood. If agency and personhood are scripted in terms of choice, then, the protagonists' sexual activity is simultaneously a choice of a sexual orientation and a protest against another, in the framework of the short story, arguably heterosexuality that objectifies and dehumanises women. Their agency and choice/rejection framework in the text is perhaps underlined by the girls' dreams of leaving the estate. While Anyango dreams of becoming a nurse (this is what she has become), Sanyu wants to be anything else other than what her father wants her to be – 'an engineer making building plans: for his mansion, for his office, for his railway to village' (JT: 165). Having rejected the version of femininity that urban poverty and heterosexual patriarchy produces in Nakawa Housing Estate, it is inevitable that the girls are also likely to experiment with or search for a more fulfilling sexual practice, ethic and existence.

The reading of the city as a site of simultaneous rejection and choice of a sexual practice recalls James Weldon's paraphrase of W.E.B. Du Bois that 'the setting for black liberation will be in the city' (quoted in Lehan: 10). It is true that Du Bois is concerned with the metaphorical importance of the city in African-American writing and struggle for emancipation. It is also true that the condition of African-American subjects that Du Bois writes about is fundamentally different from that of Ugandan women in urban centres. However, the oppressive patriarchy and heteronormativity are threads that connect the two diverse forms of suffering. Therefore, Weldon's claim is applicable to 'Jambula Tree' because of its privileging of a sexual choice and experimentation. This is because their dreams are not only anti-establishment visions but are more a rejection of also a patriarchal/heterosexual ethic. This, I argue, explains why they choose to explore and experiment with lesbianism, given that queer sexuality generally, and lesbianism specifically, are quintessentially anti-patriarchy and anti-heteronormativity.

THE CITY AND FORBIDDEN MARRIAGES

While in the above section I read the connection between the city and same-sex sexuality as a safe site of experimentation and choice of a sexual practice, in this section I posit that the city is also a site of possible performance of queer marital bliss. Beatrice Lamwaka's 'Pillar of Love' (henceforth PL) uses an urban setting not only to problematise the trials and tribulations of living as a lesbian in the Ugandan society characterised with homophobia, but also to show the possibility, albeit in fiction, of queer marital bliss. Her setting is implicitly urban – there are various textual markers that gesture to an urban setting – because her protagonists are obviously middle-class characters in a Ugandan corporate-artistic context. If Lamwaka's literary intervention in 'Pillar of Love' is to show the city as a space of possibilities and choices of sexual orientation, then, her settings (spatial and class) cohere brilliantly with her motif of the love triangle to distil important truths about Ugandan queer sexual realities. On the one hand, the love triangle – Lala-Grace-Kaya – underlines the dilemma and challenges that are a lived reality in any love relationship. On the other hand, it also implicitly suggests the need to choose. For example, the plot of the short story is structured to suggest that Lala is expected to choose between Grace and Kaya.

The conflict of the story is anchored on Lala's dilemma over whether to stay in her secret marriage to Grace or start a new love affair with the attractive man – Kaya. I argue that this is a conflict that is possible in an urban setting, since it contests the idea that marriage can only occur between a man and a woman.[2] This reminds us of Karen Martin and Xaba Makhosazana's observation about Lamwaka's 'unafraid stories of intimacy, sweat, betrayal and restlessness' (vi), here underscoring the humanness of stories like 'Pillar of Love' because they spotlight the messiness of life and love. This is an apt description of 'Pillar of Love' because the conflict of the short story underlines courage, intimacy, betrayal and restlessness in search for an ideal love. While betrayal and restlessness are signposted by the relational differences, unhappiness and challenges that Grace and Lala face – these are obviously taking a toll on their secret marriage – courage and intimacy are revealed in how Grace and Lala work through their issues as a couple. This is because the short story concludes with a reconciliation between the lovers that begs the question whether they will continue living in the closet or will make their marriage public?[3] Granted, the story of conflicted love and a secret marriage is open to a multiplicity of interpretations. On the one hand, Lala's anxiety to lead a normal life with a husband and children speaks to the insidious impact of heteronormativity on the Ugandan society. Read from this perspective, 'Pillar of Love' can be mobilised to ostracise same-sex relationships. However, the short story also paints a vision of possibility and/or choice of same-sex practices by some people Therefore, it can be argued that the text's contribution to Ugandan sexuality debates is its fictionalisation of the possibility or choice of a non-heterosexual orientation.

The city as a site where subjects can choose sexual practices reminds us of Niall McNulty's argument that '[p]lace influences literary production. Likewise, literature constructs place and our perceptions of it' (*Reading the City*: 10). Here, McNulty underscores the symbiotic relationship between creativity, subject matter and literary context. In respect to 'Pillar of Love', I agree with McNulty that the text's setting influences its content. Although the setting of the short story is not explicitly stated as urban, there are several textual markers that identity the spatiality of the short story as urban and middle class. A case in point is the opening passage: 'a bouquet of sunflowers arrives at Lala's door as she parks her Rav 4' (PL: 183). A few lines later the omniscient narrator reports that Lala 'runs to the house and heads straight to the spare bedroom' (183). However, the most explicit clue lies in the sentence: 'the last time they went to Serena Hotel for dinner was six months ago' (187). The three passages above underline the setting of the short story as urban. For example, a 'bouquet of flowers' and 'Rav 4' in the first passage are textual markers for an urban and/or middle-class lifestyle in the Ugandan context. It is middle class and urban dwellers who express affection by giving and receiving flowers. Similarly, it is the rich and city residents who drive expensive cars.[4]

The same argument can be made regarding the second and third passage. Serena Hotel is in Kampala's city centre – a fact that confirms the urban setting of the short story – and it is the rich urban dwellers that have the resources and who live near the city that dine at a five-star hotel. Similarly, it is in urban areas that households would have a spare room. The attributes of the city residents such as affluence (they buy flowers and have dinner at five-star hotels) suggest agency, possibility and choice. It can be argued that Lamwaka's depiction of women who have sex with women and those who choose to get married to other women allegorises the city as a space of possibilities. Thus, I argue that the city is a site of various opportunities, possibilities and choices – including same-sex marriages. Lamwaka deploys an urban setting to offer an ideal future scenario where people choose who to marry and what sexual orientation to practise, in spite of the sense of surveillance often associated with urban spaces.

The city as a site of possibility and choice is gestured to by the following passages. Lala reflects that 'the two year she had been living with Grace have clouded her dreams of children' (PL: 184). In another passage, she confesses that she 'hasn't received flowers from Grace in a year' (183). Later in the text she relates that they had been best friends in high school and that they had 'spent nights in Grace's bed in their family home, with nobody suspicious of anything' (PL 186). Although the above passages do not explicitly reference an urban setting, its gesture to the longevity of Grace and Lala's love relationship perhaps suggests that its longevity is made possible because of the city setting. This brings to mind Yoshinobu Hakutani's and Robert Butler's comments about W.E.B. Du Bois's thoughts about the city. They argue that for Du Bois the city 'greatly expanded possibilities for development' (9). Although the above passage is specific to the African-American condition in the 1920s and their relation to white patriarchal privilege, its key message can apply to 'Pillar of Love', especially, Hakutani's and Butler's argument that Du Bois perceived the city as a site of 'expanded possibilities'. If we read this to mean that the city opened opportunities to the African-American that rural United States of America had denied him/her, the same argument can be made about the Grace-Lala relationship and the city. Lamwaka uses the city to show the possibility of lesbian relationship existing alongside heterosexual ones. I argue that the possibilities and choice that the city imbues is the reason that Lala and Grace are able to maintain their relationship without interference from family and society.

CONCLUSION

In conclusion, we recall Achille Mbembe's and Sarah Nuttall's argument that 'to a larger extent, to write is to bring to the surface something that is not yet there or that is there only as latent, as potential' (348). The essence of Mbembe's and Nuttall's argument is the productive power of writing. In their postulation, writing has the power of bringing forward a reality that is hard to imagine. This can be applied to Arac de Nyeko and Lamwaka if one were to argue that in their respective short stories they bring to light the connection between the city and same-sex sexuality. This is because their short stories depict the city as a space of possibilities, choices and experimentation. This is highlighted by the fact that while Anyango and Sanyu thrive in the neighbourhoods of Nakawa, Mengo and London, Lala and Grace flourish as a married couple because of their middle class and urban status.

The two writers' vision of queerness as a possibility, choice and experimentation augmented by the city recalls Stuart Kellog's argument that 'fiction is much more than a plot. It is often an unwitting account of appetite, dress, weaponry, etc.; it is always a record of the author's intentions and prejudices' (*Literary Vision of Homosexuality*: 1). In a way, Kellog is rearticulating Mbembe's and Nuttall's contention that writing creates reality. Regarding the work of Arac de Nyeko and Lamwaka, the reality that their texts create is not only the possibility to choose and experiment with queerness, but also their location of this possibility in the urban centre. The beautiful prose, that Gqola has called exquisite, used to describe the allegedly forbidden love-making between Anyango and Sanyu as well as their fidelity to each other – despite factors of societal pressure, stigma and time – highlights this choice and experiment. The same applies to Lala and Grace in 'Pillar of Love'. In this text, Lamwaka deploys intertextuality – especially the love songs and poems and telepathic connection between the protagonists to show a choice of a deep love.

NOTES

1 Acknowledgements: to CAPREx, Makerere-Cambridge Africa Postdoc Fellowship and Albarola Trust for the initial research funding and the Makerere-Sida Postdoc Fellowship funding that made the research/data collection and writing of this article possible.
2 It should be noted that the Ugandan Constitution (1995) as amended and the Penal Code (2007) as amended outlaw same-sex marriages. Marriage is defined as a union between a man and a woman. It is the privileging of the heterosexual marriage that acts as one of the strongest arguments presented for the danger of homosexuality to Ugandan society. This is succinctly underlined in the preamble to the (later withdrawn) Anti-Homosexuality Act of 2014.
3 Given that even in fictional rendition lesbian marriage is closeted, it is perhaps through cunning that queerness can be practised. This underlines the paradox inherent in Ugandan queer discourses, namely the absence/presence of the practice. While society disregards its existence, it is performed sneakily in the open exemplified by the case of Lala's and Grace's parents, who believe that each girl is a good friend to the other because they easily fulfil the ethnic/tribal parameters of a good daughter. Unknown to them is the friends' sexual/marital status.
4 This argument is plausible because an average Ugandan living in the rural areas lives on less than one United States dollar a day, according to the latest World Bank and International Monetary Fund statistics, so owning a used Japanese car (RAV4) is difficult to imagine. This class marker places

Grace and Lala in the middle class, a class whose education and exposure empowers its members to claim agency including choosing a sexual orientation.

WORKS CITED

Adebanwi, Wale. 'The Writer as Social Thinker'. *Journal of Contemporary African Studies* Vol. 32, No. 4 (2014): 405-20.
Arac de Nyeko, Monica. 'Jambula Tree'. In *African Love Stories: An Anthology*, ed. Ama Ata Aidoo. Cape Town: Ayebia Clarke, 2006.
Government of Uganda. *Constitution of the Republic of Uganda*. Kampala: Government of Uganda, 2005 [1995].
——*Penal Code (Amendment Act)*. Kampala: Government of Uganda, 2007.
——*Anti-Homosexuality Act*. Kampala: Government of Uganda, 2014.
Gqola, Pumla Dineo. 'Introduction'. *Queer Africa: New and Collected Fiction*. Bramfortein: Ma Thoko's Books, 2013:1-9.
Hakutani, Yoshinobu and Robert Butler. *The City in African-American Literature*. Madison: Fairleigh Dickinson University Press, 1995.
Higgins, MaryEllen (Ellie). 'Creating an Alternative Library: Amma Darko interviewed by Ellie Higgins'. *The Journal of Commonwealth Literature* Vol. 39, No. 4 (2004): 111-20.
Kellog, Stuart. *Literary Vision of Homosexuality*. New York: The Haworth Press, 1983.
Kruger, M. *Women's Literature in Kenya and Uganda: The Trouble with Modernity*. Basingstoke, UK: Palgrave Macmillan, 2011.
Lamwaka, Beatrice. 'Pillar of Love'. *African Violet and Other Stories*. Sunnyside, SA: Jacana Media, 2012.
Lehan, Richard. *The City in Literature: An Intellectual and Cultural History*. Los Angeles: University of California Press, 1998.
Makumbi, Jennifer Nansubuga. *Kintu*. Nairobi: Kwani Trust, 2014.
Martin, Karen and Xaba Makhosazana. 'Preface'. In *Queer Africa: New and Collected Fiction*, eds Karen Martin and Makhosazana Xaba. Braamfontein: Ma Thoko's Books, 2013: i-ix.
Mbembe, Achille and Sarah Nuttall. 'Writing the World from an African Metropolis'. *Public Culture* Vol. 16, No. 3 (2004): 347-72.
McNulty, Niall. *Reading the City: Analysing Literary Space in Selected Postapartheid Urban Narratives*. MA Thesis University of KwaZulu-Natal, 2005. http://researchspace.ukzn.ac.za/bitstream/handle/10413/3800/McNulty_Niall_2005.pdf (accessed 7 March 2018).
Nakisanze, Segawa. *The Triangle*. Kampala: Mattville Publishing House, 2016.
Nussbaum, Martha. *Poetic Justice: The Literary Imagination and Public Life*. Boston, MA: Beacon Press, 1995.
Nwaubani, Adaobi Tricia. 'African Books for Western Eyes'. *New York Times*,

28 November 2014. www.nytimes.com/2014/11/30/opinion/sunday/african-books-for-western-eyes.html (accessed 7 March 2018).

Nyanzi, Stella. 'Queering Queer Africa'. In *Reclaiming Afrikan· Queer Perspectives on Sexual and Gender Identities*, ed. Zethu Matabeni. Athlone, SA: Modjaji Books, 2014, 61-6.

Okri, Ben. 'A Mental Tyranny is Keeping Black Writers from Greatness'. *The Guardian*, 27 December 2014. www.theguardian.com/commentisfree/2014/dec/27/mental-tyranny-black-writers (accessed 7 March 2018).

Stout, Janis Diane Pitts. *Sodomy in Eden: The City in American Fiction before 1860*. PhD Thesis. Rice University, 1973.

Tamale, Sylvia. 'Introduction'. In *African Sexuality: A Reader*. Cape Town: Pambazuka, 2011.

Tonkin, Boyd. *Jambula Tree and Other Short Stories*. The Caine Prize for African Writing 8th Annual Collection. London: New Internationalist, 2008.

Homosexuality & the Postcolonial Idea

Notes from Kabelo Sello Duiker's
The Quiet Violence of Dreams

IVES S. LOUKSON

INTRODUCTION

Despite its significant contribution towards the transition from apartheid to democracy in South Africa, it is clear nowadays that the Truth and Reconciliation Commission was not faultless. When *The Aversion Project* states that reconciliation and healing could not occur in the 'absence of knowledge and understanding' (Van Zyl et al.: 11), it implies that democracy in South Africa is built over troubling misunderstandings. Kabelo Sello Duiker's *The Quiet Violence of Dreams* (2001) depicts homosexuality as a privileged symbolic field that translates these misunderstandings. Though enshrined in the 1996 South African Constitution, perceptions of homosexuality are never freed from moral disgust or aversion. In this relation, centring the narrative on homosexuality takes this issue in a similar direction to that of postcolonial theory as portrayed by scholars who assert its 'subversive strategies' (Ashcroft et al. 1989: 33). The paper illustrates how homosexuality in *The Quiet Violence of Dreams* appears like the semiotic realisation's ground of the postcolonial ideal.

HOMOSEXUALITY IN *THE QUIET VIOLENCE OF DREAMS*

Moura ('La Critique Postcoloniale, Étude des Spécificités': 18) and Moudileno ('Littérature et Postcolonie': 9) insist that any postcolonial reading needs to always come back to the literary text. Consequently, this section aims to highlight what *The Quiet Violence of Dreams* is all about, before homosexuality is discussed as the central topic of the narrative. When they came to Cape Town from Johannesburg to study, protagonists Mmabatho and Tshepo believed they could make it in the post-apartheid town. Mmabatho is unwillingly transformed into a heterosexual and lesbian whore because all her black and white male partners deceive her. On his part, Tshepo misses four months of studies at Rhodes University because of psychiatric troubles. After recovery, he looks for jobs in vain. He finally finds a work as masseur at Steamy Windows, a homosexual shop. His profession labels him as 'Angelo'. Tshepo (Angelo) is found back in Johannesburg at the novel's end, where he takes care of street children in an orphanage.

The focus of the narrative on Angelo-Tshepo makes him play an explicit function in relation to Duiker's commitment in the narrative. Tshepo acts like a pretext his designer uses in order to undertake a deep introspection about post-apartheid South Africa,

> Too much has been said about my condition, my illness, whatever it is ... I'm sick of the endless explanations that come with it, the lies and cover ups, the injustice and humiliation of it all. The indifferent nurses that only communicate through prescriptions. Heavy prescriptions that dull your senses and seem to drain life force out of you ... What does 'cannabis induced psychosis mean'? There is more to it than that. This is what the medical profession will never understand. I'm looking for a deeper understanding of what happened to me,[1] not an easy answer like cannabis induced psychosis. And why don't they just say it if they truly don't understand what happened? Why blame it on cannabis? (9-10)

One thing to take note of is that Duiker employs Tshepo as a light, using him to illuminate the 'dark' or hidden places found in post-apartheid South Africa. The characters he mixes up with always carry evil traits. Written from the perspective of Angelo-Tshepo, the narrative compels the reader to perceive it as an attempt to voice what Ndebele calls 'the anonymity to which the oppressive system consigns millions of oppressed Africans' (*Rediscovery of the Ordinary*: 15).

The narrative finally appears as a radical attempt to record psychological consequences of the apartheid system in post-apartheid South Africa. The fact that Ayi Kwei Armah's fiction, *The Beautyful Ones Are Not Yet Born*, is Tshepo's favourite novel (177) clearly shows that *The Quiet Violence of Dreams* displays Duiker's resistance against the democratic South Africa because it continues to legitimate injustices. The narrative's agency could be summarised by the 'unconsciousness', in the sense Freud identified it; that is, in Lacan's words, 'the passion of knowledge and freedom' (Lacan *Le Séminaire*: Éthique de la Psychanalyse: 374). Steamy Windows appears to Tshepo as the place for the materialisation of this 'unconsciousness'.

At Steamy Windows, Tshepo disappears beneath 'Angelo'. His colleagues are Storm, Samuel, West, Carrington, Francois, Adrian, Cole and Sebastian. Shaun is their boss to whom they pay 90 Rand daily for studio fees. Tshepo performs sex with white male and white female clients; assigning his character to such a job enables Duiker to disclose the social class of clients involved in homosexuality. The clients are generally very rich people from South Africa or from abroad:

> bankers, businessmen, lawyers, stockbrokers, analysts, chartered accountants, pharmacists, engineers, doctors, surgeons, architects, editors, journalists, writers, poets, artists, academics – generally people with serious education, money and influence. (299)

Almost half of the narrative is concerned with disclosing what happens indoors at Steamy Windows. Terms common to gays' customs are well elaborated in the narrative. Names like Oscar Wilde, James Baldwin, Martina Navratilova, George Michael, David Geffen, Michelangelo, Alexander the Great and da Vinci are mentioned as ancestors of workers at Steamy Windows (253). Terms like 'blow job', 'Gay SA Magazine', 'big cocks', 'KY jelly', and 'wank'[2] are used many times by characters. This is evident testimony of the lexicological fieldwork on homosexual practices carried out by the writer.

At one point, though, Tshepo remarks, 'No thanks. This is just a stopover job. Who knows maybe I'll pursue journalism after all' (277). Duiker's portrayal of his character shows that homosexual behaviour can have social origins. Similarly, poverty and unemployment – portrayed by Phaswane Mpe as an excuse for the animosity black South Africans reserve for '*makwerekwere*'[3] (Mpe 2011: 122) – are core reasons that compel South Africans to homosexuality. Tshepo's feelings when he goes back to Johannesburg confirm that he is not just a simple character, but he is more of a tool that the writer uses to deeply mediate or address homosexuality: 'In Jo'burg everyone knows me as Tshepo. I left Angelo behind in Cape Town, still roaming its streets and exploring the underworld. I don't think I will go back there for a while. I have too many wounds that need to heal' (452).

PERCEPTIONS OF HOMOSEXUALITY IN *THE QUIET VIOLENCE OF DREAMS*

As a central topic of the novel, each character is given the occasion to display their own perception about homosexuality. *The Quiet Violence of Dreams* displays divergent mind-sets which give homosexuality its dominant nature in the narrative. Homosexuals are labelled as '*moffies*' and 'faggots' by many black South Africans. In *The Aversion Project*, *moffie* is an Afrikaans term that translates disgust felt towards a homosexual (Van Zyl et al.: 51). By calling homosexuals *moffies*, these black South Africans see themselves as pure while rejecting homosexuals as dangerous deviants. In so doing, Duiker's character observes, they fail to acknowledge that:

> The first universal human beings were born of three sexes from the Sun, Earth and Moon. There were men, women, and hermaphrodites, each of the three sexes doubled over and united as a whole. At some point in the unknowable past they were brutally cleaved in two, doomed to go through history suffering the violence and anguish of separation, constantly longing to be reunited with the lost half of the self, the better self. Being cut in half resulted in the forms of heterosexuality from the hermaphrodites and homosexuality in both female and male forms, the amnesia of the brutal separation mutating into bisexuality in others. And since then, we have all suffered the same fate. That is why some of us are what we are. That is why we are called moffies and faggots. Perhaps we took secret oaths with ourselves before we got separated, so that we would stubbornly remember that we were incomplete, the clue being that it is someone of our own sex. Perhaps we are the coarse self searching for the refined self, or vice versa. (380)

Further, when Tshepo monologues with his dead mother he tells her how his evil father let him look for himself in 'a world of vampires' (379). Associating Steamy Windows with a world of vampires echoes the way many people perceive homosexuality. Devotees of the famous 'aversion therapy' would simply say that homosexuals are sick patients that need potent treatment for conversion to heterosexuality (Van Zyl et al.: 80-82).

Many Afrikaners believe that the origins of homosexuality are to be found in what Dorrit Cohn terms 'the inner life' of the human being. This particular level of human life is hidden under the deep darkness of human flesh and blood (Cohn *La Transparence Intérieure*: 15). Homosexuality appears in this relation as some natural disposition that surfaces from the lacks, or the troubles, that the *moffies* practising it experienced in their earlier existence. A good example is the character West, whose father divorced his mother when West was still a little boy. This father yoked him to homosexuals who taught West

> to dress properly, to use roll-on instead of tones of cologne and nothing under the armpits ... to hold a magnum of champagne properly, to serve wine, to carve duck, to eat a lobster, to be a considerate guest, to jumpstart a car, to introduce [one]self with a firm but gentle handshake. (295).

West believes further that homosexuality makes him understand that any psychologically traumatised person is permanently vulnerable till they find some attention from others. For desperate persons like him, Steamy Windows offered a chance to avoid self-destruction,

> Perhaps me landing up in Steamy Windows was life saving me from self-destruction. I was going nowhere. I was drinking. I was clueless. I'd like to think that I'm a different person now that I've grown up a bit. Certainly, my worldview is wider. Life has many possibilities. We will never run out of options, of different ways of being, living, surviving. (297)

From West's point of view, homosexuality is a strategy for survival.

Representative of poor black South Africans in the narrative, Tshepo portrays homosexuality as a wonderful opportunity to make money, 'Ja, I'm keen. I can do this, I say, excitement welling up at the prospective [sic] of all the money I can make' (206). Tshepo's reaction here is evidence of the fact that, it is the lack of money that compels him to homosexuality. His expectation with homosexuality is to save as much money as he can, so that he can pay his University fees, study and become 'a someone' (270) like few black people he sees in society.

Some of the clients come to Steamy Windows because their spouses or husbands starve them sexually. Shaun is profoundly aware of this situation, advising Tshepo to bathe the client himself, to treat him/her really nicely, talk to him/her, and make the client feel special if he wants to make real money (236). Trying to understand why such important personalities come to Steamy Windows, West posits that, 'I think they come here because they know they will be appreciated, held in esteem. At home I imagine they are unhappy with their wives. They don't seem to understand what they really want, or if they do it is of no interest to them. This is what I see when I look at these men' (293).

In relation to female clients that come to Steamy Windows, West voices their perception of gays as genuine stallions who can satisfy their sexual needs the way they expect. West puts it as follows: 'They usually want a genuine escort to take them somewhere nice while their rich husbands are overseas on business or they are in desperate need of a fuck [or because] a cruel husband cheats them or starves them sexually' (293).

Even though West speaks on behalf of their clients, homosexuality at Steamy Windows appears like a kind of dustbin that retains all the odd deeds or mistakes derived from frustrations and starvations faced by individuals in their daily lives. Steamy Windows is an essential resting place where the worried or the computerised psyche finds instantaneous relaxation. This is the reason why Duiker views homosexuality as a very serious issue from which a better future is possible. He puts this in West's mouth as follows:

> What we do, it is very serious, you know. We are not just fucking these men for money. That is what I wanted to tell you. We are doing important work here. You will see that. They are showing us things, telling us things for the times ahead. (244)

West's observation about 'the times ahead' confirms that the democratic South Africa has failed to overcome rampant and repeated injustices; this failure demands new forms of resistance. The status quo about injustices suggests that instead of a radical transformation, it is a monolithic and revisionist approach that was implemented in South Africa during the transition from apartheid to democracy. The aversion therapy implemented on homosexuals for instance during this transition, ascertains the existence of a fixity that regulated the mindsets of people when dealing with homosexuality. Unable to profitably take part in the 'semiological revolution' David Herman talks about (*Logic*: 119), they fail to make good use of the various possibilities any denomination, any situation or any labels always offer. Failing to do so, Édouard Glissant sees engaging South Africans in the process of 'shocking coagulations of the being'[4] as the very psychological ground that fuels intolerance towards others (*Le Traité du Tout-monde*: 25).

As a consequence, these South Africans become effortlessly recruitable by any kind of fundamentalist ideology from local or global streams, the manifestations of which are as varied as terrorism, puritanism and extremism, just to name a few. Edward Said's *Culture and Imperialism* suggests seminal strategies to resist and challenge this intolerant mainstream which led humanity in many years of genocides, slavery and colonisation. Said suggests that the semiological revolution Herman talks about needs to settle and flourish on labels like identity, woman, nature or culture. Only this condition, Said strongly believes, will enable people that vehemently abhor gay or lesbian people like Tshepo and Mmabatho, to realise that:

> No one today is purely one thing. Labels like Indian, or woman, or Muslim, or American are not more than starting-points, which if followed into actual experience for only a moment are quickly left behind. Imperialism consolidated the mixture of cultures and identities on a global scale. (336)

From the above it appears that homosexuality is used by characters as a means either to mediate for their self-realisation or to articulate the dominant self – they work for its materialisation. The reader realises finally that Duiker succeeds in shaping homosexuality as a symbolic soil that unites very diverse and even conflicting beliefs, feelings and ideologies. The skilled reader also realises that Duiker sews homosexuality in such a way that the 'dominant self' that fosters imperialism is unveiled as the linear logic that kills the diversity that homosexuality promotes. Before dealing with characteristics of this 'dominant self' I would like to address how South Africa corresponds to the present global world. It guarantees a wider contextualisation of the issues at stake.

FICTIONAL POST-APARTHEID SOUTH AFRICA AS A MICROCOSM OF THE PRESENT GLOBALISED WORLD

In *Critiques et Vérité* Roland Barthes maintains that the writer of fiction deserves to be seen as a thinker, because to write a work of fiction is already to organise the world (*Critiques et Vérité*: 33). Barthes' position in relation to writing gives way to very diverse models of reading, on condition that the models used bring out the world organised by the writer. The actual globalised and neo-liberal world is made visible through the fictional post-apartheid South Africa displayed in the narrative. Situated in the postmodern era, the actual globalised world is characterised by telecommunications, a world market, numerically and digitally controlled tools, and aesthetically intensified marketing tactics. It includes core characteristics of neo-liberalism like market, instantaneity and velocity in goods' circulation. According to Philip Wexler, all these postmodern elements validate the idea of the present world as being typified by dedifferentiation, blurring of boundaries and the disintegration of separate domains ('Citizenship in the Semiotic Society': 168).

In the novel, the diversity of people working towards the prosperity of Steamy Windows is a suitable setting to consider as a microcosm of the contemporary marketing constellation. One can conclude that in the homosexual industry at Steamy Windows, not only skin but also national boundaries are blurred. Blacks and whites work in Steamy Windows together, and customers come from all over the world. Tshepo makes it clear to Mhabatho, who suspects him of being a racist:

> I work with a guy from Senegal ... I mean just because the Germans and French and all the other white nationalities that come here blend into the background I don't hear you saying anything about them. There's an influx of people from ex-Eastern Bloc countries to Cape Town. A lot of Russians and Czechs. (263)

Workers at Steamy Windows are labelled in such a way that they attract as many clients as possible. West, for example, is labelled as 'Kalahari West, dark hair, blue eyes, rugged marine looks, 1,75 m, 85kg, 8 inches uncut' (292). Workers are packaged as goods whose utility depends not on them, but on their various clients. When for example it is said about Sebastian that 'a client booked him' (270), he has lost his status as a human being and become a marketable object for the sexual relief of Steamy Windows' customers.

Duiker succeeds in demonstrating in his narrative how neo-liberalism, despite Foucault's assertion of homosexuality as a resistance strategy against capitalism, in fact integrates homosexuality to its advantage. In its quest to forbid homosexual intercourse Foucault argues in *Histoire de la Sexualité* that capitalism shuns homosexuality as a great nuisance against the perpetuation of those exploitations of the body which nourish capitalism (*Histoire de la Sexualité*: 12-13). Duiker's contribution to the debate about homosexuality is reasonably suspicious of Foucault's influential theories on homosexual culture that fail to resist capitalism (Said *L'Orientalisme*: 8). Duiker goes more far as Foucault, by displaying homosexuality in his narrative as a topos that enables the reader to glimpse the compatibilities between imperialism and capitalism never addressed by Foucault. Duiker also succeeds in pointing out accurate operations of the 'dominant self' which fosters apartheid (imperialism) in those days and produces forged diversity nowadays through multiplication of hypothetical new identities.

The few examples above would argue that the fictional South Africa displayed in *The Quiet Violence of Dreams* is a credible reproduction of the actual postmodern and globalised world. In his book entitled *La Création du Monde ou la Mondialisation*, Jean-Luc Nancy discusses two different approaches to globalisation. Underpinning Foucault's concept of 'biopolitics', Nancy views globalisation firstly like a process that over-empowers technology and limits or progressively kills life's possibilities in human beings (*La Création du Monde ou la Mondialisation*: 143). Secondly, globalisation is a shared or mutual exposure (in terms of making them visible and known) of cultural particularities to the whole world. Nancy points out that this type of globalisation sustains genuine diversity and even protects oppositions and differences (173).

The South Africa reflected in Duiker's *The Quiet Violence of Dreams* illustrates both types of globalisation. In a monologue in Steamy Windows, Tshepo shows how white South Africans in the post-apartheid context actively refuse to abandon their superiority complex:

> South Africa doesn't give you a chance to feel good about yourself, if you're not white, at least historically. Having gone to multiracial private schools made a difference, but my journey into myself and the true nature of people has been no different from that of township blacks, trying to find their place, their voice. I'm black and I'm proud of it, even if it is a bit silly to remind myself ... Even when I have looked my best and spoken in my best private school accent, I have confronted the harshest, the crudest prejudice from whites. They probably felt it their duty to remind me that I'm nothing but a kaffir who talks like a larney [an employer or member of the upper class]. That is how it feels when people are rude to you for no reason other than your different complexion. We still have a long way to go. (419)

As Nancy would have said, 'life's possibilities' for these white South Africans have already been killed off. That is why they keep on reminding blacks that they are not human beings or, if they must be tolerated as human beings, it is on condition that they help whites prove to themselves that they are of a superior nature. This is a litany well mastered by philosophers such as Christoph Meiners and Immanuel Kant, and addressed by George Yancy in *Black Bodies, White Gazes: The Continuing Significance of Race*.

The second aspect of globalisation is also reflected in the novel. Tshepo voices diversity as understood by Nancy when he says:

> In Angels I find familiar black and coloured faces ... I sashay to the dance floor when a groovy R&B number by Janet Jackson comes on ... In the middle of the dance floor the guys have formed a small circle while two people dance in the middle. It is a coloured and black thing. White guys in Biloxi like to dance in their own galaxies. I lounge in a chair and watch people. Two black guys French kiss next to me ... They are my age ... They go to the dance floor. I watch them dance kwaito style. I watch them dance and probably think of home Soweto. (417-18)

Homosexuals and heterosexuals evolve together in the narrative. The relationship between Mmabatho and Tshepo is an illustration. Although they have different sexual orientations, they evolve peacefully in the same environment. Not only coloured people, but also Westerners with their respective cultures meet each other in the above quotation. A derivative of the Negro Blues, Janet Jackson's groovy R&B evinces the culture of oppressed black American slaves, echoing in the participants on the dance floor. The passage above also outlines a parallel between Janet Jackson and kwaito – a South African popular music style consisting of a rowdy mix of local rhythms and international ones like hip hop, R&B and raga. In such conditions, differences are erased and music is given an impersonal status that can lead to unusual confusions about who among Westerners or Africans has the control over those two music styles played in the same bar and at the same moment. In making the oppositions invisible as evident from both kwaito and groovy R&B, the globalised world as displayed in *The Quiet Violence of Dreams* protects oppositions and disparities.

Furthermore, the varied identities associated with specific South African towns validate the country as a place where oppositions and disparities are protected, as in the following:

> Cape Town is very white, the influence of European traditions like coffee shops and bistros is inescapable. In some places in Cape Town you don't feel like you're in Africa. And this is what they call progress; obliterate any traces of the naive cultures. Jo'burg is different, the other cultures more aggressive to the domination of white culture ... In Cape Town there are certain places where you know you are not welcome and the patrons make you feel like an outcast. The culture of having a good time, of jolling is different in Gauteng. In Jo'burg people hang out. In Cape Town people go out. In Cape Town people are into drumming, doing their charts and doing drugs. Cape Town tries too hard, it looks too much to the West for inspiration when there is enough inspiration in Africa. (420)

In the same country, cities do not have the same identity. Johannesburg's identity is even contrapuntal to that of Cape Town in the above quotation. While Cape Town illustrates the first aspect of globalisation, Johannesburg displays many characteristics of the second aspect of globalisation. These evidences of globalisation highlight the fact that the South Africa on display in Duiker's *The Quiet Violence of Dreams* deserves to be considered a microcosm of our globalised world, in which very conservative cultures cohabit with rather innovative approaches or cultures.

RESISTING HYPOTHETIC NEW IDENTITIES IN THE GLOBALISED WORLD, HOMOSEXUALITY AND THE POSTCOLONIAL IDEA

In analysing the antagonism between native and imperial cultures, postcolonial criticism names avenues of expression of domination, mimicry (Bhabha *The Location of Culture*: 102-22), the 'black skin white mask' syndrome (Fanon *Peau Noire, Masques Blancs*), and the master subject (Haraway *Simians, Cyborgs, and Women*: 183-201). Each term finds an illustration in Duiker's narrative, though in a challenging relationship to the other 'self' that gives the issue of homosexuality its relevance. A glaring illustration is that homosexuality in Steamy Windows permits Cole to discover that black South Africans do not really have the power in the new configuration of South Africa. Speaking to his black colleague Tshepo, he draws the conclusion that:

> This whole brotherhood is a clever gimmick. Very convenient because it works ... You're only useful as long as you bring in money ... This thing is about power and about who has it and who doesn't. We don't have it. They come here, they pay. Okay, so we choose what we want to do with them, but we don't really have any power. It's just sex cleaned up, given a better look. You see that, don't you? (346)

Cole points to young black South Africans, the few *nouveaux riches* to whom power has been handed over, but whose existence misleads many naïve observers about the real owner of the power.

Many black people are irritated with the idea of homosexuality and, according to 'Angelo', the culture generated by their ancestors controls them in such a way that he sees them as 'schizophrenic dancing queens by night who are rigid grey suits by day' (331). The comment he makes on black men on the street brings out the various clichés attached to the perception of homosexuality in Africa: 'The ones that recognise me look away. Or they give me a dirty look so that I mustn't come by and say hi. I wouldn't anyway. But I'm always struck by how angry they seem to feel about liking men' (331).

Even though the anger displayed here can arguably prompt someone like Célestin Monga to lead the battle for true political democracy in Cameroon (*The Anthropology of Anger*), some would make the case that it is borrowed from a past that doesn't meet present-day realities: instead, they work to enact the will of their ancestors and rearticulate the archaic, as Bhabha would say. What they fail to understand is that 'if a (gay) man marries to satisfy society's prejudice, he isn't the only one who is unhappy, but spreads unhappiness to his wife and children too' (Van Zyl et al.: 52). One of the challenges for freedom from domination in the future, as Said would say, is for the colonial 'dominant self' to move to a 'sovereign self' that is rational in the sense that it is always open to difference or to movement (Nancy: 169-70). Sovereignty in this rational sense grants the 'dominant self', anywhere it is located, its freedom from fixity and from absolutism. Sovereignty in this rational sense grants the 'dominant self' its freedom to explore ways different from domination and exploitation. If given this capacity, the 'dominant self' would start to perceive the self as a simple singularity that, though similar to others, is different from them. Because the individual would no longer perceive itself as the 'dominant self', the individual would develop a capacity that would preserve the existing singularities from fixities and absolute identities with their awful consequences (Glissant: 26).

Tshepo's experience from Steamy Windows permits him to raise significant questions in relation to this new 'self' that is now needed for a more peaceful world today:

> Is it possible to draw a sincere meaning from all the things that I have known from black and white culture? ... Is it possible to feel South African and not to always source my culture to a particular race group? Can I claim Afrikaans, Coloured tsotsi taal, Indian cuisine or English sensibilities as my own? Am I a sell-out, an Uncle Tom? ... Isn't that a bigger transgression than going beyond the boundaries? Will whites ever really hear us? And will we blacks always be on the defensive? Is it possible to be comfortable with each other as we are. not wanting to alter each other? ... And us blacks, do we still look up to them instead of standing as equals? ... Do we steal and pillage from whites because we are getting revenge or have become victims of our own bitterness and anger? ... Perhaps we are moving into the territory of the oppressor. Perhaps one day whites will also speak about us with the same despicable nostalgia that we reserve for apartheid and its days. When blacks were in power, they might say. (347-9)

Just as Tshepo is here suggesting, Lacan (208) and Bourdieu (*Raisons Pratiques*: 107) also conceive artificial boundaries materialised by morals or laws that must retain the possibility of transgression. Postcolonial critics underpin this ambivalent situation of boundaries when they insist that imperialism has consolidated the hybrid nature of culture on a global scale. Seen as a fluid concept, homosexuality is therefore a perfect exemplification of this postcolonial hybrid model of culture or identity. As the twelfth-century's monk from Saxony, Hugh of St. Victor, puts it, 'the strong or perfect person achieves independence and detachment by working through attachments, not by rejecting them' (Said: 336). Societies are therefore called to learn to live with homosexuals and stop giving them 'a dirty look' (331), in Tshepo's words, because, as this essay has argued, their lives illustrate the composite, hybrid and open nature of human cultures and identities.

NOTES

1 'Me' could also mean South Africa in this specific relation.
2 Slang for masturbation.
3 South African slang which means black foreigners or strangers from Africa in South Africa.
4 My translation.

WORKS CITED

Ashcroft, Bill, Gareth Griffiths and Helen Tiffin. *The Empire Writes Back: Theory and Practice in Post-Colonial Literatures*, 2nd edition. London and New York: Routledge, 1989.
Barthes, Roland. *Critiques et Vérité*. Paris: Seuil, 1966.
Bhabha K., Homi. *The Location of Culture*. New York: Routledge, 1994.
Bourdieu, Pierre. *Raisons Pratiques: Sur la Théorie de l'Action*. Paris: Seuil, 1994.
Cohn, Doritt. *La Transparence Intérieure: Modes de Représentations de la Vie Psychique dans le Roman*, trans. Alain Bony. Paris: Seuil, 1981.
Duiker, Kabelo Sello. *The Quiet Violence of Dreams*. Cape Town: Kwela Books, 2001.
Fanon, Frantz. *Peau Noire, Masques Blancs*. Paris: Seuil, 1974.
Foucault, Michel. *Histoire de la Sexualité 1: La Volonté de Savoir*. Paris: Gallimard, 1986.
Glissant, Édouard. *Le Traité du Tout-monde*. Paris: Gallimard, 1997.
Haraway, Donna J.. *Simians, Cyborgs, and Women: The Reinvention of Nature*. New York: Routledge, 1991.
Hermann, David. *Story Logic: Problems and Possibilities of Narrative*. Lincoln and London: University of Nebraska Press, 2004.
Lacan, Jacques. *Le Séminaire: Livre VII – Éthique de la Psychanalyse, 1959-1960*. Paris: Seuil, 1986.
Monga, Célestin. *The Anthropology of Anger: Civil Society and Democracy in Africa*, trans. Linda L. Fleck and Célestin Monga. Boulder, CO: Lynne Rienner, 1996.
Moudileno, Lydie. 'Littérature et Postcolonie'. *Africultures* No. 28, May 2000.
Moura, Jean-Marc. 'La Critique Postcoloniale, Étude des Spécificités'. *Africultures* No. 28, May 2000.
Mpe, Phaswane. *Welcome to Our Hillbrow: A Novel of Post-Apartheid South Africa*. Athens, OH: Ohio University Press, 2011.
Nancy, Jean-Luc. *La Création du Monde ou la Mondialisation*. Paris: Galilée, 2002.
Ndebele, Njabulo S. *Rediscovery of the Ordinary: Essays on South African Literature and Culture*. Scottsville: University of KwaZulu-Natal Press, 2006.
Said, Edward. *Culture and Imperialism*. London and New York: Routledge, 1994.

―― *L'Orientalisme: L'orient Crée par l'Occident*. Paris: Seuil, 1980. Van Zyl, Mikki, Jeanelle De Gruchy, Sheila Lapinsky, Simon Lewin, and Graeme Reid. *The Aversion Project: Human Rights Abuses of Gays and Lesbians in the South African Defence Force by Health Workers During the Apartheid Era*. Cape Town: Simply Said & Done, 1999.

Wexler, Philip. 'Citizenship in the Semiotic Society.' In *Theories of Modernity and Postmodernity*, pp. 164-75, ed. Bryan S. Turner. London, Newbury Park, CA and New Delhi: SAGE Publications, 1990.

Yancy, George. *Black Bodies, White Gazes: The Continuing Significance of Race*. New York, Toronto and Plymouth, UK: Rowman & Littlefield, 2008.

A Warm, Woolly Silence

Rethinking Silence through T.O. Molefe's 'Lower Main' & Monica Arac de Nyeko's 'Jambula Tree'

ROBERT LARUE

> Rather than a universalized and dogmatic insistence on voice, loudness and visibility, it is important that the global queer movement begins to enhance our abilities to read and decipher the important roles of silence as a collective language of some queer communities particularly in the Global South.
>
> Stella Nyanzi ('When the State Produces Hate': 190)

Silence is not an easy thing to listen to. In the realm of social, political and cultural activism, silence, more often than not, is tantamount to inaction, and in the face of crises such as the HIV/AIDS pandemics, the rise of fascism and authoritarian regimes, and increasingly common instances of overt homophobia, we are told that both silence and inaction amount to death – a death largely left to be inferred as our own. While, in academic circles, silence is often an exciting site of discovery via numerous interpretive methodologies, silence around the homoerotic in African cultural and literary productions has become increasingly unbearable to listen to. For instance, Deborah Amory asserts that the works of those of us who study Africa 'need to be informed by an awareness of the multiple causes of political persecution and oppression: gender, race, ethnicity, class, religion, as well as sexuality' ('"Homosexuality" in Africa: Issues and Debates': 9). Similarly, Marc Epprecht implores that it 'surely behoves people who care about democracy, human rights, and good scholarship to sensitise themselves to the complexity of the historical denials of indigenous homosexualities' ('The "Unsaying" of Indigenous Homosexualities in Zimbabwe': 651). In between the critiques of silence that focus on the institutional level, Kenyan author and critic Binyavanga Wainaina diligently and movingly works to expose the damages of silence on the intimate levels at both familial and social bonds, and one's psychological health, contributing one of the most heart-wrenching critiques of the role of silence in sexual identity ('I Am a Homosexual, Mum').

Working to rethink the relationship between the languages of sexuality used in the Global North and enactments of non-heterosexual identities in the Global South, Stella Nyanzi acutely points out the paucity of critical attention paid to 'the tensions between interpretations of silence as power and the counter-position that interprets silence as powerlessness' (181). Similarly, Sylvia Tamale observes that 'by maintaining a tight grip on certain activities, and silencing the voices off those individuals and groups that engage in them, the patriarchal state makes it extremely difficult for [queer] individuals and groups to organise and fight for their human rights' ('Out of the Closet: Unveiling Sexuality Discourses in Uganda': 2).

Nonetheless, speech should not be the default means of challenging these acts of silencing. As Nthabiseng Motsemme posits, 'in privileging speech we need to be aware that those who are the most marginalised have often used invisibility and silence as means to protect themselves' ('The Mute Always Speak': 648). Taking up the call to listen to what silences speak, this essay is interested in exploring how everyday African queer enactments of silence gesture towards forms of queer identity that resist the demands for politicising themselves in the loud manner advocated for by queer movements in the Global North. As Nyanzi observes, seemingly oppressive instances of silence often have a way of paradoxically evidencing the existence of the very thing it seeks to erase. In fact, as Ashley Currier recognises, silence can often be a useful tactic in granting LGBT organisations 'temporary respite from repression, prying gazes, or unfavourable media coverage, allowing activists to assess their options' and reposition themselves and their efforts (*Out in Africa*: 11) I am interested in thinking resistance outside the organised structures of movements and organisations. It is my contention that, in an effort navigate the various forms of oppression they face daily, rather than fleeing to organised political movements, African queers often engage in practices of 'making do', as they 'introduce *artistic* tricks and competitions of *accomplices* into a system that reproduces and partitions' images of a healthy and heterosexual national identity (de Certeau *The Practice of Everyday Life*: 29, original emphases). One such strategy, I suggest, is the enactment of silence, rather than the loud pronouncements of belonging advocated for by global queer movements and voices.

A distinction must be made, however, between the politic of silencing and the self-selected acts of silence chosen by African queers.

Because the former is often state, culturally, and even academically mandated and employed, it is the latter that I emphasise, since non-institutionalised acts often do not undergo analyses. Scholars have argued against queer studies' silencing of experiences that don't clearly or neatly align with the deracialised and normativised queer politics such as the battle for hate crime legislation (Cohen 'Death and Rebirth of a Movement: Queering Critical Ethnic Studies'). Without a doubt, the oft critiqued and resisted institutional systems of silencing are problematic and damaging. But this view risks constantly positioning the silenced as without agency. It, ironically, silences those who do not desire to publicly (i.e. politically) challenge and wage war against the systems that oppress them. In other words, the expectation that the oppressed should (want to) rail against these acts of silencing, risks silencing individual choice in how one engages with their own reality. There, however, is a difference between being unable to speak or being prevented from speaking and *deciding* not to speak. Although the two are often connected, to remain silent is not the same as to be silenced. Choosing when, how or if one wants to speak can help one negotiate one's own relation to power. This choice becomes extremely powerful when it is made by one who desires to remain apart from any sort of organised political agenda.

Reading Arac de Nyeko's 'Jambula Tree' and Molefe's 'Lower Main', I trace the ways in which silence becomes an accomplice in the sustaining of queer desires. That is, I demonstrate how moments of silence assist in mediating the unspoken – or the unspeakable – and how they help present subtle shifts in the social economies in which they are enacted. While words seem the most obvious path for observing queer speaking, words often, and for various reasons, fail. More often than not, in African spaces where certain words (such as 'gay', or 'lesbian') are not completely accurate or are unavailable, enactments of silence allow for the most accurate forms of speaking. In the silences, we find that queer desire remains.

Much like the voices of minorities within the West, African voices are often homogenised and positioned as 'representatives' of an entire national – which is rendered as a continental – population. In her 2007 article, 'Why Must Authors be Tied to their Ethnicity?' Crystal Mahey insists that 'understanding literature in terms of a homogenized construct, whether it's "African," "south Asian" or "British diaspora," can be limiting – and many differences including race, class, ethnicity, gender and generation in both the writing and the writers will be eclipsed under such umbrellas'. However, in agreement with South

African author Henrietta Rose-Innes, Mahey concedes, 'the need to resign yourself to a label that effaces diversity, if one wants to reach a wide international audience, is a problem for a writers [sic] who want to explore areas not stereotypically understood as "African"'. Concurring with this sentiment, Monica Arac de Nyeko asserts that, in large, African literature has failed to reach mainstream society, yet when it does, 'the way it is perceived is very much still in the 1960s. As an African writer, if you are not writing about things like war and famine your authenticity is questioned' (quoted in Mahey).

Narrating a reunion between two black South African lesbians, 'Lower Main' is an exercise in perspective and seeing, in observing. As the story unfolds, the feelings carried by the story's narrator, Dee, for her friend, Madz, are slowly revealed as the two discuss the circumstances surrounding the end of Madz's recent relationship. Set on the patio of a café on Lower Main Road in Cape Town, the story continues the work of post-apartheid South African writing, offering an intimate image of black lesbian life within the nation while couching that intimacy within complex racial and class dynamics as the black couple (Dee and Madz) are placed within the gaze of an anonymous, white tourist couple. Yet, while Pumla Dimeo Gqola explains the story as being about 'what it means to be a subject who is constantly observed, read, consumed and packaged by some other gaze owned by those who have no consideration for your own self-making' ('Introduction': 5), I read the story also as a postcolonial articulation of queerness apart from and against a Gay International' (Massad *Desiring Arabs*). Although seemingly a story about disclosure, 'Lower Main' is also a story about silence: the frustrations of silence in the face of memory, the present, the past, and the future; and the potential of silence to create spaces for the manifestation and fulfilment of queer desire. This is to say, in response to a gaze that threatens one's (queer) self-making, Molefe offers a potentially productive and fruitful silence.

This silence, however, is not a silence of passive patience or waiting. Rather, it is a silence that becomes productive only when certain, specific, and appropriate *actions* are taken. Moreover, the silence invoked in this story is of a different frequency than is either the silencing sought and used by politicians or the silence resisted and sometimes strategically employed by queer political organisations and groups. The silence in this story is a silence easily ignored, overlooked, or dismissed, because it is of its quotidian nature and is birthed in the personal from fears of loss and interpersonal intimacy.

Within Molefe's story, a veiled sense of desire circulates through the channels of verbal disclosure in the form of storytelling. While Dee and Madz convene to discuss the end of Madz's previous relationship with her presumably white ex-girlfriend, no clear articulation of desire enters the conversation. The picture Madz paints of both her relationship and her breakup are made in (post)modernist abstract motions, befitting her artist persona, as she speaks of the period in which she stopped bathing, losing track of time in the process, without being able to directly articulate the confusion and feelings of filth that arose in her while in her relationship. As Madz recounts how 'the longer [she] didn't shower, the clearer the memory of being clean became' (Molefe: 58), the flow of the narrative, via Dee's attention, is constantly interrupted by her observations of the white tourist couple anonymously walking up and down Lower Main Road. While Dee is not the only one to notice the couple, as Madz's attention momentarily diverts to their movements, it is Dee who constantly draws attention to them as they move into her and Madz's space, threatening their intimacy.

The interruption of the couple – or, perhaps more accurately put, Dee's deflection of her desires onto the couple as they move along the street – mirrors the tensions around interracial relationships in contemporary South Africa. As Pumla Dineo Gqola notes, the story 'is about so much more than playing with bodies in an exploration of identity; it is also about what it means to be a subject who is constantly observed, read, consumed and packaged by some other gaze owned by those who have no consideration for your own self-making' (Gqola: 5). Dee's observation of and irritation with the white couple forestall the completion of her thoughts each time she inches towards fully articulating her own desire. For instance, it is after admiring Madz's beauty that she first notices the couple 'gawk[ing] at each person they see' on the street – a street Dee, herself, describes as a 'kaleidoscope of freakishness' (Molefe: 53). Or when Madz catches Dee staring at her, Dee breaks the growing tension by shifting the narrative to a description of the tourists who are discussing a poster outside a black beauty parlour (56). Both Dee and Madz remain frozen, locked in place, as the couple moves in on them. It is precisely when she seeks to silence her own articulations that she moves to offer the most complete articulations of the tourists' behaviours and motivations. Dee's tracking of the tourist couple highlights the story's double articulation of silence. On the one hand, there is the silence that keeps the desires of both Dee and Madz cloaked behind calculated or fabricated manoeuvrings, and that allows the tourist couple to close in on them as they sit at the table. Where

Dee's and Madz's silence leave them protected from the vulnerabilities of their desires, their silence also leaves them vulnerable to the couple. In opposition to this, however, is the silence through which Dee is able to resist the gaze of the couple. In and because of her silence, Dee shifts from being a hapless victim of the couple's gaze to a more vigilant observer of their actions.

If desires are left unspoken, left unverbalised, it is because Dee exhibits a deeper level of comfort with silence than with the potential fulfilment of these desires. The story ends with the following passage:

> 'Dee, my friend, this is why I am talking to you,' Madz says. She reaches toward me, clasps her fingers around the back of my neck and pulls me to her. I feel her warm breath first, then her lips, soft against my forehead.
>
> Everything disappears. A warm, woolly silence engulfs me and time seems to pause. Then slowly, it ebbs back. The door chime of the café, a scooter racing by on the street. In the distance, one of the *bergies* [a homeless person who lives in Cape Town] is awake. He shouts to a woman, 'Hey madam, sorry pretty lady ...' The tourist couple have taken a seat at the table next to us. When I notice them, they trade furtive glances. She quickly closes her notebook and slips it into her bag. He puts the lens cap back on his camera and pretends not to have been taking pictures of us. (59–60)

Not only are the terms of the two women's relationship laid bare, but Dee's *and* Madz's relationships with silence manifests themselves more clearly than anywhere else in the story. The irony of Madz declaring to Dee that this is why she has chosen to speak to her is that not much has actually been vocalised. The two speak in fragments and clipped thoughts – thoughts that are constantly interrupted by either their own acts of silencing themselves, the deflection of attention to other objects, or interruptions made by the other party. To put this differently, because it is through acts of silence that their conversation and subsequent understanding occurs, the power of silence to speak desire becomes most visible. Where elsewhere, it might be confused that Dee turns to objects as an attempt to distract her nerves, here objects function to return her to the reality of her life, reinforcing the peace she has found within the silence she has chosen. Rather than focusing on the kiss itself, she describes the objects (fingers, lips, breath) that create the space for it. In fact, if for a moment she enjoys the intimacy of the kiss itself, that intimacy proves to be too much. It throws her into a 'warm, woolly silence'.

Moreover, if the juxtaposition of the tourists' movement against Dee and Madz's fixed location risks threatening the productiveness of the two girls' silence, this threat is mitigated in a number of ways. First, Dee's recognition of the couple's collective gaze works to make bare the power dynamics of the scopic relationship. Dee's returning of the couple's gaze serves as a form of 'making do' in that, in the open space of the patio the only non-assailable form of resistance to being seen becomes seeing back. As de Certeau posits, the power gained in making do comes as the 'action[s] intervene in a field which regulates them at a first level', but 'introduce into [that field] a way of turning it to their advantage that obeys other rules and constitutes something like a second level interwoven into the first' (de Certeau: 30). Interestingly, the white couple's gender differential is equalised as the gaze of one always complements the gaze of the other – he snaps an image, while she jots down an image. Second, and most importantly, Dee and Madz are not static: though their bodies remain in one location throughout the story, their lives move closer together as the story progresses. This closeness is made possible because of the silence they share, a silence which allows them to share past, present, and future experiences and which ultimately thrusts their bodies into motion in the form of a kiss. Juxtaposing the movement of the couple against the motion(lessness) of Dee and Madz highlights the potential energy contained within silence. What is left is a revision of the concept of movement so that it is no longer simply about doing but also about 'making do'.

As with Molefe's story, Monica Arac de Nyeko's 'Jambula Tree' is interested in the consequences of a gaze that remains disinterested in individuals' self-making. A story about the consequences of the love and affection between two girls, 'Jambula Tree' relies on enactments of silence to retain, re-member, and rekindle a sense of completion from fragmented moments they continue to carry with them. Or, to say this differently, 'Jambula Tree' is a story about 'making do' in silence when other avenues have been closed. In defence of the story, many readers have been quick to universalise the two girls' relationship, arguing that, at its core, it is simply a love story. Filmmaker Wanuri Kahiu, for instance, notes that what drew her to the story was that it is a love story about 'how true love can triumph above everything' (quoted in Barlet 'Homosexuality is Not Un-African': 187). Contributing to this universalising tendency is the story's similarity to the important woman-centred African novel, *So Long a Letter* (1981), by Senegalese writer Mariama Bâ. As with *So Long a Letter*, 'Jambula Tree' grounds its story in the relationship between two female characters who share a history of intimacy, and who have been separated by life's circumstances. This separation, for both stories, results in a narrative that makes use of the epistolary form in order to maintain a degree of intimacy between two individuals. Speaking of *So Long a Letter*, Florence Stratton argues that Bâ's text 'celebrates female solidarity' by offering a hopeful tale in which the relationship between its two female characters transcends social obstacles (*Contemporary African Literature and the Politics of Gender*: 143). Similarly, in 'Jambula Tree', existing social structures are unable to destroy the bond between the story's two female characters.

However, these are two markedly different texts, with two markedly different aims. Even as it attempts to work against the suppression of gender in African literature (Stratton: 10), *So Long a Letter* is a story of a woman justifying her decision to remain committed to a marriage that had long since positioned her as excess baggage. Furthermore, the relationship between the narrator and her friend, though intimate, is not sexual. Bâ's narrator finds her ultimate message to be the assertion of 'the inevitable and necessary complementarity of man and woman' (88), which she holds as the key to healing (national) ills. In other words, Bâ's text works to reaffirm the heteronormativity of society, even as it critiques the treatment of (certain) women in that society. This is made no clearer than when the novel's protagonist, Ramatoulaye, declares, 'The success of a family is born of a couple's harmony ... The nation is made up of all the families ... The success of a nation therefore depends inevitably on the family' (89). Although, as Cinzia Mozzato contends, 'Jambula Tree' might be read as working to 'underline the relevance of ethnic difference to the creation of the Ugandan nation' ('Forms of Resistance: Writing from and about Uganda': 88), it does not move to establish, or reaffirm the nation as a heteronormative space. On the contrary, Arac de Nyeko's story sets the love and sexual desire between the story's female characters, Anyango and Sanyu, as its focus, thus demonstrating a 'willingness to unveil what is mainly regarded as obscene and is consequently expunged from social discourse and literature' (Mozzato: 85). In fact, Ken Junior Lipenga suggests the strength of the story lies in its move to 'challenge negative attitudes towards homosexuality on the [African] continent' ('Sex Outlaws': 41). Rather than establish the family as an extension of the nation, Arac de Nyeko offers the love between two girls as the very thing that will break a community when and if it is denied.

On the most immediate level, this break comes in the overt silencings that occur as individuals try to cope with the consequences of the two girls' actions: Sanyu's exile to London; the broken demeanours of both Sanyu's and Anyango's mothers (Arac de Nyeko: 104, 105). On a much more covert level, this break becomes the possibility for change in the community. If, as Lipenga suggests, the story is a challenge to 'a community that polices the role of women in what is essentially an oppressive patriarchal system' ('Sex Outlaws': 63), its challenge comes through the girls' homosexual desire – a desire that quietly moves to transgress the established boundaries. In contrast to the spectacle of gender common in the estate – evidenced by the women who sit and gossip, and by Sanyu's mother who 'bought happiness from the market' (Arac de Nyeko: 101) – the girls' transgressive desire operates in their quiet determination to in no way become like these women. Because of its foundation in a self-selected silence, it is this latter break that is of interest in this essay.

Beyond the possible reading of Anyango's epistolary structure itself as a form of silent resistance, the choice of silence as resistance becomes visible in various other ways throughout the story. One important instance of this silent resistance can be found in the text's opening moments, as Anyango describes the present state of the estate. In her description, Anyango weaves memories of her past experiences with Sanyu into her narrative, and points out that, in many ways, Sanyu will find the estate just as she left it. Still full of the women she and Sanyu 'did not want to become', the women who

> don't work. Like Mama Atim they sit and talk, talk, talk and wait for their husbands to bring home a kilo of offal. Those are the kind of women we did not want to become ... They took over their children's *dool* and *kwepena* catfights till the local councilor had to be called for arbitration. Then they did not talk to each other for a year. Nakawa's women laugh at each other for wearing the cheapest sandals on sale by the hawkers. (92)

In short, Anyango reassures Sanyu, 'Nakawa Housing Estates has never changed' (92). It is possible to read Anyango's description as suggesting the estate itself is a static patriarchal community, as it describes a group of women who reaffirm the domestic/public division of labours ('Sex Outlaws': 64). However, I would argue, beneath this apparent division rests an expression of Anyango's queer desire. The women are not the only thing that remain in the estate; Anyango has also chosen to remain there. Yet, as we see throughout the narrative, she is clearly not the same timid little girl. She has her own job and her own place, and is no longer subject to her naïve visions of life. For her, then, to declare that nothing has changed, is a subtle declaration that upon her return, Sanyu will find Anyango's love just as she left it all those years ago. By intertwining her love for Sanyu with the estate's history and people, Anyango quietly lays claim to that which has sought to deny her and her desire, while refusing to remain trapped in or by the estate's stagnation.

Moreover, the story juxtaposes the truth expressed though talking – in the form of gossip – to the truth expressed in silence by things and objects. Afraid of the silence, and wielding it as a weapon to wound one another, the women of the estate constantly talk. Talking's truth destroys. Mama Atim talks of the 'immorality' (Arac de Nyeko: 96) of others, veiling the imperfections within her own family (96), and it is because of her telling of her discovery of Anyango and Sanyu touching one another under the jambula tree in front of her house that the two girls are forced to separate. In contrast to these women, Anyango reminds Sanyu

> That's what we fought against when we walked to school each day. Me and you hand in hand, towards school, running away from Nakawa Housing Estates' drifting tide which threatened to engulf us and turn us into noisy, gossiping and frightening housewives. You said it yourself, we could be anything. Anything coming from your mouth was seasoned and alive. You said it to me, as we sat on a mango tree branch. We are not allowed to climb trees, but we did, and there, inside the green branches, you said – we can be anything. (92)

Although she begins with a recounting of shame, of a loss of innocence, the story ends with Anyango's pride in the jambula tree and all it represents. She recognises that it is not an object of shame, but of pride and life, telling Sanyu to 'rise like the sun and stand tall like the jambula tree' (105). Anyango's reliance on objects like the jambula tree become a means for her to re-member not only Sanyu's connection with the estate and Anyango herself, but also a means for Anyango to re-member the social order of the estate itself. The truth of this object, in contrast to the truth trapped in speaking, opens up paths for more intimate knowledge and bonds individuals by serving as a silent yet indelible witness to the presence of the girls' queerness. Not only do Sanyu and Anyango come to know one another most intimately when they 'walk hand in hand', they also learn of a new, deeper, and lasting intimacy between themselves in these silences, as they make contact with each other's breasts and waists under the jambula tree that sits directly in front of Mama Atim's house (96). It is this silence that has fortified Anyango in the years since Sanyu's departure It is this silence that fuels Anyango's epistle – an epistle that is itself an act of making do. It is this silence that has allowed Anyango to sustain herself and that serves to reinforce her desire. If the jambula tree represents life, it also represents a constant and silent queering of the ordinary. The tree, resting in front of Mama Atim's house, carries with it its history with Anyango and Sanyu. Each day it serves as a constant reminder of the queer desire it sheltered, and of Anyango's defiance of the social norm as she chooses to grow strong and immutable like the tree. And each day it remains, it stands as the community's tacit acknowledgement of Anyango and Sanyu's desire and love, even as they have outwardly rejected that desire's presence. The recognition of the tree's queer symbolism is held within Anyango's closing call for Sanyu to 'rise like the sun and stand tall like the jambula tree in front of Mama Atim's house' (105), because she knows that, no matter what happens, the tree will always carry with it its part in the two girls' love.

The fact that, in both of these stories, the actions that define each are performed outside in the open (Dee and Madz sit on the open patio; Anyango and Sanyu are caught touching one another in the open, under the jambula tree in front of Mama Atim's house) cannot be overlooked. By taking place outside, in the open, the stories offer a challenge to the idea that there is a desire to hide – whether this be because of fear or shame – as is often suggested by proponents of visibility. Given the presence of war circulating in the background of 'Jambula Tree', the resistance held in the placing of these events outdoors becomes that more poignant. As Sofia Ahlberg notes, 'love does not conquer all ... but the enormous effort to narrate love in times of war is an act of resistance unparalleled by any other' ('Women and War in Contemporary Love Stories from Uganda and Nigeria': 409). The choice of silence should not be equated to a desire for invisibility, at least an invisibility that suggests a disavowal of one's self. But neither should these outdoor settings be seen as a part of a politics of inclusion that 'would have us adopt the oppressive rhetoric and ideals' of the dominant culture 'for a seat at the table' (Cohen 'What is this Movement doing to My Politics?': 113). Neither Dee, nor Madz, nor Anyango present a desire to be included. Where Anyango and Sanyu openly reject, and fear, being included into the group of women in their estate, Dee and Madz offer indifferent reactions to their society – while the café is 'not [Dee's] kind of vibe', Madz likes it because it is 'laid back and unadorned' (Molefe: 53). In the place of inclusion, then, the openness suggested by the outside settings proposes collective autonomy, in which individuals are granted a degree of sovereignty while still participating in a collective body.

To be clear, the silences I have moved to delimit are not utopian. They are laden with pain. Yet, what is remarkable and highly instructive is that this pain is not debilitating. Rather, the silences in these stories suggest attempts at what Taiye Selasi calls 'working from a position of pain' (Bady and Selasi 'From that Stranded Place': 158). Though the individuals have chosen silence, they have not chosen inaction or passivity. Although Selasi is specifically concerned with explaining the experiences of a class of Africans who exist in the 'new' diaspora (160) – i.e. the descendants of immigrant African professionals – these stories and their silences share her attempt to cope with the constant rejection of her identity and to lay claim to a space of her own in the face of that rejection. These silences are not inert, impotent or barren. Rather, enactments of silence not only often serve as the driving force for the action but also as a challenge to those who are mere voyeurs to these personal experiences.

WORKS CITED

Ahlberg, Sofia. 'Women and War in Contemporary Love Stories from Uganda and Nigeria'. *Comparative Literature Studies* Vol. 46, No. 2 (2009): 407-24.

Amory, Deborah P. '"Homosexuality" in Africa: Issues and Debates'. *Issue: A Journal of Opinion* Vol. 25, No. 1 (1997): 5-10.

Arac de Nyeko, Monica. 'Jambula Tree'. In Karen Martin and Makhosazana Xaba (eds) *Queer Africa: New and Collected Fiction*. Braamfontein, SA: MaThoko, 2013: 91-105.

Bâ, Mariama. *So Long a Letter*, translated by Modupé Bodé-Thomas. Oxford: Heinemann, 1981.

Bady, Aaron and Taiye Selasi. 'From that Stranded Place'. *Transition*, No. 117 (2015): 148-65.

Barlet, Olivier. '"Homosexuality is Not Un-African: What is Un-African is Homophobia": An Interview with Wanuri Kahiu on *Jambula Tree*'. *Black Camera* Vol. 5, No. 2 (2014): 186-90.

de Certeau, Michel. *The Practice of Everyday Life*, translated by Steven Rendall. Berkeley: University of California Press, 1984.

Cohen, Cathy J. 'What is this Movement doing to My Politics?' *Social Text 61* Vol. 17, No. 4 (1999): 111-18.

——'Death and Rebirth of a Movement: Queering Critical Ethnic Studies'. *Social Justice* Vol. 37, No. 4 (2011/2012): 126-32.

Currier, Ashley. *Out in Africa: LGBT Organizing in Namibia and South Africa*. Minneapolis, MN: University of Minnesota Press, 2012.

Epprecht, Marc. 'The "Unsaying" of Indigenous Homosexualities in Zimbabwe: Mapping a Blindspot in African Masculinity'. *Journal of Southern African Studies* Vol. 24, No. 4 (1998): 631-51.

Gqola, Pumla Dineo. 'Introduction'. In Karen Martin and Makhosazana Xaba (eds) *Queer Africa: New and Collected Fiction*. Braamfontein, SA: MaThoko 2013: 1-7.

Lipenga, Ken Junior. 'Sex Outlaws: Challenges to Homophobia in Stanley

Kenani's "Love on Trial" and Monica Arac de Nyeko's "Jambula Tree"'. *Assuming Gender* Vol. 4, No. 1 (2014): 41-71.

Mahey, Crystal. 'Why Must Authors be Tied to their Ethnicity?' *The Guardian*, 11 July, 2007. www.theguardian.com/books/booksblog/2007/jul/11/why mustauthorsbetiedtoth (accessed 27 January 2018).

Massad, Joseph A. *Desiring Arabs*. Chicago: University of Chicago Press, 2007.

Molefe, T.O. 'Lower Main'. In Karen Martin and Makhosazana Xaba (eds) *Queer Africa: New and Collected Fiction*. Braamfontein, SA: MaThoko, 2013: 53-60.

Motsemme, Nthabiseng. 'The Mute Always Speak: On Women's Silences at the Truth and Reconciliation Commission'. *Current Sociology* Vol. 52, No. 5 (2004): 909-32.

Mozzato, Cinzia. 'Forms of Resistance: Writing From and About Uganda'. In *Experiences of Freedom in Postcolonial Literatures and Cultures*, Annalisa Oboe and Shaul Bassi. New York: Routledge, 2011: 79-90.

Nyanzi, Stella. 'When the State Produces Hate: Re-Thinking the Global Queer Movement through Silence in The Gambia'. *Thamyris/Intersecting: Place, Sex & Race*, No. 30 (2015):179-93.

Stratton, Florence. *Contemporary African Literature and the Politics of Gender*. London: Routledge, 1994.

Tamale, Sylvia. 'Out of the Closet: Unveiling Sexuality Discourses in Uganda'. *Feminist Africa*, No. 2 (2003): 1-6.

Wainaina, Binyavanga. 'I Am a Homosexual, Mum'. *Africa is a Country*. January 19, 2014. http://africasacountry.com/2014/01/i-am-a-homosexual-mum (accessed 27 January 2018).

Breaking/Voicing the Silence

Diriye Osman's *Fairytales for Lost Children*

ASUNCIÓN ARAGÓN

The relationship between queer studies and African studies presents a long thread of dis-encounters. On the one hand, queer studies have regularly taken Western countries and their identity politics as a referent and, on the other, African studies have often avoided placing queer subjects in the academic agenda. Additionally, as Taiwo A. Osinubi aptly notes 'North America-based Africanists allied with North American queer studies worry about the seeming indifference of American queer studies to African studies as well as the indifference of queer studies to Africa and African studies' ('Queer Prolepsis and the Sexual Commons': 13).

Despite all this, in the last few years, queer studies have proliferated in some African universities and the portrayal of LGBTI characters has spread in African literature and films, particularly in South Africa but also in Nigeria, Zimbabwe, Ghana and Kenya. These texts offer an array of the complexities of queer lives and experiences that debunk the homogenisation of African queer people or the stereotypical trope that 'Africa is a homophobic continent'. Such a monolithic image of one single homophobic Africa is a fallacy. As Keguro Macharia pointed out in *The Guardian*, 'Homophobia in Africa is not a single story'. Moreover, homosexuality has to be historically and geographically contextualised, since it is inextricably interwoven with categories such as ethnicity, religion, class, nation, diaspora or globalisation. Hence, as Macharia contends 'we must understand homophobic acts within their specific local histories as these intersect with broader global histories'.

The queer characters in African novels and films assert that to be loved, cherished and accepted is a basic human need. However, they also denounce how for many of them acceptance is bound with silence. Sometimes silence is not golden and though it might seem that you are waving you are just drowning. As Audre Lorde suggested, 'your silence will not protect you' (*Sister Outsider*: 41). The contemporary

British-Somali writer, critic, and visual artist Diriye Osman, a young gay Muslim man who grew up in a very religious Muslim household, also defends this belief and, like many other African queer people, challenges the cultures of silence and invisibility surrounding their lives and everyday practices.

In 2013, Osman made his debut with the publication of *Fairytales for Lost Children*, a collection of short stories that, as the author concedes, was born 'out of silence' ('No Longer Silent: Chronicling Queer African Lives'). *The Guardian* considered it one of the books of 2014. That year *Fairytales for Lost Children* was also awarded the Polari First Book Prize, given to a first book that explores the LGBT experience. Diriye Osman became the first African author to receive the award. Despite its title, the book is an adult collection of LGBT stories interspersed with tattoo-like black and white illustrations, most of them of women. Designed by Osman as modern riffs on ancient folktales ('No Longer Silent'), it also contains Arabic calligraphy that corresponds to the title of each tale. The stories are presented very similarly to the medieval form of fairy tales. In the publication of this work, every detail was cherished: the texture, the quality of the paper and the cover: a photograph of Osman donning an Elizabethan dress, face painted and wearing jewellery. As a visual artist, Diriye Osman is genuinely interested in imagery, and this pictorial feature pervades his writing. As he acknowledges in an interview with Anna Jäger:

> For me, my writing stems from painting images ... Visual art is a language and so it felt natural, necessary even, to incorporate illustrations that would add flavour and nuance to the visual quality of the prose ... I don't think I could write a book that doesn't incorporate visual art in some way. It's how I make sense of the world. ('On Mermaids and Microwaves')

Taken together, the characters in these 11 short stories grow older as the book progresses: this is literally a coming of age collection, but they are always Somali queer people, lesbians, gays, transgenders, living under dire needs in London, Nairobi or Mogadishu. They are human beings who are trying to overcome displacement, alienation, stigmatisation or solitude through optimism and the exercise of freedom.

One of the main themes of the book is the troublesome issue of homosexuality and family acceptance. Osman delves into the consequences of coming out to their family for LGBT people, and much of the plot in these 'fairy' tales depicts the outcome of this thorny question. The result is undoubtedly predictable in a homophobic society: most characters in the stories are not accepted by their family, and many of the protagonists have been traumatised and have lost their minds, at least temporarily. Nevertheless, contrary to what one would expect out of this gloomy and despairing situation, Diriye Osman is not interested in presenting LGBT people as victims but as survivors. Thus, positive feelings flow in all the tales whispering that hope is always out there for those who struggle for freedom. As Osman contends: 'After all, freedom isn't freedom unless you do something with it' (Neelika Jayawardane 'Diriye Osman: How to be Gay, Muslim, African').

Quite significantly, the book opens with the story 'Watering the Imagination', a piece commissioned by Bernardine Evaristo who was guest-editing an issue of the journal *Poetry Review*. The story is about a Somali mother's love and acceptance of her lesbian daughter. 'My eldest daughter, Suldana, is in love with another woman ... I respect her privacy and allow her to live' (*Fairytales*: 3). This mother, who does not know why her daughter is a lesbian, nor who her lover is, supports her daughter. She does not speak about lesbianism – these things in Somali culture go 'unsaid – but together with her daughter she builds stories of dreams and hopes that, wrapped around stones, they throw into the ocean as a way of sharing their 'most intimate secrets without shame or fear' (4). The story encapsulates the idea that there are many ways to break the silence and give voice to the unspeakable.

This short story contrasts sharply with the disavowal proclaimed by most family members in the other tales of the book. Thus in 'Shoga', the plot is narrated by a teenager who is proudly gay but his grandmother, Ayeeyo, warns him that she will practice an exorcism if he grows up to be gay, as he explains:

> 'Saar' was a brand of Somali exorcism. The 'possessed' – which was code for the mentally unstable – were put through their paces. Healers would beat drums to release spirits from the possessed, who would shimmy and shake, and if they got too frisky, would face the kind of beat-down usually reserved for criminals. Such superstition has always been rife in the bush and my gran, a country gal through and through, knew its effectiveness at deterring unacceptable behaviour. (33)

When the protagonist falls in love with his grandmother's houseboy and comes out to her saying 'I am a shoga, a faggot' (41) she slaps him so hard that he falls. Their affections become deeply shaken: 'She stopped speaking to me altogether and we became two strangers bound by blood and bad history' (41). The end of this tale is depressing not just for this rejection but also because these individuals are all they have, the only surviving members of a Somali refugee family living in Kenya. Thus, after the protagonist leaves for England, Ayeeyo dies alone. She never accepted any of his calls from London, and the thought of his grandmother dying alone breaks his heart. However, as we have already commented, the author is not interested in the victimisation of his characters but in their struggle for survival despite the loss, pain or solitude that affect their lives. Thus, at the end of the tale, the protagonist comments: "'Insha Allah, everything will work out" ... I kept repeating this statement louder and louder until it created an incantatory effect. I repeated this statement until it shifted from mantra to fact, until it became something I could hold onto, something I could believe in' (43).

The disavowal of the family is also depicted in the tales 'Ndambi' and 'Earthling'. In both cases, the protagonist is a Somali lesbian who is rejected by her sister. In the first one, 'Ndambi', the narrator is accused of living in sin because 'it is haram for a woman to love another woman' (69). In a witty dialogue, the protagonist rebuts all the litany of reproaches uttered by her sister on her lesbianism. The narrator is far from feeling upset; she is a young, empowered lesbian who calls herself Ndambi, meaning the 'most beautiful'. In a text full of irony, Diriye Osman criticises homophobic ideas and lesbianism as the mark of a satanic possession, or a mental illness that can be cured (particularly if you marry a man). Obviously, the pairing of heterosexuality and marriage does not lead necessarily to a state of bliss, as the protagonist exemplifies with her sister's life:

> My sister never finished high school because she wanted to play house with an illiterate bundu-boy from Bosaaso, who subsequently made her drop five babies before she was thirty, before dumping her ass for an Egyptian teenager with an air-tight clit and cash to stash. (79)

The short story 'Earthling', Victorian slang for lesbian (94), is narrated in a darker tone as it explores the intricacies of family, lesbianism and mental breakdowns. The protagonist, a Somali photographer, called Zeytun, has just been discharged from a psychiatric hospital in London after attempting suicide, and is heading to her local internet café to get some news about her sister, Hamdi. We soon learn that their relationship was broken when Hamdi's fiancé made her choose between him or Zeytun because of the latter's lesbianism: 'Two women "fornicating" was unnatural and repulsive, not to mention "haram"' (80). In a desperate move to get married to this man from their clan, Hamdi disowned her sister. In the story, the issue of marriage is again questioned, just as is the value given to Hamdi's heterosexual relationship in contrast to Zeytun's lesbian love. As the protagonist tells her sister: 'I love Mari because she makes me happy. You love Libaan because he validates you' (80).

The disavowal of Hamdi marked the beginning of a mental breakdown for Zeytun. Hamdi was her muse, her closest living family member. In her aural hallucinations, Zeytun started hearing voices shouting homophobic insults: 'this smelly Somali lesbian is sitting next to me'; 'dykes are such nasty creatures'; 'hell, that's where you're headed, you dirty bitch', or 'lesbians are nothing but cheap whores' (77-8). Homophobia becomes part of Zeytun's mental breakdown; it has been introjected in her mind.

However, this is not an irrelevant anecdote since there is no doubt that in most societies verbal abuse, intimidation and harassment are constant in the daily lives of many LGBT people who suffer abuse from the state, strangers, acquaintances and even family. Carroll and Mendos' 2017 report, *State-Sponsored Homophobia*, published by the International Lesbian, Gay, Bisexual, Trans and Intersex Association, records that 72 countries have criminal laws against LGBTI people. 32 of these states are African and, in 24 of these countries, the law applies to women as well as men. In the UK, Nick Antjoule's Galop National LGBT 'Hate Crime Report 2016' revealed that 4 in 5 LGBT people had experienced a hate crime related to their gender identity or sexual orientation in their lifetime (79 per cent), up to 2.1 million LGBT people in the UK.

The British Stonewall report by Guasp et al., 'Homophobic Hate Crime', stated that harassment, insults and intimidation are most common. According to the survey, three in four LGBT people experienced verbal abuse as part of a hate crime (75 per cent). Furthermore, the intersection of racism and homophobia is blatant. The report reveals that black and minority ethnic lesbian, gay and bisexual people represent 22 per cent of victims physically assaulted, two and a half times the figure for white people (9 per cent). In view of that, to some extent, one is not surprised to read that in her psychosis Zeytun heard murder threats and thought that she was going to be raped and dismembered just for being a lesbian: 'Their abuse had a psychotic intensity. They were insane. They didn't even know her. Why would they attack her so randomly? For being a lesbian? Did she look that butch? Was there a mark upon her forehead that disclosed her sexuality?' (*Fairytales*: 81). The rejection by her own family has a profound impact on her mind; she is a lesbian, a 'khaniisad'. In contrast to her family's estrangement, the love of her partner Mari flourishes. Mari becomes her sanctuary, her life jacket; as Zeytun remarks, 'she is the reason the voices can't attack me here'. (83). Mari, half Somali/half Japanese, identifies totally with Somalia. Thus, the food she cooks, the clothes she wears, the way she does her hair exhibit her regard for Somali culture. The fact that Kinsi, Mari's mother, a fully Somali woman, accepts her daughter's lesbian relationship also questions the arguments given by Zeytun's family about homosexuality being something repudiated by Somali culture. As Zeytun disputes with Hamdi, homosexuality is not against Somali beliefs: it is against Hamdi's personal beliefs. The support and love of Mari and Kinsi symbolise the silver lining of this story; they mark the road to freedom for Zeytun, 'the lack of noise in her head, the sense of clarity' (99), a state of mind that, as she confesses at the end of the story, is almost there: 'I'm almost free' (99).

In the summer of 2004, Diriye Osman had a psychotic episode. Traumatised by his aural hallucinations he stopped speaking. In the short story 'Your Silence will not Protect You', Osman elaborates on his painful personal experience of having a bout of depression and coming out to his family. Again, issues of sexuality, family and acceptance are present from a more autobiographical and intimate point of view. All these themes are pivoting around the concept of silence in a literal or metaphorical sense. Thus, at the beginning of the story the narrator resorts to silence in self-protection after a painful psychotic episode. In Somali culture, mental illness is a taboo subject; hence, the protagonist reckons, 'I wanted to recover without feeling any guilt and shame over my condition' (106). In his reclusion, his oldest sister became his closest friend, and it was to her that he first came out; he had uttered 'the unspeakable' (108), but she seemed to support him as long as he kept his being gay in silence. For most African families homosexuality is a taboo subject, it is not mentioned in family discussions (Madu 'Health Complaints of High School Students in the Northern Province and Taboo Themes in their Families'). This is commonplace in most societies. In 2006, Christian Grov et al. published a study addressing the coming-out process for gay, lesbian and bisexual persons in New York and Los Angeles. The findings of this research showed that young people of colour are significantly less likely to tell their parents about their homosexuality. Thus, approximately 80 per cent of white women reported being out to their parents, compared to 61 per cent of African-American women, 72 per cent of Latinas, and 68 per cent of women identifying as other races (Asian/Pacific Islander). Similarly, 77 per cent of white men indicated they were out to their parents, compared to 62 per cent of African-American men, 51 per cent of Asian/Pacific Islander men, and 69 per cent of Latinos ('Race, Ethnicity, Gender, and Generational Factors Associated with the Coming Out Process among Gay, Lesbian, and Bisexual Individuals': 118).

In Diriye Osman's short story, the protagonist's sister considers homosexuality a dark secret to be kept in silence. Accordingly, under the guise of tradition, suppression is exacted and silence demanded. When the protagonist starts dating a man his sister tells him to stop it, but now the narrator enjoys 'an open, healthy, guilt-free life' (110), and he is adamant about keeping it. When his sister outs him to the rest of the family, the homophobic insults do not come from aural hallucinations but from them: his brother bullies and threatens him relentlessly, but he cannot keep silence anymore: indeed, his mental health depends on this. In a sense his father's belief that his homosexuality, what he calls 'this gay business' (108), is a side effect of his mental illness and not the other way round is certainly quite ironic. In fact, Diriye Osman has commented on the schizoid consequences that living a life full of silences and lies already had on him:

> My life-long guilt and repression, however, split my selfhood into wildly opposing polarities: the asexual, mysterious vault crammed with secrets to appease my Muslim family, and the hedonistic, sexually adventurous man who danced and drank and made mad, intense love. These polarities – coagulated fear and shame versus freewheeling youthful energy and passion – were headed towards a collision that ultimately resulted in a psychotic episode followed swiftly by hospitalization in a psychiatric unit. ('How Art Can Save a Life')

The traumatic rejection by their relatives makes the lesbian and gay characters in *Fairytales for Lost Children* question the concept of family. As the protagonist ponders in 'Your Silence Will Not Protect You', 'I had always thought of family as a fixed, all-powerful entity. I was raised in a culture where family was the most important thing. But as a gay man I had to learn that nothing in life is fixed, especially families' (113). Even if they are desperately craving the love and tolerance of their families, they are disowned. Therefore, after being banished from their blood relatives, these characters, LGBT people, start creating new families of their own where they are loved and valued.

Coming from very close-knit Somali families that have escaped the horror of wars, refugee camps or corrupt policemen, these diasporic queer characters experience isolation and exile in many different ways. Specifically, they are geographically exiled from their Somali culture; simultaneously there are emotionally isolated from their Somali community for being homosexual and end up by being exiled in their own minds as a result of all the social stigma and psychological stress they suffered.

However, as the title of the story announces, 'silence will not protect you'. Osman follows the pathway paved by Audre Lorde in her essay with the same title. She defended her persistent belief that we must speak out whatever is important or meaningful to us, even if we are misunderstood or harmed since we cannot avoid being hurt in many different ways: we all die even if we have never spoken out what is significant for us. As she confesses, 'of course I am afraid, because the transformation of silence into language and action is an act of self-revelation, and that always seems fraught with danger ... But you're never really a whole person if you remain silent' (*Sister Outsider*: 42).

Thus, the humanity and dignity of LGBT characters prevail in the book *Fairytales for Lost Children*. Diriye Osman, a proudly gay Muslim man, is giving voice to the untold stories of queer people not just from his native Somalia but Africa. Moreover, there is a universal voice in his writings, a truthful voice speaking from the heart, a balsamic healing narrative for those who have been cast out and feel lost. In this collection of short stories we find tales reverberating with songs of experience but, there are also some fully harmonic songs of innocence with contagious joyfulness. A powerful blend of innocence and experience, beauty and horror is encapsulated in the short story that gives the book its title: 'Fairytales for Lost Children'. As the author remarks 'I realized it was important for me to write this story in this way because gay children are so often underrepresented in, if not wholly absent from, fiction' ('The Queering of Sleeping Beauty'). In this story, Osman pays homage to those 'fairy' children who are invisible and lost in heteronormative stories with not-so-happy endings for them.

Xirsi, a ten-year boy who loves Disney films and fairy tales, narrates the story: 'To me they were holy texts, each idea and image sacred ... I was Muslim but fiction was my true religion. The God of Imagination lived in fairytales' (20). When Xirsi goes to school, he falls in love with the blond and blue-eyed six-year-old Ivar. In his imagination, he becomes the Sleeping Beauty and Ivar his Prince Charming. He knew that his love was not easy: 'The object of my affection preferred Action Man to Princess Aurora' (20). There were obstacles in his way, and he was conscious that he was not allowed to love a boy, but he was indeed allowed to dream. All this childish innocence of love and dreams is intertwined with the nightmare that surrounds the daily lives of Somali people. In fact, Xirsi and his family had recently escaped from Somalia.

The memories of the protagonist are framed in blood and terror. In Somalia, these images were of 'brains splattered across the roadside' (16), 'young gabdo [sic] raped and mutilated', or 'an old man tortured until he bled to death' (20-21). Similarly, in Kenya, the panic of being deported by corrupt policemen besieged Xirsi's home. Love, death, innocence and fear are inextricably stitched together into the fabric of this story. The narrative is also imbued with politics in a double way. On the one hand, we are shown Miss Mumbi, the kindergarten teacher who wanted to decolonise her 'Disney-addled' pupil's minds using Kenyan languages and infusing 'each fairytale with Kenyan flavour' (19). In her African political reappropriation of Disney princesses, Rapunzel became Rehema, who had 'an Afro that grew and grew ... The Afro wrapped itself around the moon and pulled Rehema out of the fort ... Even after her death, the Afro lived on' (19). Similarly, Snow White and the Seven Dwarfs turned into Kohl Black and the Seven Street Boys. Kohl was 'plumpness personified: thick thighs, lips, Afro' (23). Coffee-coloured eyes, and darker than liquorice skinned, she was *'supuu'* (beautiful), but her stepmother considered her 'subhuman' (23). The heroine's stepmother was called Immaculate and 'as her name suggested [she] was obsessive. She was obsessed about her size and skin-tone' and suffered from 'Envylitis' (23).

On the other hand, feminism has shown us that the personal is political and the queering of the fairy tales has been a standard feature in the works of many feminist authors such as Angela Carter, Emma Donahue and Jeanette Winterson, among others. However, this short story does not just undoubtedly subvert heteronormative gender ideas; it is equally challenging to racial politics and stereotypes, probably in the footsteps of James Baldwin and his *Little Man Little Man* (1975). Indeed, Diriye Osman's representation of a young African gay boy loving a white boy and identifying himself with a Disney princess involves the opening of a new window for many LGBT children. Furthermore, in the context of the politics of representation, all the queer children around the world, whose desires are not fulfilled in the fairy tales they read, are to some extent given voice in this short story.

This collection of 'fairy tales' is not a children's book but a kaleidoscope of stories around the coming of age of LGBT people. In this context, the politics of identity is questioned particularly in stories such as 'The Other Wo(man)'. The main character Yassin is a young African art student living alone in London who is trying to come to terms with his own political and sexual identity. Adrift in the world, he feels lost, he could not claim a sense of belonging to the Somali culture or the Muslim religion because he was gay and, in both cases, he would be excluded from these communities because of his queerness. In his identity quest, he thought of himself as 'Somali first, Muslim second, gay third' (137). However, this polyhedric sense of identity is also unstable and mutable in time, as the protagonist reckons 'that was only a matter of timing: born Somali, raised Muslim, discovered gay' (137). In his experimenting with sex and identity, Yassin defends his multiple and complex persona. Undoubtedly, the intersectionality of categories such as religion, nation, race, gender or sexual orientation shapes our identities and Yassin is determined in holding all them together.

One of the main themes of *Fairytales for Lost Children* is sexuality, and accordingly, sexual activity is explicitly depicted in it in a sex-positive way. Hence, Diriye Osman describes 'sexlicious' queer scenes in many stories. In 'Ndambi', a woman plays 'games' with her body, and enjoys the 'Jade Love Egg', a practice originated in China taught to a very small number of women that gave them extraordinary skills as lovers (72): 'I tease myself ... until my throat is dry, until I'm panting' (73). In 'Shoga', the protagonist illustrates his sexual intercourse with Boniface: 'He opened me up using lips, fingertips, tongue-tricks' (38). In the story 'My Roots are Your Roots' the author portrays with sensuous overtones the details of the lovers' encounters: 'He licks my lips. A bead of sweat from my forehead drops onto his nose and glints there, a diamante piercing' (155).

All those lost 'children' wandering in the diaspora ultimately find their homes. The idea of home conveys a complex trope and multiple topoi. As the protagonist in 'Ndambi' tells us, home is at once a place in the imagination – 'my Eden, my Janna' (74) – and it is also a family 'all of whom have rejected me, all of whom I still love'. Home is equally evoked in former lovers, in cities and countries like London, Kenya or Somalia, 'the land where my soul will eventually be laid to rest' (74). However, home is essentially an 'embodied' concept: 'Home is in my hair, my lips, my arms, my thighs, my feet and hands. I am my own home' (74).

Diriye Osman finely crafts the scattered lives of those queer survivors in their quest for freedom, and he achieves this in a beautiful prose full of poetry. This collection of short stories oozes freedom, hope and survival. He is indeed following Audre Lorde's advice on transforming silences into speech since, as she said in her poem *A Litany for Survival*,

when we speak we are afraid
our words will not be heard
nor welcomed
but when we are silent
we are still afraid.
So it is better to speak
remembering
we were never meant to survive.
(*The Collected Poems of Audre Lorde*: 256)

Therefore, in a very intimate and personal prose, Diriye Osman is breaking all the silences walled up by feelings of intolerance, fear or shame to speak out his mantra for survival and to shout to the world that 'we own our bodies We own our lives' (156).

WORKS CITED

Antjoule, Nick. 'The Hate Crime Report 2016: Homophobia, Biphobia and Transphobia in the UK', London: Galop, 2016.

Carroll, A. and L.R. Mendos. *State-Sponsored Homophobia 2017: A World Survey of Sexual Orientation Laws: Criminalisation, Protection and Recognition*, 12th edition. Geneva: International Lesbian, Gay, Bisexual Trans and Intersex Association, 2017.

Grov, Christian, D.S. Bimbi, J.E. Nanin and J.T. Parsons. 'Race, Ethnicity, Gender, and Generational Factors Associated with the Coming Out Process among Gay, Lesbian, and Bisexual Individuals'. *Journal of Sex Research* Vol. 43, No. 4 (2007): 115-21.

Guasp, April, A. Gammon and G. Ellison. 'Homophobic Hate Crime: The Gay British Crime Survey'. London: Stonewall, 2013.Jäger, Anna. 'On Mermaids and Microwaves'. *Chimurenga Chronic*, 9 May 2014. http://chimurengachronic.co.za/on-mermaids-and-microwaves (accessed 14 August 2017).

Jayawardane, Neelika. 'Diriye Osman: How to be Gay, Muslim, African'. *Africa is a Country*, 8 December 2014, http://africasacountry.com/2014/12/diriye-on-being-gay-muslim-and-african (accessed 14 August 2017).

Lorde, Audre. *Sister Outsider*, Berkeley, CA: Crossing Press, 2007.

——*The Collected Poems of Audre Lorde*, New York: W.W. Norton, 1997.

Macharia, Keguro. 'Homophobia in Africa is Not a Single Story'. *The Guardian*, 26 May 2010, theguardian.com/commentsfree/2010/may/26/homophobia-africa-not-single-story (accessed 14 August 2017).

Madu, S.N. 'Health Complaints of High School Students in the Northern Province and Taboo Themes in their Families'. *South African Journal of Education* Vol. 22, No. 1: 65-9.

Osinubi, Taiwo Adetunji. 'Queer Prolepsis and the Sexual Commons: An Introduction'. *Research in African Literatures* Vol. 47, No. 2 (2016): 7-23.

Osman, Diriye. *Fairytales for Lost Children*, London: Team Angelica, 2013.

——'How Art Can Save a Life', *Huffington Post Blog*, 14 July 2014, www.huffingtonpost.com/diriye-osman/how-art-can-save-a-life_b_5582637.html (accessed 14 August 2017).

——'The Queering of Sleeping Beauty', *Huffington Post Blog*, 3 February 2015, www.huffingtonpost.com/diriye-osman/the-queering-of-sleeping-_b_6599428.html (accessed 14 August 2017).

——'No Longer Silent: Chronicling Queer African Lives', 23 October 2017, www.diriyeosman.com/single-post/2017/10/23/Chronicling-Queer-African-Lives (accessed 5 April 2018).

Reading for Ruptures

HIV & AIDS, Sexuality & Silencing in Zoë Wicomb's 'In Search of Tommie'

LIZZY ATTREE

Although Cape Town is one of the epicentres of the HIV/AIDs pandemic, it was not until 1999 that Capetonian writers took on this devastating subject. Ten years later, in her only story featuring HIV infection, Zoë Wicomb weaves the taboo subject into 'In Search of Tommie'[1] a story of last days and the search for identity and meaning. It is the first story by a South African author to represent the life of an HIV-positive gay black African man (from Langa). HIV is silenced in the story, not only in the sense that it is not spoken about out loud, particularly by the protagonist TS himself, but also in the sense that between the differently related characters: TS and his mother, TS and his half-sister, TS and his sometime boyfriend, Joe, the word is not used. In two other texts from Cape Town, Rayda Jacobs's novel *Confessions of a Gambler* and Derrick Fine's non-fiction *Clouds Move*, HIV has a very different volume and significance For the purposes of this article, both Jacobs's and Fine's texts feature as points of comparison to demonstrate the level of silencing of HIV/AIDS in South African literature, especially in relation to the cosmopolitan Cape in which they are all set. In addition to a comparative reading, this article also focuses on the differences between depicting gay characters in fiction and non-fiction.

In 'In Search of Tommie' TS alludes to his illness while narrating the story of his '*vark*' (pig) father, Tommie, who left his mother and had another child in England. TS shares his father's name but refuses the identification until his story returns to him in the form of a semi-fictionalised autobiography written by an English woman who could be his half-sister. Allusions to T.S. Eliot and other literary references are thrown into the story by his latter day boyfriend or partner Joe who provides TS with part of his identity as a *moffie* and leads him to contact his potential relative, Chris, in England. It is only through TS and Joe's relationship that TS is able to contact Chris in the UK after reading her book as suggested by his ex-boyfriend. Using mimicry and the urgency of time, which as he is ill is short, TS 'ensnares' Chris (just as her mother is said to have 'ensnared' his father) who also shares the narrative voice at times, providing a cynical counterbalance to TS's conviction that they are related. It is Chris who eventually crystallises the reader's suspicion that TS is dying of AIDS: 'Of course, that was it: the poor guy was ill, probably dying' (79), although AIDS is still not the term used.

The spotlight falls primarily on TS as his interior monologue guides the narrative of 'In Search of Tommie'. In the opening two sentences blood is mentioned immediately. TS describes a 'conviction' as a 'powerful feeling, it was, like fresh blood' (67). He appears to capture two ideas simultaneously: it is ambiguous whether the conviction is that he is ill, or if his conviction is that he has a sibling after reading the book. I favour the former, primarily because in the continuing paragraph he goes on to further elaborate what must be the early stages of tuberculosis, explained away as 'just the rain, unseasonable [which] made his chest wheeze' (68). Wicomb's subtle authorial technique addresses the taboo of HIV-positive status through indirection, but pushes the point further when the reader too is exposed to what seems to be a more serious plight in the lines: 'Things had taken an unfortunate turn, when there was so little time left, so little energy' (68). The link to T.S. Eliot then becomes apparent – an apparently throwaway comment by Joe about TS's choice of name, the significance lost on TS himself – when he writes that 'he had become addicted to heading off into stories'. The power of literature then becomes strangely significant and important to TS, as the reading programme he embarks on, 'meeting the truth in books', takes on a consoling role directly described at one point as a form of escape from his current predicament, in which he has 'so little energy': 'Let's blow, says the book, and off they go ... into the great unknown' (68).

The silencing of HIV is notable in the context of the voicing of other taboo subjects, such as sexuality, which is spoken of more freely than the disease which lurks in TS's 'bad blood' (68-9).[2] TS refers to Joe as 'his Joe' (68) although he knows that 'Joe wouldn't be his for much longer ... Joe had always wanted children. Perhaps he would find a woman' (68-9), suggesting that somehow Joe is more flexible, ambivalent, even emotionally detached from their relationship and its delimitation of his sexuality whereas TS's position is more entrenched. He finds the idea of sex with women, for reproduction in particular, to be abhorrent – 'For TS the idea of reproduction was horrible, the thing that dogs or pigs did; he had never had anything to do with women

'... he did not like women's bundled-up softness. Or the crying' (69). TS explains that he and Joe 'had a history' (69) and implies that Joe is paying for his expensive medication, but '[h]e and Joe didn't talk about the drugs that was paid for' (69). There is an unspoken commitment between the two men that appears stronger than a purely sexual relationship but which at the same time involves a certain amount of dependency by TS on Joe. Theirs is a long and binding friendship, even kinship, which extends beyond sexual engagements and its consequences; it seems not to involve guilt or obligation on either side.

On seeking them out, the references to sickness are ever-present: 'a strange wobbliness – perhaps a new symptom of his sickness – seemed to invade his body' (74), and yet the disease is never named. The only indication that it could be a sickness with a stigma associated is TS's thought that 'she [Chris] may not want to have anything to do with people like him' (74). It is telling that the silenced taboo here is not that TS is gay (or that he is mixed race), but that he is ill. Nevertheless, it is the reader-critic/critical reader who amplifies the voice of the disease in this case. HIV is not the focus of the narrative although it plays a pivotal role in Chris's silent acceptance of her new found relative, indeed prompts her not to reject him but to acknowledge him as kin out of sympathy – connecting them across a hitherto unbridgeable cultural and genetic divide.

Though they do finally meet in the Cape, it is the presence of the disease itself, providing a space of intersection for Chris and TS, that seems unusual in South African literature – 'Was it the tenderness of the light that made her [Chris] straighten up and turn around?' (79). Wicomb is perhaps playing with a different sort of light[3] with this question. The fierce sunlight of the Cape is rarely described as 'tender', but in light of his illness, a certain 'tenderness' changes Chris's perspective on TS; she sees him in a different, softer light because he is HIV positive. This is a silent, almost imperceptible shift, crucial to the conclusion of this unlikely meeting that pivots on a form of cosmopolitan sympathy. It is amusing that instead of mentioning TS's sero-positive status, Chris plays on their racial and cultural difference in the last line of the story when she jokes 'What the hell, eh, she laughed. Just as long as you make sure, my brother, that I don't have to eat authentic African offal' (80). It's easier to mention their ethnic, racial or national difference, than the looming presence of HIV.

The elision of the importance of a sibling genetic or 'blood' connection in finally confirming or defining their relationship is also distinctly cosmopolitan. Kwame Anthony Appiah notes: 'We have obligations to others, obligations that stretch beyond those to whom we are related by the ties of kith and kind, or even the more formal ties of shared citizenship' (*Cosmopolitanism*: xv). Likewise with Joe's relationship with TS, their *moffie* bond is born of companionship and need not be defined in formal or literal/legitimate terms to sanctify its lasting significance. 'In Search of Tommie' stands out in Karina Magdalena Szczurek's collection, *Touch: Stories of Contact*, as one of the few dealing with the outcomes of sexual contact, not only in terms of homosexuality, progeny, scattered siblings and paternity but also in terms of HIV infection. The rest of the collection seems not to live up to its promise of 'touch', from the tame imagery of ruffled white bed sheets against loveless grey walls depicted on the front cover, to the declaration on the back cover that all author royalties will be donated to the Treatment Action Campaign 'for the fight against HIV and AIDS'. The collection overall does not speak of the expected sexual and emotional intimacies and cross-pollination or contamination suggested by the sub-title 'Stories of Contact' – which sounds a little like a colonial encounter. Perhaps the image of the empty bed speaks of absence, or perhaps more profoundly of loss,[4] but overwhelmingly the collection fails to really connect humans physically and emotionally; – perhaps that was the point?

Going beyond the collection in which it features, how does Wicomb's story compare with Rayda Jacobs's novel *Confessions of a Gambler*, or Derrick Fine's non-fiction work *Clouds Move*, also set in the Cape? And how is HIV/AIDS situated in these texts? What is the difference between the handling of HIV/AIDS in fiction and non-fiction in the South African context? The selection of writers from such diverse corners of society is exemplary of the cosmopolitan nature of the Cape: Wicomb's Griqua background relocated to Strathclyde in Scotland, Jacobs's Muslim roots born in Diep River and spending 27 years in Canada, Fine's white Jewish liberal background, gay and HIV positive, living in Kommetjie – these all converge in the Cape. This resonates with Appiah's suggestion that the possibility of a cosmopolitan community is based on individuals from varying locations entering into relationships of mutual respect despite their differing beliefs: 'people are different, the cosmopolitan knows, and there is much to learn from our differences' (*Cosmopolitanism*: xv); indeed, 'our understanding of toleration means interacting on terms of respect with those who see the world differently' (145). That three such different texts, from three such different authors, are all recognisably Capetonian, does not mean that HIV features in the same way in each text. Although writing about HIV/AIDS links these generically distinct texts, I suggest in this article that the presence of the disease in a short story, a novel and an autobiography written by such diverse authors can also be linked to their cosmopolitanism as it is the cosmopolitan nature of the texts (their broad, open-minded and inclusive narratives) that allows the authors to feature HIV in the first place.

*****

The significance of literature in the context of HIV/AIDS lies not only in Steven Kruger's identification of the potential for literature, particularly fiction, to 'intervene politically' (Aids Narratives: 61) in social and political discourses, but also in what Alex de Waal identifies as an indirect means of discovering what kinds of discussions are sparked by news about AIDS:

> No researcher has investigated what people actually talk about, as opposed to how they receive official education messages. We can, however, approach this question indirectly, through those professional observers of everyday life: novelists. A small sample of African novels in English provides a first cut at exploring this topic, and it is clear that AIDS is approached indirectly, in diverse ways, through other issues. (AIDS and Power: 32)

Literature provides access to a complex web of cultural, intimate information that other forms of research cannot. Didier Fassin remarks that 'works in the social sciences rarely mention subjectivity' (*When Bodies Remember*: 261), or rather the creative capacity subjects have for re-defining, re-imagining and re-inscribing their reality. As Alex de Waal reiterates: 'We need to *imagine* HIV/AIDS before we can think practically about it' (*AIDS and Power*: 117).

In South Africa, as Deborah Posel comments, 'the birth of a nation [is] accompanied by the death of its people' ('A Matter of Life and Death': 1). Posel goes on to ask, in a time of AIDS: 'what place, therefore, does an analytic of death occupy within the theorization of modernity?' (2). Indeed, what place does the analytic of death or the space of death occupy within South African literature? Posel has stated: 'In reconfiguring death and dying, AIDS has become a major factor in the refashioning of modernity itself ... The idea of death is therefore also the condition of meaning and the production of culture – even if it in no way exhausts or even dominates the proliferation of meaning' (5-6). Her significant research in the field of sociology has built upon these important questions, but how can they usefully be applied to reading fiction? The positive elements of cosmopolitanism as part of healthy multi-cultural nation building seem integral to modernity, and capture the cultural, ethical and social elements of globalisation, which is the driving force of the twenty-first century; yet the HIV/AIDS pandemic was thriving at the height of the nation-building project in South Africa, causing massive social and physical disintegration. For example, in the midst of the period in which the three literary texts were published (between 1999 and 2007), in 2005 in South Africa 5.5 million people were infected with HIV (UNAIDS/WHO Epidemic Update).

Speculation that the HIV/AIDS epidemic could have an impact parallel to apartheid on South African society has recently been asserted by at least one major book-length study, which notes: 'The scale of the HIV epidemic is enormous and its social consequences will be felt as deeply as those of apartheid, in the years to come' (Abdool Karim *HIV/AIDS in South Africa*: 453). Historically, since its discovery in the early 1980s, HIV/AIDS has triggered multiple socio-cultural responses that Paula Treichler has termed an 'epidemic of signification' (*How to Have Theory in an Epidemic*: 171). The most dominant of these is rooted in the language of differentiation. Sander Gilman explains that the process of differentiation is bound up with the idea of the 'pathological': 'the potential illness, age, and corruption of the self is projected onto others so that the world becomes seen as both corrupt and corrupting, polluted and polluting. The threat and its result become one' (*Difference and Pathology*: 23). Yet literature can offer a space that enables close identification with another through the depiction and articulation of suffering that is often otherwise silenced or rendered unspeakable. Linguistic representation walks a tightrope in exposing and 'excavating silence' (Brink 'Stories of History': 33), as well as provoking or recovering repressed trauma in the face of pain and death. So what part has HIV/AIDS played in re-fashioning this strand of literature, stories of modernity and death in South Africa? And how is the cosmopolitan configuration of the Cape affected by the presence of HIV/AIDS – a source of division, differentiation, repression, amnesia and (often hard-won) sympathy?

David Attwell writes of South African letters that 'the predominant mode, it is said, is the literature of witness, documentary, and protest – varieties of realism' (*Rewriting Modernity*: 169), and this is borne out in the literary publications that feature HIV/AIDS which, though largely fictional, are mostly realist witnessing texts, often containing an element of protest. Fiction, biography and autobiography are powerful forms of witnessing that have increased in number since 1999, before which, South Africans appeared reluctant to confront the spectre of HIV/AIDS in literary or published form, perhaps because the feelings and reactions that HIV/AIDS inspires are often 'too unreal for words' (Dellamora *Apocalyptic Overtures*: 154), but also because the impact of the epidemic has been so overwhelming. When HIV did begin to appear in South African literature it took a fictional form.[5] Part of the reason for favouring fiction over 'fact' (for both writers and critics) is because, as André Brink writes: 'The enterprise of fiction ... reaches well beyond facts: inasmuch as it is concerned with the real (whatever may be regarded as "real" in any given context) it presumes a process through which the real is not merely represented but imagined' ('Stories of History': 30). In my mind, this emancipatory capacity of literature opens up spaces for utopian impulses, creating spaces in which HIV/AIDS can not only be articulated but managed, imagined and distanced from the immensity of the suffering it causes and outside the boundaries and tyrannies of medical, developmental, economic, social and political discourse. In Wicomb's fiction this fragile space allows HIV, race and sexuality to become purely part of the fabric of the Cape cosmopolitan world rather than simply the site of social and political struggle.

An integral part of cosmopolitanism lies in the imagination. Kwame Appiah writes: 'The idea behind the Golden Rule is that we should take other people's interests seriously, take them in to account. It suggests that we learn about other people's situations, and then use our imaginations to walk a while in their moccasins' (*Cosmopolitanism*: 63). The subjectivity of the Cape cosmopolitan is exposed in Wicomb's short story to be as broad and open in imagination as it is narrow and restricted by circumstance. Yet in Wicomb's story the presence of HIV/AIDS provides a space in which to connect two characters across a racial, economic and emotional divide. Much of 'In Search of Tommie' is rooted in 'conversation', speech, communication, dialogue. We hear the silences, or rather the silent voices, internal monologues, and amplify them. TS's conversations with himself provide the reader with invaluable insight into his state of mind but also his isolation and loneliness, living with his mother in Langa. The conversations TS has with Joe, his mother and Chris exemplify and enact the intimacy and distance between them. But it is his brief conversation with Chris that transforms and connects them – ironically not through what they say to each other, but what is left unsaid. Appiah suggests that

> conversations across boundaries of identity – whether national, religious, or something else – begin with the sort of imaginative engagement you get when

you read a novel or watch a movie or attend to a work of art that speaks from some place other than your own. So I'm using the word 'conversation' not only for literal talk but also as a metaphor for engagement with the experience and ideas of others. And I stress the role of the imagination here because the encounters, properly conducted, are valuable in themselves. (85)

The silent engagement and acceptance of TS's illness by Chris is not the only imaginative encounter occurring in the short story; of course the reader is also intimately involved in the silent unspoken world of TS via his interior monologues and, through the dexterity of Wicomb's written words, is drawn into an alliance of sympathy with those who are HIV positive – communicating all that falls between the cracks and remains unspoken.

*****

Literary representations of HIV and AIDS in the Cape have included Rayda Jacobs's description of Reza's illness and death in *Confessions of a Gambler* (gay son of protagonist narrator), and Derrick Fine's autobiographical story, *Clouds Move*, which describes his life to date as an HIV-positive gay man living in Kommetjie. Jacobs writes in her novel the tale of the premature death of Reza, who dies in his thirties, whereas both Fine and Wicomb describe the processes of living with HIV, re-fashioning identities, making new connections, coming to terms with treatment and survival. When compared to Wicomb's short story 'In Search of Tommie', Jacobs's and Fine's works are comparable because their stories deal with HIV and sexuality, the infection and premature death of young gay men. Wicomb's writing also significantly details the way in which last days are reconfigured through literature by actions that are arguably motivated by impending death. TS's search for roots, for a sibling, for a more meaningful connection between himself and the world he only comes to recognise and make sense of through reading Chris's book, are all propelled by his knowledge that 'Joe wouldn't be his for much longer' (68). In TS's search for his father Tommie, he reclaims a kind of agency over his own identity, gaining more control over his own narrative.

The reclamation of the diseased body, and the traumatised, afflicted self is part of the still developing process of writing HIV/AIDS in postcolonial South Africa that mirrors what Gikandi has called 'territorial repossession' ('The Politics and Poetics of National Formation': 384). Destabilising the myth of the 'nation' as a unified, monolithic, naturally healthy entity, narratives about HIV/AIDS deconstruct hegemonic (often patriarchal) discourses of the postcolonial nation. Such reclamations have particularly significant implications for the patriarchal nation when the diseased body is either masculine or feminine. In this theorisation I draw on Meg Samuelson's illuminating work on the appropriation of women's bodies to bolster national imaginaries of 'wholeness and unity ... while repressing the ruptures that women's manifestly different experiences ... may reveal' (*Remembering the Nation, Dismembering Women?*: 232). It is the rupture caused by the unflinching description of the sick body that fractures national imaginaries, but it is the restoration of subjectivity to these sick bodies and those who interact with them, that confirms our humanity and creates space for utopian impulses to arise from the survival of hope and beauty, in the face of death. The recognition and representation of the infected body, not vulnerable to infection but already infected (and sometimes surviving), speaking and articulating their suffering is an act of rupture, a move from the imaginary and the symbolic towards sympathy and empathy with the suffering individual. This rupture breaks a long-held silence in South African literature about HIV/AIDS and its effects on the body.[6] Rayda Jacobs achieves a similar rupture in describing Reza's fate in *Confessions of a Gambler*:

> I stood looking at him for a few moments – the full lips, the sunken cheekbones, the bony shoulders poking through the pyjamas. A thought came to me cold and calm without panic. My son was going to die. His life was going to end as quietly as it had begun. (99)

The novel contains a strong element of compassion in its description of Reza's suffering from HIV/AIDS. Instead of focusing on the spectacle of HIV/AIDS, Jacobs's protagonist matriarch, Abeeda, reflects on the fate of her son – once a baby, whom she: 'carried ... under [her] heart' (47). This language of love, physical connection and motherhood is a powerful weapon with which to confront those who would rather not speak of HIV/AIDS or who blame and deny their families in these times of crisis. In *Confessions of a Gambler*, it is gambling that is referred to as a disease[7] and arguably the presence of the casino and Abeeda's addiction to gambling that provides the risqué edge to the book. This element of Abeeda's life suffuses the novel with a sense of *haraam* (unlawfulness/sin), provoking the judgement of both friends and family. However, this is accommodated within a wider (modern) moral framework that allows for discrepancies in one's devotional life:

> 'Are you saying it's all right for Mummy to go to the casino?' Munier asked.

> 'Of course not, but I don't think we should make it such a big issue. Mummy's not a child. And we all sin.'
>
> 'We don't have to add to our sin,' Munier continued. (76)

In fact when God is mentioned by Braima, Abeeda's ex-husband and Reza's father, Abeeda exclaims: 'I wanted to scream. "Always it's about God – isn't it? Well, there's no time to play the holies. He has AIDS. That's real. I need your help, not make it worse"' (33). The sole reference to the clichéd idea of AIDS as a 'plague' in this novel is to the Old Testament, which doesn't seem to fit in the cosmology of this somewhat compromised Islamic universe. Abdul, a spiritual advisor and friend, reassures Abeeda: '"I read this book," he said to me once, "that the God of pestilence and plagues was the God of four thousand years ago … the author's implying that as man evolved, so had God"' (162-3). It seems that, according to Abdul, 'plague' is no longer relevant in this post-apartheid, cosmopolitan, twenty-first century Islamic view of South Africa, and neither is homophobia.

Interestingly, despite the constant moralising and inclusion of Qur'anic indictments of the behaviour of both Abeeda and her son Reza, the text of *Confessions of a Gambler* is very straightforward and down-to-earth about Reza's suffering from AIDS: 'the truth is that he's gay, and he has AIDS, and I'm not going to hide it' (140). Not once is the disease referred to metaphorically. There is no judgement of his condition, and when the subject of blame does come up, Abeeda is emphatic that there is no one to blame: 'It's no one's fault. He's a good son' (34); 'Don't blame yourself for this, Braima. It's not you' (138). In Abeeda, Jacobs depicts a strong modern independent Muslim woman who believes love for her children overcomes all else, even homosexuality, which is taboo in the Qur'an:

> my sons didn't meet my eyes. They were quiet because I'd silenced them. But they didn't agree with me. For all their modern ideas, they still went by the Book. But the Book also talks about compassion. I'm a mother. I carried my son under my heart. I wasn't going to rob him of his last moments with his companion and friend. (47)

In fact it is remarkable that an Islamic-informed text written by a woman vehemently overthrows censorship in this way. It is also worth noting that Wicomb's text does not even begin to question where TS may have contracted HIV and who may be to blame for his infection: that is a search that TS is uninterested in, unable or unwilling to initiate, or perhaps he already knows the source – it is simply outside the scope of the narrative, and is thus rendered irrelevant.

A comparable companion or friend can be found in Derrick Fine who does not shy away from the ravages that AIDS enacts on his body and those he loves. Openly gay, Derrick has been living with HIV since 1999 and writes that 'starting as a jarring wake-up call, testing HIV positive has taken me on an eight-year journey to a life-affirming identity of living, and loving and being loved, with HIV as one part of who I am' (*Clouds Move*: 207) He wrote and published *Clouds Move* in 2007 and declares that the book 'is not just my story, but the story of many people close to me ... many people living with HIV [and] many people affected by HIV' (3). His aim is to 'reduce stigma around HIV and AIDS' and in doing so he tells a moving tale of his life, coming out aged 26 to his sister and two years later to his father, testing HIV positive at 41, the death of his mother and father, his commitment to his life partner Andile in 2004 and their marriage in 2006.

HIV, sexuality and race are all featured very clearly and boldly in Fine's book which follows in the footsteps of Edwin Cameron's *Witness to AIDS* and Adam Levin's *AIDSAFARI*, both published in 2005, but *Clouds Move* is styled as a self-help book, with questions, discussion and workshop suggestions printed at the back. Derrick describes the process of gradually revealing his HIV-positive status to friends and finally family, drawing strength from the support he receives, and taking anti-retroviral medications from the very beginning. He describes the side effects he experiences as minimal, including 'bitterness in the mouth, dry lips and occasional flaky skin or small rashes' (25). He encounters many others who are obviously ill and in denial or who die without facing their infection, such as Lizo, whose lips are described as 'very red, discoloured and dry. He has a nagging, lingering cough that he disguises as due to continuing to have the odd cigarette I don't buy it' (41). He admits to tuberculosis, but a few months later Lizo dies suddenly. AIDS is not mentioned at his funeral in Nyanga.

During 2002 Derrick comes off his antiretroviral therapy (ARVs), and meets Andile the following year through a lonely hearts advertisement. Andile also tests positive and he and Derrick face the future together, setting up the Openly Positive Trust that publishes *Clouds Move* and provides support to the HIV-positive community. After a stressful period liaising with the Department of Health over the contents of the national toolkit ('To the other side of the mountain – the faces and voices of people living with HIV and AIDS in South Africa'), Derrick contracts shingles which re-starts his ARV programme: 'Two months from hell follow. Enormous immobilising pain (post-herpetic neuralgia) limits my mobility and capacity to be active at work' (113).

The cloud, though, has a silver lining as Derrick and Andile decide to hold a commitment ceremony on Kommetjie beach at the end of 2004 in front of family and friends. By 2005, following the loss of a close friend and an ex-boyfriend, Derrick is back on ARVs for life, and the book continues to detail the changes to his pill regimen and his eventual marriage (civil union) with Andile in 2006. Fine shares the details of the physical effects of the disease and, like Jacobs, he de-stigmatises his homosexuality and HIV, defending his gay lifestyle and presenting a practical, loving way to live happily and be HIV positive.

In contrast, in Wicomb's text, as mentioned earlier, the only sign that TS's body is afflicted is in the reference to his 'bad blood', some wobbliness, a coughing fit, and tiredness. Wicomb's protagonist still has a relatively healthy body, occupying a state of limbo like Fine, between sickness and health. *Clouds Move* as a personal story goes deeply into the different emotional and physical aspects of HIV infection, whereas 'In Search of Tommie' provides a brief window into TS's life in which, although HIV is not at the centre of the story, its presence re-focuses a key moment in TS's life and perhaps also drives the need to find his origins and a sibling – to invest his 'bad' blood with another more positive kind of significance. Wicomb's story differs substantially from those of Jacobs and Fine, in that the presence of HIV is muted, but nevertheless its presence acts as a catalyst to alter the relationship between TS and Chris. Indeed, by including the subject at all, Wicomb is also breaking a long-held silence in acknowledging the presence and effect of HIV/AIDS and allowing its presence to be quietly spoken.

*****

Each text examined in this article breaches the 'immense wall of silence' identified by Adam Levin (*AIDSAFARI*: x), and each rupture in the coherent 'healthy' national imaginary has a particular volume and significance. 'In Search of Tommie' is the most muted on the subject of HIV infection from the Cape, compared to *Confessions* and *Clouds*. It is perhaps this subtlety that makes Wicomb's story the most effective as a work of literature and of imagination, demonstrating the power of literature by 'meeting the truth in books' (68), however complex and obscured 'the truth' is. Nonetheless the disease and its effects are distinctly present in Wicomb's text. Difficult to ignore, HIV/AIDS has become an increasingly large part of the African present, disrupting the African renaissance and the utopian dreams of a 'free' South Africa. It is arguably also part of South Africa's cosmopolitanism, one of its key links to the globalisation of the twenty-first century world.

The hazard of cosmopolitanism and the global network it now comprises is the negative impact such connectedness can create, meaning that we can 'through negligence as easily as malice [send] things that will cause harm: a virus, an airborne pollutant, a bad idea' (Appiah *Cosmopolitanism*: xii). Although the trajectory of the representation of HIV/AIDS in South African literature has crept closer and closer to the personal over the last ten years, 'In Search of Tommie' is the first story to represent the life of an HIV-positive gay black African man (from Langa) and, though not written by such a man, its presence is nevertheless significant in literary terms, as Treichler notes: 'The activities and ideas that we organize around the sign AIDS – including the chronicles that we write – have the power to change the fate of the epidemic' (*How to Have Theory in an Epidemic*: 329).

Indeed it is not until Masande Ntshanga's *The Reactive* was published in 2014, that a black HIV-positive character features as the protagonist narrated in the first person in a novel from South Africa. Literature that features or mentions HIV/AIDS whether loudly and explicitly (like Moele's *The Book of the Dead*) or quietly (as Wicomb does) has begun to create new languages and linguistic codes, finding increasingly more-complex and subtle ways of writing about HIV/AIDS, linking South Africa with a cosmopolitan community of writers and readers who have written about and experienced HIV/AIDS far beyond the shores of the Cape, presenting the diversity and tragedies of the Cape in compelling, individual and dynamic ways.

NOTES

1   First published in *Wasafiri* Issue 59, Autumn 2009. The text referenced throughout is the version published in Szczurek's *Touch* in 2009.
2   It is interesting to note that an alternative reading of the reference to 'bad blood' can be traced through Wicomb's consistent consideration of 'mixed blood' or 'miscegenation' with particular reference to Sarah Gertrude Millin's *God's Step-Children*; indeed the subtitle for Book II is 'Mixed Blood . J.M. Coetzee has written about 'the poetics of blood' in the chapter 'Blood, Taint, Flaw, Degeneration: The Novels of Sarah Gertrude Millin' in his *White Writing*. Thanks to Dorothy Driver for pointing out the potential for inter-textual connection between Wicomb and Millin at the Wicomb Conference in Stellenbosch, April 2010. Unfortunately, further in-depth discussion of this issue falls outside the bounds of this article. It is worth noting that the symbolism of 'bad blood', the idea that mixing blood is

dangerous, was the root of apartheid ideology and can be linked to fears of disease, contamination and 'infection' not just in the literal sense, but also in the metaphorical sense; the idea that white supremacism could be 'diluted' or disrupted by inter-racial mixing was a founding principle of the National Party, which sought to police the privacy of the bedroom as much as the public streets of South Africa. Fears of the spread of tuberculosis and sexually transmitted diseases through 'contact with natives' fuelled the division of mining compounds, cities and townships, and the requirement for permission to travel from rural areas based on the *dompass*, which required certain vaccinations (smallpox in the early days) before permitting the movement of valuable labour in to 'whites only' areas.

3   Wicomb's novel *Playing in the Light*, is about 'passing' as white, playing with racial categorisation based on skin colour during apartheid.

4   As in the photography collection by Santu Mofokeng titled *Child-headed Households*: the photographs, such as 'Mkanzi Family Bedroom' powerfully acknowledge AIDS without depicting it directly. We are invited to investigate the detail of the domestic interior – the symbols of the children's day-to-day reality – which contain vacant spaces, empty beds and chairs that symbolise the absence of parents.

5   The major fictional examples are: *Nobody ever said AIDS* edited by Nobantu Rasebotsa, Meg Samuelson and Kylie Thomas, *Welcome to Our Hillbrow* by Phaswane Mpe, *Confessions of a Gambler* by Rayda Jacobs, *Beauty's Gift* by Sindiwe Magona, *The Book of the Dead* by Kgebetli Moele. Non-fiction: *Three Letter Plague* by Johnny Steinberg, *Khabzela* by Liz McGregor, *AIDSAFARI* by Adam Levin, *Witness to AIDS* by Edwin Cameron, and *Clouds Move* by Derrick Fine.

6   For more on this see Lizzy Attree 'The Body in South African Fiction and Film' in *Images of Africa*: 191.

7   'Compulsive gambling is a disease, and it's progressive. That means it gets worse with time. You can't cure it' (*Confessions of a Gambler*: 90). Perhaps this is a metaphor for sexual behaviour and HIV/AIDS? That is, self-control can prevent danger. Although Abeeda's adultery with her sister's husband does 'pay off' in the end, she only gets her 'winnings' when she has exercised a period of self-restraint. This mirrors the abstinence argument in HIV/AIDS prevention – the most effective and least observed of the ABC rules: Abstain, Be faithful, Condomise).

WORKS CITED

Abdool Karim., S.S. and Q. Abdool Karim (eds). *HIV/AIDS in South Africa*. Cape Town: Cambridge University Press, 2010.

Appiah, Kwame Anthony. *Cosmopolitanism: Ethics in a World of Strangers*. New York: W.W. Norton 2006.

Attree, Lizzy. 'The Body in South African Fiction and Film'. In *Images of Africa: Creation, Negotiation and Subversion*, ed. Julia Gallagher. Manchester: University of Manchester Press, 2015: 188-200.

Attwell, David. *Rewriting Modernity: Studies in Black South African Literary History*. Scottsville, SA: University of KwaZulu-Natal Press, 2005.

Brink, André. 'Stories of History: Reimagining the Past in Post-Apartheid Narrative'. In *Negotiating the Past: The Making of Memory in South Africa*, eds Carli Coetzee and Sarah Nuttall. Cape Town: Oxford University Press 1998: 29-42.

Cameron, Edwin. *Witness to AIDS*. Cape Town and London: Tafelberg Publishers and I.B. Tauris, 2005.

Coetzee, J.M. 'Blood, Taint, Flaw, Degeneration: The Novels of Sarah Gertrude Millin'. In *White Writing: On the Culture of Letters in South Africa*. New Haven, CT and London Radix, Yale University Press, 1988: 136-62.

Dellamora, Richard. *Apocalyptic Overtures: Sexual Politics and the Sense of an Ending*. New Brunswick, NJ: Rutgers University Press, 1994.

de Waal, Alex. *AIDS and Power: Why there is No Political Crisis – Yet*. London: Zed Books, 2006.

Fassin, Didier. *When Bodies Remember: Experiences and Politics of AIDS in South Africa*. Berkeley, CA: University of California Press, 2007.

Fine, Derrick. *Clouds Move*. Cape Town: Openly Positive Trust, 2007.

Gikandi, Simon. 'The Politics and Poetics of National Formation: Recent African Writing'. In *From Commonwealth to Post Colonial*, ed Anna Rutherford. Sydney: Dangaroo Press 1992: 377-89.

Gilman, Sander. *Difference and Pathology: Stereotypes of Sexuality, Race and Madness*. Ithaca, NY: Cornell University Press, 1985.

Jacobs, Rayda. *Confessions of a Gambler*. Cape Town: Kwela Books, 2003.

Kruger, Steven. *Aids Narratives: Gender and Sexuality, Fiction and Science*. New York: Garland, 1996.

Levin, Adam. *AIDSAFARI: A Memoir of My Journey with AIDS*. Cape Town: Zebra Press, 2005.

Magona, Sindiwe. *Beauty's Gift*. Cape Town: Kwela Books, 2008.

Millin, Sarah Gertrude. *God's Step-Children*. London: A. Constable, 1924.

Moele, Kgebetli. *The Book of the Dead*. Cape Town: Kwela Books, 2009.

Mofokeng, Santu. *Child-headed Households*. South Africa, 2007.

Ntshanga, Masande. *The Reactive*. Cape Town: Umuzi, 2014.

Posel, Deborah. 'A Matter of Life and Death: Revisiting "Modernity" from the Vantage Point of the "New" South Africa'. Draft Paper delivered on 7 February 2003 at the Bio-Politics, States of Exception and the Politics of Sovereignty Workshop at WISER (Wits Institute for Social and Economic Research), University of Witwatersrand. http://wiserweb.wits.ac.za/PDF%20Files/biopolitics%20-%20posel.PDF (accessed 22 October 2010).

Samuelson, Meg. *Remembering the Nation, Dismembering Women? Stories of the South African Transition*. Scottsville, SA: University of KwaZulu-Natal Press, 2007.

Treichler, Paula. *How to Have Theory in an Epidemic: Cultural Chronicles of AIDS*. Durham, NC: Duke University Press, 1999.
UNAIDS/WHO. *AIDS Epidemic Update*. Geneva: Joint United Nations Programme on HIV/AIDS and World Health Organization, 2006.
Wicomb, Zoë. *Playing in the Light*. New York: New Press, 2006.
——'In Search of Tommie'. In *Touch: Stories of Contact by South African Writers*, Karina Magdalena Szczurek (ed). Cape Town: Zebra Press, 2009: 67-80.
——'In Search of Tommie'. *Wasafiri* Vol. 24, No. 3 (2009): 51-55.

Queer Temporalities & Epistemologies

Jude Dibia's *Walking with Shadows* & Chinelo Okparanta's *Under the Udala Trees*

KERRY MANZO

Nigerian gay and lesbian literature has recently experienced something of a 'coming out,' signalled on the one hand by the publication of two novel-length explorations of the complex identity negotiations of same-sex desiring subjects in the context of a homophobic Nigerian society, and on the other hand by scholarly attention to these works as 'emergent' forms. Yet, Jude Dibia's *Walking with Shadows* (2005) and Chinelo Okparanta's *Under the Udala Trees* (2015) – hailed as the first Nigerian gay and lesbian novels, respectively – are not the first literary treatments of homosexuality in Nigerian history. There have been previously the well-known character of Joe Golder in Wole Soyinka's *The Interpreters* (1965), the arguably queer Elvis Oke of Chris Abani's *Graceland* (2004), and the characters of Daisy and Ruth in Tess Onwueme's *Tell it to Women* (1992, 1997). What makes Dibia's and Okparanta's works resonate as significantly different from earlier works, however, is their exploration of the dual problematics of identity formation and subjectification of non-heteronormative sexualities. In these works, the same-sex desiring protagonists struggle to reconcile ostensibly private self-knowledge and desires against publicly circulating normative sexual discourses, only to find that 'private' desires are, from their inception, subject to public speculation and control within an already constituted normative discourse field. It is only when one's desire is outside the bounds of the recognisable that the public nature of private desires becomes apparent. Thus, a central problem in these works is how to locate an epistemological stance that would not merely pit private desire against public sexual discourse, but rather to shed light on the ways in which the knowledge of a normative public attempts to speak in place of individual self-knowledge.

Public discourses of homosexuality and anti-homosexuality at the local and national levels in Nigeria tend to be citational, arguing on behalf of either an originary heterosexual past or a past in which alternative sexual identities had a 'traditional' role. In both cases, the strength of the argument is presumed to stand on the idea of a citational chain stretching back to time immemorial in which the presence or absence of homosexuality is consistent over time. Only now, the argument goes, do we see something different happening in the realm of sexual knowledge. Based on this logic, many anti-homosexual politicians and lobbyists in Nigeria point to Western imperialism as the source of homosexual contamination (Ekine 'Contesting Narratives of Queer Africa': 78), while LGBTI activists counter by pointing to Western evangelicals' importation of homophobia and the idea that homosexuality is 'un-African' (Mac-Iyalla 'Changing Attitudes through the Example of Jesus': 76). On the other hand, at the transnational level, LGBTI rights-based discourses reflect a belief in individuals' possession of a 'true' private self, an essential inner core that is sexual identity. This 'shared 'gayness'' allows international LGBTI rights advocates and non-government organisations to argue from a moral mandate, yet at the same time, by positing a universal essential identity that is stable across cultures, these same movements are excused from participating in the worlding of actual LGBTI lives internationally (Hoad *African Intimacies*: xiii). Thus, whether citational or essentialising, public discourses of homosexuality, anti-homosexuality, and LGBTI rights tend to be both homogenising and hegemonising. My analysis below suggests that by disengaging from the citational chain in favour of engaging allegorical and allusive relationalities and by locating the conditioning of self-knowledge in public discourses that work to direct and constrain difference, Dibia's and Okparanta's works counter dominant sexual discourses temporally and epistemologically.

In these two works, the protagonists face social censure when their homosexual desires are revealed. The arc of both stories is a journey towards self-acceptance and a liveable life. In much of their themes and character, *Walking with Shadows* and *Under the Udala Trees* do not differ strongly from other contemporary Nigerian writing. Being twenty-first century works by authors born after the Nigerian Civil War, they are periodised as belonging to the 'third generation' of Nigerian writing. Third-generation writing – broadly characterised – explores the problems of 'ethnic and national identity in the contested site of Nigerian nationhood' (Adesanmi and Dunton 'Nigeria's Third Generation Writing': ix), often employing intensely personal motifs such as sex, violence, and trauma as allegorical renderings of historical violences of colonialism and postcolonialism. Dibia's and Okparanta's works differ from this general trend primarily in that the latter is inverted, such that historical violences serve as allegorical renderings of the intensely personal motifs of anti-homosexual violence, homosexual desire, and the trauma that comes from both.

This article is divided into three sections. The first section examines the texts' representation of 'coming out' or being 'outed' as a process of subjectification and interpellation by dominant normative discourses. The second section analyses the texts' engagement with the temporality inherent in citational homosexual and anti-homosexual discourses. I argue that Nigerian LGBTI literature in its emergent form is future-anticipatory and speaks to a desire to transform gender and sexual knowledge through allusive connection to the past and solid grounding in present realities. Finally, the third section offers a queer analysis of the figure of the child in Dibia's and Okparanta's works, wherein the child is re-imagined as a means to disrupt national and transnational normative sexual discourses.

PUBLIC DISCOURSE/PRIVATE DESIRE

In *The Black Atlantic*, Paul Gilroy suggests that rather than proceeding from a position that argues for or against essentialism or anti-essentialism, racial identity or racial non-identity, one might look for the source of racialised subjectivity in the social practices and forms of power that operate on the black body. This anti-anti-essentialist position asks us to look for how '[the signs of blackness] produce the imaginary effect of an internal racial core or essence by acting on the body through specific mechanisms of identification and recognition that are produced in the intimate interaction of [performance]' (102). Gilroy uses Foucault's idea of power to open a path to critical understanding of the ways in which black cultural signs are used as commodities to create a sense of racial identity. Here, I would like to rework Gilroy's argument to suggest that 'homosexuality' or 'gayness' in *Walking with Shadows* is produced as an effect of the dominant society's discursive practices. Whereas same-sex desire is portrayed as inherent to the individual, 'homosexuality' or 'gayness' are instead the result of the same-sex desiring subject's interpellation within a regime of sexual truth.

In Dibia's work, the protagonist Adrian struggles to maintain a bourgeois life as a husband and father after a disgruntled ex-employee – whom Adrian recently fired for engaging in fraudulent practices – reveals to his friends and family that Adrian is gay. While Adrian had hoped that by making a choice to marry and have a child he could leave his desire for men in the past, relegating it to the status of a trace or 'shadow' in his present life, it is less of an 'absent presence' than a *present absence* for those around him. Having heard the accusations of a stranger on a phone, Adrian's family and co-workers press to hear it from Adrian himself. In confrontation after confrontation, Adrian must speak the 'truth' of himself. Whether it is his wife asking, 'Are you gay?' (19), his brother asking, 'It's all lies, isn't it?' (49), or his boss asking, 'Is there something you would like to tell me, Adrian?' (72), he is pressed into the confessional mode. The confession functions as a crucial element of 'coming out' as constituted within Western and other minoritising sexual discourses, wherein gay self disclosure, even when performed as an affirmative political act, exists in relation to both the silence of the closet and dominant society's play of ignorance (Sedgwick *Epistemology of the Closet*: 8). Thus, while the silence around 'the closet' defines the boundaries of acceptable sexual behaviour, so, too, does the compulsion to convert certain sexual desires into discourse via confession. In essence, the repetition of these confessionals constitutes performative moments through which Adrian effectively becomes 'gay' through discourse and simultaneously enacts his subjection to the existing regime of truth.

Interposed with these confessional moments are private confessions in which various characters express the sentiment that they already knew Adrian was not like everyone else. Adrian's wife, Ada, recalls the sense that she 'knew something' was different even before their marriage, and she attributes this sense to Adrian's neatness and 'prettiness ... those subtle signs' (36). Likewise, Adrian's brothers, Chika and Chiedu, recall that Adrian was 'quiet and reserved' as a child (126). Suggestively, in these moments, no one is struck with memories of when Adrian was just like everyone else, times when he was 'passing'. Yet, was Adrian always that different, or are these memories merely discourse effects of the othering? In other words, is it possible that the salience of being *named as different* has recalled memories which likewise pose Adrian as different? Further, is it possible that Adrian comes to identify as gay and essentially different because the discourse has made him so? This is not to say that Adrian does not desire men. But is it this desire that makes him 'gay' or the process of selective and retrospective memory in combination with societal practices of naming the other? While there exists the temptation to suggest that the novel comes squarely down on the side of essentialising gayness, it may be also possible to read Adrian's conversion to this position as a product of normativising discourses, rather than as the ideological position of the author. In effect, the novel suggests that people are retrospectively seeking signs of 'gayness' in Adrian's past and retroactively apportioning to those signs a meaning as an effect of an imagined internal sexual core.

While *Walking with Shadows* takes place in a twenty-first century globalised Nigeria, *Under the Udala Trees*, published ten years later as Nigeria's first 'lesbian' novel, goes back to Nigeria's civil war (Biafran War) to connect the schisms of the past with those in the present. The Biafran War (1967-1970) was largely the result of deep societal and tribalist schisms left over from the colonial period. The Biafran War has been the subject of numerous literary works, including Chinua Achebe's 'Girls at War', Buchi Emecheta's *Destination Biafra*, Flora Nwapa's *Never Again*, Ken Saro-Wiwa's *Sozaboy* and Chimamanda Adichie's *Half of a Yellow Sun*. Whether written close to the events of the war or decades later, these works chronicle the sufferings and injustices of the war visited on ordinary people. While earlier works, such as those by Achebe, Emecheta, Nwapa and Saro-Wiwa, trouble Nigerian nationalism by bearing witness to the atrocities visited on the people in the name of nationhood (Morrison 'Imagined Biafras': 24), later works tend to enact witnessing as part of a process of healing and recuperation of national solidarity (Hawley 'Biafra as Heritage and Symbol': 16). By contrast, Okparanta allegorises the war in order to critique both ethnocentric and heteronormative aspects of nationalist discourses by linking the chauvinisms of the war with the homophobia of the present.

Anti-homosexual sentiment and ethnic chauvinism are connected in the thematic and historical elements of the text, but are perhaps most clearly linked in Mama's lesson on Leviticus 9, 'thou shalt not sow thy field with mingled seed' (76). Mama's intended lesson here is that Ijeoma's relationship with Amina is an 'abomination' not only because they are both girls but also because Amina is Hausa. Mama uses this moment to recall the 'lessons' of the war, saying, 'are you forgetting what they did to us during the war? Have you forgotten what they did to Biafra? Have you forgotten that it was her people who killed your father?' (76). Mama's motivated re-memorialising of the incidents of Ijeoma's father's death – his suicidal refusal to flee the bombing planes and the fact that the ethnicity of the pilots could not possibly be known (8-9) – also points to the constructedness of the past and the linking of the 'lessons' of history with the fallacious moralising of the present. In addition, the trope of bodily violence – found, for example, in the descriptions of the 'tangled' and 'twisted' limbs of Ijeoma's father after the bombs fell (19), the rape and dismemberment of the Levite's daughter (79), and the half-burned face of Adanna 'burning and burning and turning to ash' in the flames (209) – links the war, the Bible and anti-homosexual sentiment in the text, while the notion of the text as allegory suggests that all three may indicate 'something more than we [can] easily put our fingers on' (81). I suggest here that this 'something more' can be read as a tendency towards fractious identity politics at the heart of Nigerian nation building.

Okparanta is highly conscious of herself as attempting to intervene in existing discourses on homosexuality in Nigeria in a way that does not participate in reifying the straw man of Western influence. Nor is she interested in locating traditional referents for Nigerian homosexuality. Ijeoma neither identifies herself via Western categories of sexual minorities, nor via traditional categories. Rather, Okparanta locates subjectivity of the woman-desiring-woman in the lived present, *subjectified* by heteropatriarchal discourses of nationalism, ethnocentrism, and religion. Ijeoma, like Adrian, becomes Other when her private desires conflict with public discourses. The recourse to the lived present, itself a product the immediate past codified as experience, sets the terms of the Nigerian 'conversation.' Okparanta seeks to initiate a conversation in a space transected by multiple normativising discourses, yet still leaves open the possibility for transformation in the face of an indeterminate future. Because the woman-desiring-woman is always already subjectified by heteropatriarchal discourses, however, the lived present leaves little space for transformation on its own. Thus, in Ijeoma's lifetime, she and her lover Ndidi do not see a lessening of homophobic violence, though they can imagine, perhaps even foresee, a future in which 'love is allowed to be love' in Nigeria (321). It is only through ongoing conversation – which is not just about participating in discourse, but about bringing about a conversion in society's discourses, however slow – that process of conversation and conversion may be accomplished.

QUEER POTENTIAL IN THE PRESENT

Written from the historical and social perspective of the author's present, Dibia and Okparanta's works set the terms of the conversation(s) into which they seek to intervene in the 'now' that is the moment of enunciation. In *Walking with Shadows*, Adrian works for a transnational mobile telecommunications company that has recently established branch offices in Nigeria, a fact which associates the narrative with the Obasanjo administration of the early 2000s, when privatisation and a return to structural adjustment led to a boom in foreign investment in the mobile market (Falola and Heaton *A History of Nigeria*: 236). While in the case of *Under the Udala Trees*, the novel begins in the past, the narrative brings the reader to the narrator's 'present' of 2014, ending with an author's note that criticises the Same-Sex Marriage Act passed that very year. Consequently, these texts are not 'timeless' and not 'universal', but specifically located in local contexts contemporary to the text's construction. Anchored in the present, the texts evoke the past through allusion to pre-colonial social and belief systems. Allusion allows the texts to draw a line of continuity with past indigenous systems while refusing to repeat the sign of tradition, 'in the guise of a pastness that is not necessarily a faithful sign of historical memory but a strategy of representing authority in terms of the artifice of the archaic' (Bhabha 'Cultural Diversity and Cultural Differences': 156). To put it differently, an appeal to tradition as a sign of an originary Nigerian queerness would only repeat the power of structures of traditional patriarchal authority. On the other hand an appeal to the universal as a justification for a rights claim would only repeat the power of Western discourses of queerness. Between the universal and the particular, the local and the global, these texts operate in an indeterminate space, in which discourses of the past can be re-imagined as sites of queer potential in the present.

Thus, in *Walking with Shadows,* the protagonist Adrian's chance encounter with Yahaya at the club Champagne – a known venue for gay male cruising – alludes to ethnographical accounts of the 'gay' Hausa subculture of northern Nigeria.[1] Yet the text resists the temptation to make Yahaya speak in the name of originary Nigerian queerness. Rather than speaking of tradition or acting as the sign of tradition, Yahaya assures Adrian that his lifestyle as a married man who 'like[s] men' is 'just the way things *are*' (emphasis added) (118). Yahaya's assuredness contrasts with the assertions of Adrian's wife, Ada, who justifies her abhorrence of her husband's 'gayness' in her strong belief that 'homosexuality *was* a borrowed trait' (emphasis added) (150). Whereas Ada seeks an origin in the discourse of anti-homosexuality, Yahaya refuses the alternative discourse of indigeneity and locates his justification in the present, as 'the way things are.' Similarly, Okparanta's *Under the Udala Trees* alludes to indigenous queerness in anthropological accounts of female husbands among the Igbo. Yet, rather than using these accounts of 'the traditional' as justification for the right to female desire, they perform an imaginative remaking of female husbands to locate the possibility of woman-woman desire in traditional systems without asserting their historical reality. Okparanta allusively addresses the notion that same-sex desire is unimaginable in Nigerian native and pre-colonial systems, even when such systems and practices mean that both the possibility and potential for non-heteronormative sexual practices are at hand.

DISRUPTING EPISTEMOLOGIES AND TEMPORALITIES

Thus far, I have argued that Dibia's and Okparanta's works can be read as taking an anti-anti-essentialist perspective, in which public sexual knowledge works to construct private identity via multiple dominant discourses. Additionally, I have argued that Nigerian LGBTI literature is presentist and future-anticipatory, looking to the past solely for inspiration and not for traditionalist definitions. In this section, I bring these threads together, extending my analysis through a close reading of the figure of the child in Nigerian LGBTI literature.

In her contribution to *De-Scribing Empire,* Jo-Ann Wallace argues that 'both nineteenth-century English colonialist imperialism and many twentieth-century forms of resistance to imperialism' circulate through the figure of 'the child', making it 'the site of overdetermined and often contradictory investments' (172, 177). In colonialist literature, and especially nineteenth-century children's literature, the figure of the child signifies 'potential or futurity' as both a subject in formation and subject in need of discipline, and is transposed onto the figure of the colonised person in the form of the figure of 'the primitive'. Postcolonial literature, she argues, recoups the colonialist figure of the child in order to re-inscribe the site as both aspirational and explanatory, offering the child as the symbol of the possibility of 'a future condition of empowerment' (183). In Nigerian postcolonial literature, the lines of determination running through this figure are complicated even more, as the figure of 'the child' is additionally linked, via the àbikú figure – the child 'born to die' and be reborn again in a metaphysical cycle of maternal torment – to national regeneration and degeneration, as well as to individual reincarnation. Dibia's and Okparanta's works tap into these multiple and contradictory figurations to present 'the child' as the site of homosexual identity formation, a site for the negotiation and healing of personal trauma, the knot of the national hetero-reproductive order, and a site of potentiality for changing that order.

In *No Future*, Lee Edelman introduces the concepts of *sinthomosexuality* and queer negativity in order to reject the politics of futurity represented by compulsory reproductive heteronormativity and the figure of the child. In this argument, if politics as futurity 'gives us history as the continuous staging of our dream of eventual self-realization' (10), this staging always only ever has us looking to a future that looks largely the same as our present. Edelman suggests the queer subject finds liberation from the politics of futurity by embracing the *jouissance* of the living present. Queerness as such 'refus[es] the coercive belief in the paramount value of [reproductive] futurity', thereby 'dispossess[ing] the social order of the ground on which it stands' (6). In making his argument, Edelman invokes the Lacanian *sinthome*, or symptom – a joy (*jouit*) that is beyond and does not demand meaning in the symbolic order – in order to propose the category of *sinthomosexuality*. As a form of catachrestic identity the *sinthomo*sexual marks the location of that which refuses intelligibility, and so appears in Western literature as a threat to the symbolic order that must be tamed through symbolic acts. Hence, *Sinthomo*sexuality denotes a binding force that knots together the threats to the symbolic order, in the forms of the threat to meaning, the threat to the children (and hence to the reproductive order), and the threat of death.

In Dibia's and Okparanta's works, others' suspicions over the origin of same-sex desire and the nature of homosexual identity link the protagonists to the figure of the child as both subject in formation and the subject in need of discipline, though in the eyes of those others the formation of the child protagonist is a malformation, and s/he is evidence of a failed disciplinary apparatus, an apparatus that must be reapplied with increased vigour to achieve the desired result. In Dibia's *Walking with Shadows*, not only is Adrian punished and isolated as a child for his deviation from the norm, his brother invites a pastor to whip the adult Adrian into conformity, suggesting that homosexuality is being read as perpetual immaturity. Further, the many confrontations with suspicious others provoke Adrian, the protagonist, to revisit traumatic childhood memories in which he recalls a heightened sense of *différance*, which he reads as *difference* and as the sign of an essential gay identity. Because Adrian's sense of himself does not fit easily into the existing order, rather than accepting a deferral of its meaning, he accepts the order's differentiation of himself from it as an ex-centric or abject being. Adrian subsequently comes to identify as 'gay' not as a direct identification with Western sexual counterpublics, but as an effect of the existing national heterosexual public's prerogative to name its difference.

Ijeoma, narrator and protagonist of *Under the Udala Trees,* similarly tracks the origin of her desire to her childhood and a causal sequence of events that fell into place to determine her desire (4-5). As with Adrian, Ijeoma is subject to discipline from the heteronormative order. Having learned of Ijeoma's relationship with another girl, Ijeoma's mother lectures her nightly from the Bible. Unlike the child Adrian – whose strong desire to meet the terms of the existing order is symbolised by a baptism that he experiences as the death of his old self and rebirth into a new, more 'manly' existence – the child Ijeoma is precocious and persistent in her refusal to fully accept terms of the discipline, such as when she suggests to her mother that the morality tales of the Bible might 'just [be] allegories of something else' (81) or that it was an act of cowardice for the Levite in Judges to allow an innocent girl to be raped to save himself (80). Thus, for Okparanta, the failure of the disciplinary apparatus results from its foundation on moral and logical errors, which are opposed to something, if not congenital, then something more rooted in truth and authenticity of the self.

Even as Adrian and Ijeoma use memory as a vehicle to come to terms with and find acceptance for themselves within themselves, the act of reclamation of childhood through memory produces an ambivalence. While memories of childhood serve as a means for the protagonist to find both comfort and personal acceptance in an essential queerness, they also legitimise the heteronormative order's suspicions of childhood, and hold it open if not as a site for correcting queerness, then as a site to be monitored for its emergence. Although the suspicion visited upon the child as a result has precedents in European sexual knowledges imported to Nigeria under colonialism, it also has roots in indigenous Yoruba and Igbo beliefs about spiritual possession and reincarnation, wherein the child has the potential to either uphold the existing order or to destroy it.

While in much of Nigerian literature, futurity and potentiality of the nation are linked to the bourgeois child via the *Bildungsroman* structure (Hron, 2008: 30), anti-futurity and pessimism for the nation are linked to the figure of àbikú (Igbo: *ogbanje*), the mischievous child spirit that torments its parents in a painful cycle of birth and death. Àbikú are said to inhabit the wombs of pregnant women so that they may be born into the human world. Once born, they will soon after choose to die for no other reason than to torment the parents. The àbikú will then return to the same woman's womb to be born again, and so on and so on. In some cases, the àbikú will allow itself to live into childhood, or the parents will secure the resources of a powerful *dibia* (or *babalawo*), or magical healer, to bind the child to life. Still, the àbikú is always merely an itinerant visitor to this world, threatening at any moment to choose death over life, or to evade the binding magic.

Prominent in such works as Ben Okri's *The Famished Road*, Chinua Achebe's *Things Fall Apart*, and Wole Soyinka's childhood memoir *Aké*, the àbikú serves as an allegory for the nation's tendency to cycle through political births and deaths, to hover between becoming and collapsing. The àbikú is a timeless crosser of boundaries, never content to stay in one place, always testing the limits of life and the social world (Ogunyemi 'An Abiku-Ogbanje Atlas': 666). Always seeking appeasement through gifts and parental capitulation to its desires lest it choose to die and begin the cycle anew, the àbikú also confuses and confounds the parent-child relationship, upsetting the balance of power and leaving the parent helpless before the child. In this way, the àbikú figure is a threat to the stability of both the family and futurity. This figure may be contrasted with the figure of the bourgeois child in Nigerian literature, who represents a will towards futurity, possibility and continuity. The bourgeois child embodies those ideals that hold together the national hetero-reproductive order, even as the àbikú represents those ideals that threaten it.

In both novels, the heteronormative world locks on the queer child, as it does on the àbikú, as a destabilising force at the heart of its project. The suspicious eye cast upon the queer child contains within it the same hesitancy of purpose and fear of reprisal as that which is cast upon the àbikú. Further, the protagonists, while not àbikú themselves, are allusively connected to the àbikú concept and, like àbikú, work to destabilise the institutions of heteronormativity that would impede them from the full expression of themselves. In *Walking with Shadows*, the leitmotif of death and rebirth connects the protagonist to the àbikú figure, beginning in the novel's first line of the prologue, where Adrian's child self declares his intention to die so that he may be reborn. For young Adrian, death and rebirth are the doorways through which he must pass in order to shed one sexual identity and put on another. At the end of the novel, he 'resurrects' the child he once wished to death, so that he may integrate that part of himself into himself (216). In *Under the Udala Trees,* the connection to àbikú is established in the title, which alludes to a belief that good children wait in the branches of udala trees to be born. The udala tree thus stands for reproductive heteronormativity, the imperative to have children to 'carry on the family name' (310), the mandate that keeps Ijeoma locked in an unhappy marriage for many years. The counterpart to the udala in this regard is the iroko tree, in whose branches àbikú are said to hide. In a dream, Ijeoma sees an udala tree. Her daughter hangs from a noose tied to its branches, strangled to death. Behind the udala tree, she sees other trees, including iroko. She wakes and realises that she and her child are 'choking under the weight of something larger than [them], something heavy and weighty, the weight of tradition and superstition and all of our legends' (311-12). Ijeoma then leaves her husband and returns to her female lover.

In the end, it is not through identifying with àbikú themselves, but by upsetting the duality of life and death, good and evil, heterosexual and homosexual – represented by the àbikú concept – that both protagonists ultimately find a path forward, and a place from which to project a radical vision of the future. While neither Adrian nor Ijeoma end their tales in an anti-futuristic full embrace of the now as *jouissance*, they do find comfort in the living present as imperfect, but liveable.

CONCLUSION

Lindsey Green-Simms writes, 'twenty-first century Nigerian writing ... resist[s] the dominant in ways not previously done before and [tells] diverse stories about same-sex desire that are neither monothematic nor moralistic' ('The Emergent Queer': 142). This article appends this claim by arguing that these texts resist and address *multiple* dominant publics and their associated discourses in order to draw attention to the ways in which public knowledge constrains private self-knowledge. The recognition that this field of emergence is neither binary nor simplistic – that it is, in fact, a complex milieu characterised by multiple normative sexual discourses, including citational local and national discourses of homosexuality and anti-homosexuality, and transnational LGBTI rights-based essentialising discourses – is fundamental to developing complex and nuanced readings of the emergent literature that don't merely repeat the signs of tradition or essentialism. To accomplish this, I have suggested critical attention to the ways in which shifted temporalities, anti-anti-essentialist epistemologies and queer figurations put pressure on both citational and essentialising discourses.

NOTE

1 Rudolf P. Gaudio uses the term 'gay' to refer to 'men who are conscious of themselves as men who have sex with men, and who consider themselves to be socially (if not temperamentally) distinct from men who do not have this kind of sex' ('Male Lesbians and Other Queer Notions in Hausa': 117). Communities and social practices of men who have sex with men, according to anthropological and ethnographic accounts, predate colonial occupation and are still a prominent feature of life in Hausaland.

WORKS CITED

Adesanmi, Pius and Chris Dunton. 'Nigeria's Third Generation Writing: Historiography and Preliminary Theoretical Considerations'. *English in Africa* Vol. 32, No. 1 (2005): 7-19.

Bhabha, Homi K. 'Cultural Diversity and Cultural Differences'. In *The Post-Colonial Studies Reader*, eds Bill Ashcroft, Gareth Griffiths and Helen Tiffin. New York: Routledge, 2006: 155-7.

Dibia, Jude. *Walking with Shadows: A Novel*. Nigeria: BlackSands, 2005.

Edelman, Lee. *No Future: Queer Theory and the Death Drive*. Durham, NC: Duke University Press. 2004.

Ekine, Sokari. 'Contesting Narratives of Queer Africa'. In *Queer African Reader*, eds Sokari Ekine and Hakima Abbas. Oxford: Pambazuka Press, 2013: 78-91.

Falola, Toyin and Matthew M. Heaton. *A History of Nigeria*. Cambridge, UK: Cambridge University Press, 2008.

Gaudio, Rudolf Pell. 'Male Lesbians and Other Queer Notions in Hausa'. In *Boy-Wives and Female Husbands: Studies of African Homosexualities*, eds Stephen O. Murray and Will Roscoe. New York: St. Martin's Press, 1998 115-28.

Gilroy, Paul. *The Black Atlantic: Modernity and Double Consciousness*. Cambridge MA: Harvard University Press, 1993.

Green-Simms, Lindsey. 'The Emergent Queer: Homosexuality and Nigerian Fiction in the 21st Century'. *Research in African Literatures* Vol. 47, No. 2 (2016): 139-61.

Hawley, John C. 'Biafra as Heritage and Symbol: Adichie, Mbachu, and Iweala'. *Research in African Literatures* Vol. 39, No. 2 (2008): 15-26.

Hoad, Neville Wallace. *African Intimacies: Race, Homosexuality, and Globalization*. Minneapolis: University of Minnesota, 2007.

Hron, Madelaine. 'Ora Na-Azu Nwa: The Figure of the Child in Third-Generation Nigerian Novels'. *Research in African Literatures* Vol. 39, No. 2, 2008: 27-48.

Mac-Iyalla, Davis. 'Changing Attitudes through the Example of Jesus: Transition Interviews Nigerian Gay Rights Activist'. *Transition* Vol. 114, No. 1 (2014): 70-83.

Morrison, Jago. 'Imagined Biafras: Fabricating Nation in Nigerian Civil War Writing'. *ARIEL: A Review of International English Literature* Vol. 36, Nos 1-2 (2005): 5-26.

Ogunyemi, Chikwenye Okonjo. 'An Abiku-Ogbanje Atlas: A Pre-Text for Rereading Soyinka's *Aké* and Morrison's *Beloved*'. *African American Review* Vol. 36, No. 4 (2002): 663-78.

Okparanta, Chinelo. Nigerian-American Writer Chinelo Okparanta. *Conversations with African Poets and Writers*, The Poetry and Literature Center at the Library of Congress, 3 Feb. 2015. Transcript.

——*Under the Udala Trees: A Novel*. New York: Houghton Mifflin, 2015.

Quinn, Molly Rose. 'Chinelo Okparanta on Faith, War and Being Gay in Nigeria'. *Literary Hub*, 21 September 2015. https://lithub.com/chinelo-okparanta-on-faith-war-and-being-gay-in-nigeria (accessed 28 May 2016).

Sedgwick, Eve Kosofsky. *Epistemology of the Closet*. Berkeley, CA: University of California, 1990.

Wallace, Jo-Ann. 'De-Scribing the Water-Babies: "The Child" in Post-Colonial Theory'. In *De-Scribing Empire: Post-Colonialism and Textuality*, eds Chris Tiffin and Alan Lawson. New York: Routledge, 1994: 171-84.

Dilemma of an African Woman Faced with Bisexuality
A Reading of Armand Meula's *Coq mâle, coq femelle*

STELLA ONOME OMONIGHO

INTRODUCTION

The issue of sexual orientation has become a major topic in African society and attracts the intervention of the government in some countries. The subject is so polemical that it is at the root of a great ideological division even among intellectuals. Although several writers avoid the subject in their works, Armand Meula in his play *Coq mâle, coq femelle* ('Male Rooster, female rooster') has highlighted the traits of three sexual orientations and their complications in Africa, a continent of conservative tradition and practice. In the play, he highlights the subject through three characters: a couple (Vicky and Conrad) and the homosexual partner of Conrad (Jean-Luc). Vicky, pregnant with her fourth child, discovers in a shocking manner the double sexual nature of her husband. Conrad is torn between his family on one hand and the desire to be with his 'female cock', Jean-Luc, on the other. They decide all three to live together so that Vicky can accept Jean-Luc as her husband's co-wife and so that the homosexual partners can legalise their union But because of the government's declaration against homosexuality in the country, the pact is broken; Vicky returns with her children to her parents while Jean-Luc gets angry with his partner Conrad who finally confesses that he prefers a family to a homosexual relationship.

This article centres on the dilemma facing an African woman, married with children, who discovers after nine years of her marriage that her husband is bisexual or homosexual. That is the image of a woman presented in Armand Meula's *Coq mâle, coq femelle*. What will she do? Will she abandon her marital home to her husband's homosexual partner? Will she stay and live as a co-wife/husband of Jean-Luc under the same roof? How will she explain to her family that her husband and the father of her children is homosexual?

BISEXUALITY

According to Alfred Kinsey sexuality is a continuum, and almost all heterosexuals tend to have amorous feelings towards people of the same sex, in varying degrees. In his book *The History of Sexuality* (1976, 1984), the philosopher Michel Foucault argued that homosexuality is an invented concept: a few generations ago, homosexual behaviour existed but was not called or seen as a sexual orientation. Many researchers are in favour of labelling it as a sexual behaviour rather than an orientation.

Bisexuality, at the same time, is defined by Judd Marmor as: 'Sexual or romantic attraction for both sexes or, more broadly, for romantic, sentimental or sexual relationships with same-sex or opposite-sex' (quoted in Drescher 'Judd Marmor, Psychiatry and Homosexuality'). It is also said that people who experience sexual attraction to people of the same and different sex at some point in their lives are bisexual. Some bisexual people do not like this name because they believe the term is obsolete and limiting. Consequently, they are also called pansexual, non-preferential, sexually fluid, queer or simply strange. Regardless of the name, for this article, the term bisexual will be maintained to refer to people who have sexual attraction or love for both sexes. Bisexuals can also be people who primarily have heterosexual sexual relations and sexual desires but also have traits and experiences with the same sex. In his research, J.R. Little ('Contemporary Female Bisexuality') identified 13 types of bisexuality: alternating bisexuals, circumstantial bisexuals, relational, conditional, emotional, integrated, exploratory, hedonistic, recreational, isolated, latent, motivational and transient bisexuals. Among these different types, the notions of isolated and relational bisexuality are appropriate concepts for an analysis of the situation and personality of the husband in Meula's *Coq mâle, coq femelle*.

An isolated bisexual, in the terminology of J.R. Little, is one who is 100 per cent directly gay or lesbian now but has had several sexual experiences with another sex in the past. In *Coq mâle, coq femelle* Conrad is a young man who is married with children but who at some point in his life decides to follow his passion for being gay. Not wanting to have sex with the opposite sex, he reveals his new orientation to his wife Vicky by introducing Jean-Luc, his gay partner. The relational bisexual on the other hand, is one who has a primary relationship with only one gender, but engages in occasional or secondary relationships with people of the opposite sex. Armand Meula presents a situation that is between the relational bisexuality and the isolated bisexuality in the character of Conrad, who escapes to cohabit with his homosexual partner during a period of three months without any word to his family. He reappears after the three months to embrace his wife with the intention of giving the baby at its birth to his homosexual partner.

The play opens with Conrad's refusal to have sex with his wife despite her pleas. He refuses under the pretext of the well-being of the foetus in the uterus of his pregnant wife:

> **Vicky** (*Implorant, elle essaye de l'aguicher*): S'il te plaît, chéri. Sois galant, conduis-moi au panthéon de l'extase. Comble-moi de ton émulsion voluptueuse. Faisons-le une fois, chéri, juste cette fois. Faisons-le maintenant, je t'en supplie. Viens, viens en moi ! (*elle essaye de l'attirer vers elle. Il la repousse*)
> **Conrad:** Non, Vicky !
> **Vicky:** Tu sembles avoir perdu toute envie de moi. Et ce but de vie qui a germé dans mes entrailles n'est certainement pas l'unique cause de cette anorexie. (14-15)

> **Vicky** (*crying, she's trying to tease*): Please, honey, lead me to the pantheon of ecstasy. Fill me with your sensuous seed. Let's do it once, honey, just this once. Let's do it now, please. Come, come inside me! (*She tries to lure him to her, but he is repelled*)
> **Conrad:** No, Vicky!
> **Vicky:** You seem to have lost any desire for me. And this new baby life that we wanted, now growing in my womb, is certainly not the sole cause of this sexual famine.]

He is no longer interested in the opposite sex. He has a new passion for his own sex but does not want to reveal his secret because he needs the child who will be borne by Vicky for Jean-Luc his partner. This rejection also marks the beginning of Vicky's dilemma. She asks herself why her husband does not want her in spite of her supplication.

> **Vicky:** Tu as disparu de notre vie pendant trois mois, douze longues semaines, sans laisser la moindre trace, sans envoyer le moindre signe de vie. Tu nous as abandonnés, les enfants et moi, dans une angoisse insupportable. Aujourd'hui, plus de deux mois après ta réapparition, j'ignore toujours les véritables raisons de cette disparition mystérieuse. (18)

> [**Vicky:** You disappeared from our life for three months, 12 long weeks, without the slightest trace, without sending any sign of life. You abandoned the children and me, leaving us in unbearable anguish. Today, more than two months after your return, I still don't know the real reasons for your unexplained disappearance.]

Meula presents Conrad before his meeting with Vicky as showing latent traits of the bisexuality that he apparently had before his marriage:

> **Conrad:** ... Je n'avais connu aucune expérience sentimentale avant de te rencontrer.
> **Vicky:** Tu étais de nature timide, prétextant que tu n'étais pas encore prêt à affronter une relation amoureuse.
> **Conrad:** C'est toi qui, peu à peu, m'a appris à connaitre la femme, à l'apprécier, à l'aimer ... tu m'as donné le courage de fonder une famille, de faire des enfants, alors qu'en vérité, je ne savais me servir de cet engin (*il désigne le dessous de sa ceinture*) que pour évacuer les impuretés de mon organisme. (28)

> [**Conrad:** ... I had no romantic experience before I met you.
> **Vicky:** You were shy by nature, claiming that you were not ready for a loving relationship.
> **Conrad:** It is you who taught me to know women, to appreciate them, little by little, to love ... you gave me the courage to start a family, to have children, while in truth, I did not know the use of this gear (*he indicates below his belt*), except to release the impurities from my body.]

Trevor Gates and Pamela Viggiani, in their study on understanding the stigma of lesbians, gays and bisexuals ('Understanding Lesbian, Gay, and Bisexual Worker Stigmatization'), reveal that fear of labelling and receipt of different treatments were possible reasons why people prefer to remain discreet about their sexual identity, especially in situations like Conrad's in Meula's play, in which the character disguised his true orientation for years.

DILEMMA IN SOCIAL THEORY

According to Anthony Giddens in *The Transformation of Intimacy*, the dilemma is a situation in which a difficult choice must be made between two or more alternatives, especially those that are also undesirable. On his part, John Platt defines the dilemma exemplified in this play as: 'A situation in which the conduct of a certain behavior or defect contributes to the increase of private profit at half-time to a short-term but do not drive the behavior to a higher profit in the long run' ('Social Traps'). The situation of Vicky's dilemma in this play is demonstrated by the fact that she had to choose between her homo(bi)sexual husband, and divorce. She feels situationally trapped.

Dilemma of an African Woman Faced with Bisexuality **169**

Presenting Jean-Luc to Vicky, Conrad proposes the co-habitation of the three under the same roof:

> **Conrad:** ... Vicky, je n'ai pas l'intention de te quitter. Je veux continuer à m'occuper de toi et des gosses. C'est pour cela que nous devons tous êtes réunis sous le même toit.
> **Vicky:** Et quel statut avais-je ? Celui de femme de ménage ?
> **Conrad:** Celui de femme, tout court. Ou plus exactement, de première femme, puisqu'en fait, j'épouse Jean-Luc en secondes noces ... N'oublie pas que nous sommes mariés sous le système polygamie.
>
> [**Conrad:** Vicky, I have no intention of leaving you. I want to take care of you and the kids. That's why we should all be under the same roof.
> **Vicky:** And what status do I have? That of a maid?
> **Conrad:** Absolutely that of a wife. Or, more accurately, the first wife, since in fact I have taken Jean-Luc as my second wife ... don't forget – we are married polygamously.]

She refuses her husband's proposal and asks him what will become of the children if they get wind of their father's new sexual orientation. She does not want them to know what he has become. Conrad is challenging her with a divorce as his response to her refusal to cohabit with his homosexual partner, and this further increases her dilemma:

> **Conrad:** Que préfères-tu alors ? Que je divorce de toi afin d'épouser Jean-Luc ?
> **Vicky:** ... J'ai grandi dans la polygamie. Et je n'y ai rien trouvé d'amusant. J'ai souffert du conflit permanent entre les femmes et les enfants de mon père...En t'épousant, j'avais cru être délivrée de l'enfer. J'avais remercié sept fois le ciel de m'avoir donné un mari attentionné, délicat, compréhensif, respectueux. Voilà qu'aujourd'hui mon bonheur s'écroule. (*En sanglots*) Comment pourrais-je m'en sortir sans revenu avec trois enfants, que dis-je quatre enfants à ma charge ? où vais-je trouver ce veuf riche et solitaire qui acceptera de nous prendre sous son toit ne serait-ce que pour rompre la monotonie dans sa maison ? Que vais-je devenir? .. Je ne sais pas. Je ne sais plus ... (53-55)
>
> [**Conrad:** What do you prefer then? That I divorce you in order to marry Jean-Luc?
> **Vicky:** ... I grew up in polygamy. And it was no fun at all! I suffered from the constant conflict between my father's wives and his children ... Marrying you, I thought I would be delivered from hell. I thanked God time and again for having given me a caring, sensitive, understanding and respectful husband. Now today my happiness has disintegrated. (*In tears*) How could I manage to care for three – no four – children with no income?

Do you think I can find some rich solitary widower willing to take us under his roof to disturb the peace and quiet of his home? What will become of me? ... I do not know. I just don't know anymore.]

When an individual finds him/herself in a situation where s/he begins to ask so many questions, it is the moment of the climax of the character's dilemma. Vicky confesses that she is in a social trap. She does not want to cohabit with homosexuals even if one is her husband and, in addition, her financial status will not allow her to do otherwise. Her status as a full-time housewife with three children in an African society where tradition limits women's freedom will not allow her to do exactly what she wants. The uncertainty of the future, especially the future of her children without their father, compels her to remain in the trap against her will.

The situation of this social trap is a dilemma with which many African women live. They are surrounded and limited by the feelings of insecurity and uncertainty, and are sometimes overwhelmed. They are afraid to make definitive decisions. African women are also limited because of the norms of social morality – in the case of domestic violence, for example, where the woman is beaten almost every day: she refuses to attract the attention of the police or even to leave her marital home because she has accepted the African tradition of dogmatic submission by the woman. Some others are limited by considering the future of their children who they believe can suffer socially and psychologically because of divorce. According to Patience Akumu,

> most African countries have constitutions that guarantee female equality and are signatories to key international conventions. However, there is a silent proviso that has a strong influence on the attitudes of African countries towards the rights of women. This is the proviso that an African woman can enjoy her rights within certain limits. ('"African Culture" is the Biggest Threat to the Women's Rights Movement')

This is obvious when her husband begins to feel threatened by her decisions.

Stephanie Coontz argues that historically, marriage has played a central role in women's oppression, lack of economic and political power, and the limitation of opportunities (*Marriage: A History*). She argues that this oppressive trend has survived to modern times, especially in developing countries. In sexual relations, an African woman must not openly discuss sex as an abomination and must not report what happens in her home. This implies a form of violence against women who are restricted from sharing their views about certain topics concerning sexual relations. The society prefers them being silent about it even to the detriment of their mental health. A woman should be free to discuss any issue, be it sex or not, as it impacts on her emotions.

According to D. Kamor ('Homosexuality as Transgression Beyond Limits'), another dilemma faced by the African woman is traditional African points of view. The underlying assumption is that bisexual/ homosexual relations are abominable acts punishable by gods and the supreme God. This notion puts the African woman in a precarious situation of collaboration with a 'delinquent' to 'desecrate' the land. Understanding the implications of this dilemma faced by African women in bisexual/homosexual marriages will help society in supporting them instead of castigating or condemning them.

CONCLUSION

Vicky in *Coq mâle, coq femelle* is faced with a problem that threatens not only her marital home but the safety of her unborn baby. In Africa traditional women learn not to be heard, but to accept the decisions of their husbands without asking questions and to help their husbands achieve their life goals and dreams. At marriage, African women lose many privileges – sexual freedom, freedom of expression and self-confidence. While the woman in marriage may face several challenges, she is led to believe that the secrets and weaknesses of her husband must be treated with all privacy and secrecy (Fadzayi 'Of Success and Stigma: The Dilemma of the African Alpha Female').

The impact of modernity, education, and social media on the liberation of women and on gender equality has combined to create a new generation of women. Women who know their rights work to ensure that their rights are protected. These women, however, face several dilemmas, one of which is the dilemma of accepting or rejecting a bisexual/gay husband. What will society say? What about the future of our children and our family? What are the consequences of my decisions and how can I deal with them? Ann Ferguson ('Gay Marriage: An American and Feminist Dilemma') argues that the dilemma of accepting or rejecting homosexual relationships poses a dual threat: undermining the rights of the gay partner on the one hand, and jeopardising the normative status of the traditional heterosexual nuclear family, on the other. This dilemma is partly responsible for the non-responsiveness and reluctance of African women to either accept or reject bisexual/homosexual husbands.

WORKS CITED

Akumu, Patience. '"African Culture" is the Biggest Threat to the Women's Rights Movement'. *African Arguments*, 2015. http://african arguments. org/2015/03/09/african-culture-is-the-biggest-threat-to-the-womens-rights-movement-by-patience-akumu (accessed 6 April 2018).

Coontz, Stephanie. *Marriage: A History*, London: Penguin. 2006.

Drescher, Jack. 'Judd Marmor, Psychiatry and Homosexuality'. *Journal of Gay & Lesbian Psychotherapy* Vol. 10, No. 2 (2006): 117-25.

Fadzayi, Mahere. 'Of Success and Stigma: The Dilemma of the African Alpha Female'. 2014. https://fadzayimahere.wordpress.com/2014/05/09/of-success-and-stigma-the-dilemma-of-the-african-alpha-female (accessed 22 May 2017).

Ferguson Ann. 'Gay Marriage: An American and Feminist Dilemma'. *Hypatia* Vol. 22, No. 1, (2007): 39-57.

Foucault, Michel. *Histoire de la sexualité*, I, II, III. Paris: Gallimard, 1984.

Gates, Trevor and Pamela Viggiani. 'Understanding Lesbian, Gay, and Bisexual Worker Stigmatization: A Review of the Literature'. *International Journal of Sociology and Social Policy* Vol. 34, Nos 5/6 (2014): 359-74.

Giddens, Anthony. *The Transformation of Intimacy*. London: Wiley, 1993.

Kamor, D. 'Homosexuality as Transgression Beyond Limits', *Daily Trust*, 7 April 2009.

Kinsey, Alfred. *Sexual Behaviour in the Human Male*. Bloomington, IN: Indiana University Press, 1998.

Little, J.R. 'Contemporary Female Bisexuality: A Psychosocial Phenomenon'. Unpublished doctoral dissertation, 1989.

Meula, Armand. *Coq mâle, coq femelle*. Paris: L'Harmattan, 2012.

Platt John. 'Social Traps'. *American Psychologist* No. 28 (1973): 641-51.

Featured Articles

African Oral Literature & the Environment

NDUBUISI OSUAGWU

Over the years, I have, in introducing my students to the study of African oral literature, striven to explain to them the concept of the form and also given them background lectures on the African environment including the people's cosmology. I have been conscious of the fact that the idea of the environment is all-encompassing and includes the African climate, vegetation, ecosystem, demography, economy, politics and the various dimensions of social relations. These constitute the African milieu which yields African literature, including its oral forms, and the environmental sensibilities the literature naturally articulates.

All literature is about its milieu: the flora and fauna of the human communal location which yields food, shelter and the abundant offerings nature makes to existence; the community, in the fullness of its culture, world view, customs and tradition, laws, social, economic and political relations in the fullness of their manifold manifestation. Literature as a vehicle and a reflection can only articulate, at a time, a few of the dimensions of the sensibilities arising from the manifold projections of the all-embracing milieu. This is understandable, given its formal limitations and the profundity of the milieu which the limited capacity of the artist as a human person can carry, comprehend, or articulate in a single creative endeavour.

What then is the basis for the choice the artist makes in terms of what themes to, or not to, address in a given creative endeavour? The answer (often) is fashion, dictated by the trajectory of a combination of, at least, social, political and economic experiences. These throw up immediate concerns for society and constitute contemporary issues – the trend of thought, the fashion of the time. This explains the preponderance of given concerns in the reflection of the social trend of thought at various stages and periods of social/human development. It explains the nature of the sensibilities expressed in pre-colonial, colonial, negritude and post-colonial African literature; in renaissance, romantic, Harlem renaissance and such other literature.

As in fashion, these periodic shifts in concern are driven by a few people who start them off; others follow with conviction; still, some others follow for the mere sake of currency (a sense of 'belonging', 'being among', or the desire for the 'cool' feeling of 'amongness'). Yet, there are those who just stand aloof, and others who adopt a critical or cynical attitude. Often, the questions and cynicism that arise are dictated either by experience, or a suspicion of the cunning hands of politics at play in the manipulation of the morality that underlies the shift in concern. Nadine Gordimer, in her allegorical essay, 'Three in a Bed: Fiction, Morals and Politics', underlines the suspicious romance between literature and politics. According to her:

> Morals are the husband/wife of fiction. And politics? Politics somehow followed morals in, picking the lock and immobilizing the alarm system. At first it was in the dark, perhaps, and fiction thought the embrace of politics was that of morals, didn't know the difference ... And this is understandable. Morals and politics have a family connection. Politics' ancestry is morality – way back and generally accepted as forgotten. The resemblance is faded. In the light of morning, if fiction accepts the third presence within the sheets it is soon in full cognizance of who and what politics is. (116)

She adds:

> The first dismaying discovery for the writer is ... best expressed by Magris's cynicism: 'The lie is quite as real as the truth, it works upon the world, transforms it': whereas the fiction writer, in pursuit of truth beyond the guide of reasoning, has believed that truth, however elusive, is the only reality. Yet we have seen the lie transforming; we have had Goebbels. And his international descendants, practicing that transformation on the people of a number of countries. (119)

To a large extent, unfortunately, the growing reference to literary endeavours in relation to their milieu, their environment, in terms of ecoliterature – ecopoetry, ecofiction, ecodrama, ecocriticism – appears to be an effort by some art practitioners to key into the equally growing global fashion. In some cases, it is driven by the desire to contrive a relevance for the arts in the new-found obsession with the climate and the environment as the centre-piece of contemporary consciousness by global funding agencies. Some in this group basically attempt to speak in the new-found language designed to appeal to the desires of sponsors and operators of fund centres. The hope is to squeeze some of the funds out of their otherwise art-hating hearts and hands. Chinyere Nwahunanya seems to justify this tendency when he suggests that:

The challenge before the writer then would be to capture the tensions and peculiarities of our environment, through a functionally useful language that produces an environmentally friendly literature. Once this happens, the writer would become more relevant to his environment, and with government support and encouragement his efforts would be rewarded, since he also needs to make a living from his writing. ('Language, Literature and the Environment': 12)

The danger in Nwahunanya's suggestion is the possibility of compounding and even escalating the spectre of creative mercantilism. That would sacrifice art for pecuniary benefits. It would expose it to the cash-and-carry desires of the very big money (governments, multinational corporations and their public and private agencies) whose policies and activities have, all through history, proven to be largely anti-people. The same big money has been generally implicated, through their actions and omissions, in the degradation and rape of the environment. His suggestion creates the impression that 'reward' and the need 'to make a living from his writing' should be a major consideration for the artist in his choice of theme. The artist should also measure his relevance by his ability to attract support and encouragement (funding?) from government, in compensation for his satisfaction of its desires. It is a scary scenario of grievous disservice to art, as it would appear to encourage an inappropriate alliance between art and the oppressor. Appropriately, art should ally with the oppressed public, the proven victim of the many governmental policies that have encouraged multinational corporations to levy war on the same environment.

Furthermore, rather than aid naturalness or the free-flow of creativity, Nwahunanya's prescription would engender drudgery in the creative process and make art more mechanical than entertaining in its teaching. At best, it would become more propagandist than aesthetic in its attempt to contrive a relevance within the eco-context. Iniobong Uko's reference to Sekou Toure's 'The Political Leader as a Representative of a Culture' (cited in Frantz Fanon, *The Wretched of the Earth* 167) is quite instructive:

> To take part in the African revolution, it is not enough to write a revolutionary song: you must fashion the revolution with the people. And if you fashion it with the people, the songs will come by themselves, and of themselves. (Uko: 'Towards Pragmatising the Nigerian Environment': 14)

Indeed, let the songs of ecoconsciousness 'come by themselves, and of themselves'; let the art emerge from the spontaneous feelings engendered by the immediacy of experience. Let them not be a product of some mechanical contrivance for relevance in some banality hoisted by some oppressor seeking for satisfaction of some materialistic lust.

Otherwise, in literature, the environment is the totality of the milieu, including the climate, vegetation, the living and non-living presence of nature and their relations in the unending struggle for survival. There is therefore really nothing new in the 'econess' of the expression of a literary endeavour, except the newness of the coinage itself, which merely limits the scope of its appreciation. It is in the same way that one would refer to its concerns, its themes within its milieu, in terms of the preponderance of the social, political, cultural or religious sensibilities that it articulates.

The new trend in ecoconsciousness has created a level of concern and discomfort within the community of African writers and critics for various reasons. There are indeed those who see the eco-trending in literature and, in particular African literature, as neo-colonialist, or wilful surrender to a new trick by the erstwhile colonial masters who, by the way, are the major proponents and, in a sense, sponsors of the current call to ecoconsciousness. Significantly, while they support the consciousness, they look in the direction of the 'Third world' and their erstwhile colonial enclaves (still underdeveloped) for the solution. It is of little importance to them that it has been largely through their mindless drive to conquer nature that the earth in its environment and ecosystem faces destruction.

In his remarks on the Earth Summit of 1992, held in Brazil, Baba S. O. Wey Agbeyangi captures the conflict of interest and its attendant suspicion of deceit:

> Between January and June 1992, environmentalists, world leaders converged in the Brazilian city of Rio in a grand carnival to save the world and ecosystem. In focusing on the short-circuited construct of sustainable development, the earth Summit conveners once again missed the point: the world is as much as we give, not what we take. ('Beyond Sustainable Development': 66)

According to him:

> The basic instruments that were adopted at Rio bespeak the point. There was a lot of defending at the summit. North nations defended their right to industrial activity (which really was not the point) with the attendant threat of carbon emissions on the stratosphere, and South nations insisted that the North set up a revolving ecological protection and alternative development fund if they wanted them to go along in placing embargo on the continued practice of exploiting forest resources as fuel. (66)

In other words, whereas the 'North nations' recognise the danger to the world of their drive for industrialisation, they are unwilling, or at best reluctant, to make the needed sacrifices to protect the environment. Such sacrifices must come from the 'South nations' that must abandon their own needs for industrialisation and collectively retain the forest reserves for the already industrialised nations of the North. Herein lies the danger – the interplay of global politics and the trending ecoconsciousness.

Gordimer asks: 'For when have writers not lived in time of political conflict? Whose Golden Age, whose Belle Epoch, whose Roaring Twenties were these so-named lovely times?' ('Three in a Bed': 117). Indeed, the suspicious and cynical would want to know: whose eco-trending economic and political interests are really driving the current ecoconsciousness in our literature and its criticism? Are we about to mistake the rough grab (rape) of politics and big business for the loving embrace and caress of morals, in the sense of Gordimer's allegory?

Obviously, the suspicion and its kindred cynicism seem to arise from experiential and ideological depths. As William Slymaker, in 'Echoing the Other(s): The Call of Global Green and Black African Responses', observes:

> For some black African critics, ecolit and ecocrit are another attempt to 'white out' black Africa by coloring it green. To some African critics and writers, who directly participated in the liberation of their nation states from colonialism, what ecocriticism offers is not another theory of liberation like Marxism. Rather, it appears as one more hegemonic discourse from the metropolitan west ... Black African writers take nature seriously in their creative and academic writings, but many have resisted or neglected the paradigms that inform much of global ecocriticism. (648)

Nwahunanya seems to more clearly articulate the 'great need' for African literature to redirect its focus and embrace the new fashion, to 'belong', to 'key-in' to the trending ecoconsciousness when he declares:

> An ecocritical focus by our writers is now inevitable. Presently, all over the world, literature is expanding its purview and extending its horizons to shift attention from purely socio-political and economic issues to issues relating to how human activity blights and impacts on the physical environment. An environmentally conscious literature would probably improve the reader's response, and reinvigorate his interest, especially where readers are getting bored with recycled socio-political problems to which those addressed have been indifferent. ('Language, Literature and the Environment': 8)

He gives three major reasons, here, as to why a shift of focus has become 'inevitable': it is now the fashion 'all over the world'; readers have become (suddenly?) bored with socio-political problems; those addressed (social and political leaders, one imagines) are indifferent. The idea of an inevitability of a shift, simply to join the bandwagon, does not seem to encourage uniqueness in the character of our literature. Are our experiences not peculiar and specific? Should our literature not mirror such experiences in their specific peculiarity? Is there, and should there be, a standard world list of thematic concerns to which every literature, including ours, must conform? It would appear that a shift merely for the purpose of conformity with fashion is hardly persuasive.

Besides, there is no indication that the 'boredom' ostensibly experienced by the reader arises from the said 'recycling' of socio-political problems; it may well be that the 'reader', including the (leadership) addressed, does not read them, in the first place, or the level of the sense of urgency articulated is not high enough to jolt him. In any case, there is no indication that (to the general reader) a shift from the more existential bread and butter socio-political problems to the ecocritical foci will truly reinvigorate his interest and elicit improved response. The indifference of the addressed seems to arise more from both their general refusal to read and greed-induced stiff neck.

Given the disposition of African writers and critics, one strongly suspects that soon enough, and should the onslaught persist, ecocriticism will develop ideological variants among its African disciples, very much similar to feminism and its variants – not the least, womanism – to satisfy the ideological reticence of African critics. Indeed, Slymaker further observes that:

> For many African writers and critics whose origin and interests lie in the manifold cultures south of the Sahara and north of Pretoria, Eurocentred or Euroafricanised ecodiscourses are another literary theatrical fashion emanating from the Western academic elites, something like an 'art d'eco' that is culturally analogous to art deco as a decorative style created and marketed in Europe and America. ('Echoing the Other(s)': 684)

It seems therefore that there are major ideological issues to resolve. These are issues that have endured from the very beginning of African literary criticism. Tejumola Olaniyan and Ato Quayson summarise these perennial, yet burning ideological concerns as follows:

> These questions include the relevance for African deliberations of Western derived models of the relationship between man and nature, the relationship

between knowledge and power (even when posed in the guise of concern for welfare of the earth), and the links to be made between the ecoactivism of people such as the martyred Ken Saro-Wiwa and the ways in which literary critics think about issues of equity and justice. ('Ecocriticism': 681)

Yet, African literature has from its origin reflected the 'eco-consciousness' of African people. In particular, African oral literature in its manifold forms has been more profuse and more profound in this regard. The African world view which yields the basic ingredients of the literature is generously suffused with such understanding of the symbiotic and balanced co-existence among the various manifestations of nature: human beings, other animals, the vegetation, the rivers, the mountains and the creatures inhabiting them, and, of course, the spiritual or metaphysical dimensions of nature. These give rise to the existence of the large corpus of oral literary creations which articulate this world view's overwhelming consciousness of the environment in all its ramifications.

In his 'Festivals, Ritual, and Drama in Africa', Tejumola Olaniyan discusses the use of festival theatre ritual in the African society and observes that:

> In many African communities, the foremost indigenous cultural and artistic institution is the festival. Organized around certain deities or spirits, or to mark generational transitions or the passage of seasons whether of climate or agricultural production, festivals are sprawling multimedia occasions – that is, incorporating diverse forms such as singing, chanting, drama, drumming, masking, miming, costuming, puppetry, with episodes of theatrical enactments ranging from the sacred and secretive to the secular and public. (355)

Olaniyan clearly underlines the eco-sensibilities inherent in the very many dimensions of festival theatre that exist in many African communities. These are forms of oral literature created by the people with sensibilities or consciousness of the environment drawn from their cosmology. Beyond the ritual dramatic and festival theatrical approach to the African expression of ecoconsciousness, there is an overflowing corpus of myths and legends which emphasise the environment and champion its cause. Myths are often more readily exploited to achieve this purpose of eco-conservation, especially given their effective and useful element of awe. Several of such myths exist among many communities in Africa and serve to protect and preserve such features of the environment as rivers, mountains, forests and a variety of animals and plants.

Among the Okpala people in Ngor-Okpala, Nigeria, myths are

woven around forests, rivers and animals, some of which are totems. The myths forbid acts that are capable of threatening the continued existence of such parts of the environment. One of such myths, for instance, preserves the small, rare bird which the people call *Chiri Nwam* (apparently an ideophonic name derived from their interpretation of the bird's unique song). It is their belief that anyone who kills the bird, or removes its young ones from the nest, ends in tragic circumstances. Their local interpretation of the bird's song is normally employed to emphasise the warning of disaster, from the bird itself.

Chiri nwam, chiri nwam achiforom,
Okpukpu nwam, okpukpu nwam gbagburu gi.
(You) collect my chicks, collect my chicks leaving none for me,
My chicks' bone, my chick's bone (will) choke you to death.

Children are potentially the natural hunters for birds, in general, and such birds, in particular. The interpretation of the bird's (cursing) song is naturally directed to them as the audience and it has great effect on their attitude to *Chiri Nwam* and such other mythical birds, including the equally rare *Gelegele odu asaa* (a small bird with seven tails), and animals.

Significantly, the curse song of the bird strengthens its myth as a bird of the spirits which its owners (the spirits) are bound to protect. Anyone who attacks, kills or eats it provokes its spirit-owners and risks disastrous consequences. The myth draws from the people's world view on curses and their potency which imply the involvement of supernatural forces. There is a mortal fear by the people of circumstances that could attract a curse, the fulfilment of which is normally beyond human control. They would rather deal with their fellow human beings who they can more easily predict and/or control than with supernatural forces that operate outside their prediction or control. It is that element of awe that the people invoke in order to protect and preserve that little and otherwise endangered bird. This scenario is pervasive in African society, which effectively exploits myth making and its basic elements of the supernatural as a natural means of environmental conservation and attainment of balance in nature and the ecosystem. It is replicated in the many rivers where it is a taboo to fish, the many trees that cannot be felled at whim and the many animals that can neither be hunted nor eaten as meat.

Totemism and the attendant myths create a spiritual and or kindred aura around the relationship between the people and their chosen totems. The monkey in Lagwa, Mbaise, the pig in Ihiagwa, Owerri, the leopard in Okpala, Ngor-Okpala – all in Imo State, Nigeria; the Iguana in Isoko, Delta State, Nigeria, are all totems to the people. They neither hunt, nor permit anyone to hunt or kill these animals; they do not eat them, either. The killer of a totem animal is deemed to have killed one of the people, which is an abomination. The 'murderer' is required to perform the normal traditional burial rites as for a deceased person in the community. In each totemic case, there is a myth and also a collateral kindred relationship which develops and creates such peaceful co-existence that neither the people, nor the animals hurt the other. There is, rather, a conducive environment for a flourishing population on each side of the relationship.

In most African communities, the forest, including all it holds, is held in deep awe arising from the people's belief of it as the sacred abode of the gods, ancestors and supernatural forces (including spirits, good and bad). Conscious, strenuous and extensive efforts, including myth making, are made to preserve it in its natural state. For instance, among the Ukpom Edem Inyang people in Oruk Anam, Akwa Ibom State, Nigeria, there exists a forest which the people believe to be the abode of their ancestors and shelter for spirits and other supernatural presences. It is a taboo for anyone to cut down any part of that forest. The myths woven around the forest protected it, until the late 1960s when some persons began to clear it. It was claimed that while the clearing was going on, the entire community was invaded by ghosts and spirits, including long dead ancestors and wild animals. The people abandoned the community and could only return after the control of the situation had been achieved through sacrifices of appeasement.

Like myths, folktales are extensively exploited by the people to provide early childhood education on the need to preserve the environment and sustain the natural balance in the ecosystem. Such tales often exploit the world-view-inspired awe of the supernatural to achieve effect. The popular Igbo tale, 'Akwa Eke', further illustrates the premium the people place on the need for self-discipline in their relationships with the environment. The story is about an unnamed pregnant woman who, in the course of her foray in the forest, found a python's egg in the hollow base of a huge tree. The python had gone in search of food. The woman was exceedingly enticed and salivated at the idea of enjoying the delicacy. She could not resist the urge and took the egg home. At home, she tried very hard to cook it but it would not cook. She tried to roast it; it would also not roast. She then chewed a lot of *okro* with which she eventually swallowed the egg. Shortly after, the dispossessed python returned and began to search for its missing egg. It called out to the egg in the following lament:

    Akwa eke, o rima, akwa eke o rima
    Ndo rimama, ndo rima
    Akwa eke m' dobere n'ukwu ozuru
    Ndo rimama, ndo rima
    Python's egg, o rima, python's egg, o rima
    Pity rimama, pity rima
    Python's egg (that) I kept in the hollow base of a tree
    Pity rimama, pity rima

The egg heard the python's song and in ridicule of the pregnant woman in whose stomach it was, responded as follows:

    Nwanyi ime ndo, ndo, ndo o, ndo, ndo
    Nwanyi ime ndo, ndo, ndo o, ndo, ndo
    I nu ka nne n'akpo m, ndo, ndo o, ndo, ndo
    I nu ka nna n'akpo m, ndo, ndo o, ndo, ndo
    I sie m n'ite m'ju, ndo, ndo o, ndo, ndo
    I ruo m n'oku m'ju, ndo, ndo o, ndo, ndo
    I tapia okwuru loo m, ndo, ndo o, ndo, ndo
    Pregnant woman, pity, pity, pity oh, pity, pity
    Pregnant woman, pity, pity, pity oh, pity, pity
    You hear (my) mother calling me, pity, pity, pity oh, pity, pity
    You hear (my) father calling me, pity, pity, pity oh, pity, pity
    You cooked me in (a) pot I refused, pity, pity, pity oh, pity, pity
    You roasted me in fire I resisted, pity, pity, pity oh, pity, pity
    You (then) chewed okro and swallowed me, pity, pity, pity oh, pity, pity

The python's repeated lament and the egg's equally repeated jeering response enabled the python to establish communication with its egg, successfully trace and identify the egg's location. On arrival at the pregnant woman's home, the python struck through the door and killed the woman.

For the people and the audience of children for whom the tale is meant, self-discipline is essential for survival; the lack of it can lead to very tragic consequences. This is an especially important consideration in dealings with the environment. The fate of the pregnant woman would naturally, in the people's world view, attract empathy and understanding considering their belief that pregnancy predisposes the carrier to extra cravings of the palate, making her have a 'sweet tooth' of sorts. Yet, the teaching of the tale elevates self-discipline above circumstance. The tale understands the woman's circumstance but would not acquit her, even if the python is a dangerous animal; the woman ought to have avoided trampling on its rights and therefore provoking it.

Iniobong Uko notes that the 'phenomenon of ecocriticism was first evolved by Cherill Glotfelty and Harold Fromm in their seminal book, *The Ecocriticism Reader: Landmarks in Literary Ecology* (1996).' Paraphrasing Glotfelty, she states that:

> Ecocriticism takes as its subject the interconnections between nature and culture, specifically the cultural artifacts, language and literature. As a critical stance, it has one foot in literature and the other on lands ... it negotiates between the human and nonhuman. (21-2)

From the foregoing, it is obvious that concern with the environment and the need to preserve it has been acute in African society, without the suspicious prompting of the Western world. It is their capricious drive for nature conquest and industrialisation (especially through the agency of their multinational corporations) that constitutes the greatest threat to the environment, in the first place. Nwahunanya, quoting D. H. Lawrence in 'Morality and the Novel' (1925), reminds us that 'the business of art is to reveal the relation between man and his circum-ambient universe, at the living moment'. He then asks: 'To what extent has literature helped or succeeded in addressing the problems of the physical environment, especially with regard to the impact of human activity on it?' (9). With respect to African literature, the answer appears to be obvious: quite a lot. As already shown here, there exists a large corpus of literature championing the cause of the environment and naturally strengthening the institutionalisation of ecoconsciousness, without the banality that has attended the current trend. The ecoconsciousness of the people is not a new trend; it has endured from their pre-historic times and been institutionalised in the large corpus of their literature, especially in the oral form. Written African literature can only enrich and extend the frontiers; It should indeed do so but without the distracting appearance of deriving its thrust or motivation from the neo-colonialist drive for profit or a sense of 'amongness' in a 'new' trend.

This scholarship does not repudiate the desirability of African literature, especially its written form, to address issues of the environment or deepen the people's con—sciousness of the ecosystem. Such a concern should be a matter of course as the literature articulates the sensibilities of the people on those issues that critically impact on their daily existence and hopes for the future. Indeed, the literature acquits itself and has not failed to discharge its remit creditably, in this regard. As Uko notes, partly in agreement with Enajite Ojaruega (32):

> Modern African literature has always been a literature of engagement as writers deploy their artistic resources toward addressing important issues concerning the people and the corporate existence of their various societies ... This utilitarian function is often directed toward any pressing problem that the writers want to enlighten the society about and also seek a possible solution to. Therefore, it is not surprising that African writers have also taken up environmental, ecological, and related issues as they attempt to sensitise the public about the deteriorating environment in the forms of decreasing biodiversity, environmental pollution, and other forms of degradation or acts of ecocide. (22)

The point that this scholarship makes is that the banality which ecoliterature and its attendant ecocriticism represent, is ultimately unnecessary and an avoidable red herring. African literature, especially in its oral forms, has an innate capacity for, and has indeed been championing the cause of, ecoconsciouness derived from the African milieu, itself. The apparent drive by ecocritics and writers to 'belong' must be circumspect; it must not be a pursuit of 'amongness' for its fashionable sake, or for the funding lucre attainable through its posturing. Creativity need not be aligned with the pursuit of fashionable emphasis. Indeed, as Gordimer warns:

> The transformation of the imagination must never 'belong' to any establishment, however just, fought for, and longed for. Paternak's words should be our credo: 'When seats are assigned to passion and vision on the day of the great assembly Do not reserve a poet's position: It is dangerous, if not empty.' (121)

WORKS CITED

Agbeyangi, Baba S. O. Wey. 'Beyond Sustainable Development'. In *12 June 1993 Revolution (How Conurbation will Change the Face of the Earth)*, Alade Mammah (ed.), Lagos: Mace Associates, 1994.

Gordimer, Nadine. 'Three in a Bed: Fiction, Morals, and Politics'. In Tejumola Olaniyan and Ato Quayson (eds). *African Literature: An Anthology of Criticism and Theory*. Malden, MA: Blackwell, 2007.

Nwahunanya, Chinyere. 'Language, Literature and the Environment: (Towards the Use of Language to Produce an Environmentally Friendly Literature)'. *CALEL: Currents in African Literature and the English Language*, Vol. vii, May (2016): 1-2.

Ojaruega, Enajite. 'Eco-activism in Contemporary African Literature: Zakes Mda's *Heart of Redness* and Tanure Ojaide's *The Activist*' *Eco-Critical*

Literature: Regreening African Landscapes, Ogaga Okuyade (ed.). New York: African Heritage Press, 2013: 31-46.

Olaniyan, Tejumola. 'Festivals, Ritual, and Drama in Africa'. In Tejumola Olaniyan and Ato Quayson (eds). *African Literature: An Anthology of Criticism and Theory*. Malden, MA: Blackwell, 2007.

Olaniyan, Tejumola and Quayson, Ato. 'Ecocriticism'. In Tejumola Olaniyan and Ato Quayson (eds). *African Literature: An Anthology of Criticism and Theory*. Malden, MA: Blackwell, 2007.

Slymaker, William. 'Echoing the Other(s): The Call of Global Green and Black African Responses'. In Tejumola Olaniyan and Ato Quayson (eds). *African Literature: An Anthology of Criticism and Theory*. Malden, MA: Blackwell, 2007.

Uko, Iniobong. 'Towards Pragmatising the Nigerian Environment: The English Language and African Literature as Determining Paradigms'. *CALEL: Currents in African Literature and the English Language*, Vol. vii, May (2016): 13-31.

'From the Street to the World of Art'
Writing Women's Liberation in Nawal El Saadawi's *Zeina*

SIMONE A. JAMES ALEXANDER

Renowned Egyptian writer and feminist Nawal El Saadawi's phenomenal novel *Zeina* is strategically set against the backdrop of revolution in Cairo. Revolutionary in its own rights, the novel chronicles female resistance to patriarchal mandates. The poignant and searing critique of the masculinist Egyptian regime should come as no surprise. Mona Eltahawy reminds us that, according to a 2013 Thomson Reuters Foundation poll of women's rights following the Arab Spring, Egypt 'was judged to be the single worst country for women's rights, scoring badly in almost every category, including gender violence, reproductive rights, treatment of women in the family and female inclusion in politics and the economy' (Eltahawy *Headscarves and Hymens*: 24). Shedding light on the precarious position in which feminists in the region find themselves, Khadidiatou Guéye is quick to point out that in the Arab region most women writers' 'feminist ideologies clash with the Muslim background of their cultures' ('Tyrannical Femininity': 160). While religion is undoubtedly one of the tools of female oppression, Eltahawy surmises: 'Whether our politics are tinged with religion or with military rule, the common denominator is the oppression of women' (18). A consummate feminist and the leading spokeswoman on the status of women in the Arab region, El Saadawi exposes, even as she challenges, the male-centric, patriarchal regime that perpetuates female oppression.

The illegitimate daughter of Bodour, a young university student-turned-literary-critic and distinguished professor, and Nessim, a young revolutionary, Zeina, the eponymous heroine, is abandoned by her mother on the streets of Cairo when Nessim is killed during one of many demonstrations of the repressive patriarchal system. Forced to carry this secret, Bodour writes a fictionalised account of her life, which mysteriously gets stolen. In a novel where female bodies are subject to the worst form of subjugation, colonisation, and body theft, the novel's title, *The Stolen Novel*, is apt. The theft of Bodour's text/body appears to be an act of revenge for the idea of the book germinated 'specifically on a night that passed like a terrifying nightmare or an ephemeral dream of paradise when she had eaten the forbidden fruit' (32).[1] The theft that results in body silencing further underscores another punitive act, female transgression, as Bodour's immoral indulgence is brought to the fore. Although Petra Kuppers' analysis pertains to fatness and the fat body, her critique about the culture in which we live 'in which a young girl has to speak about the split between controlling mind and loose body' is germane to my analysis ('Fatties on Stage: Feminist Performances': 280). The cultural expectation is that a girl must submit to established patriarchal rules of feminine behaviour. Bodour's transgression manifests further in her trespassing in the masculine sphere of intellectual thought. 'Jealous of her mind and the words she put down on the page', Bodour's husband, Zakariah, felt that 'her self-confidence … bordered on arrogance. He wanted to break this arrogance (*Zeina*: 123). Bodour's psychiatrist, whom she shares with friend, Safaa (Safi) al-Dhabi, pontificates that women are not revered for their intellect: 'Any woman with a mind cannot find the man who deserves her. All the men are made of tinsel. Nothing stays except your mind, work, writing and health' (122).

Commissioning Badreya as her double, Bodour rids herself of the invisible chains on her mind and body.[2] The novel is her/Badreya's intellectual creation that serves to challenge the perception that women's bodies function solely as vessels for male gratification and procreation.[3] Thus, we witness a parallel between creativity and procreation, a juxtaposition of mind and body via the conflation of the lost book and the lost child: 'At night, Bodour cried for her stolen novel. She lost it in her sleep, together with the daughter she had carried in her womb' (37). The expulsion-cum-dismissal of the female creative process is likened to a forced abortion. Bodour was 'tearing out her own liver, wrapping it, dripping with blood, in a soft woollen blanket … She rubbed her palms clean on the ground and tore out her liver from her chest, depositing it on the street and following the dark, endlessly long road' (38). Likening her daughter to her liver, Bodour stresses that motherhood is vital to her existence, to her sense of self. This forced expulsion that results in Bodour's disembodiment and her inability to compensate for the lost novel/daughter, functions as a critique and a challenge to patriarchal mothering. Both Bodour and Safi register their resistance to patriarchal mothering by unequivocally expressing their desire to have a daughter like Zeina who does not subscribe to patriarchal code of conduct and expectations of womanhood. Safi stresses that unlike Zeina, Mageeda al-Khartiti (Bodour's daughter with Zakariah) lacks originality in that 'she imitated her father's style of writing and her mother's literary criticism'; Bodour agrees, admitting that her mothering is compromised: 'Mageeda is her father's daughter, Safi. She looks exactly like him when he was young. I sometimes feel she is his daughter not mine. I wish I had a daughter who took after me' (83-4).

Whereas the conflation of body and mind (book) serves to empower Badreya/Bodour, her male psychiatrist is unable to provide her with an effective cure, he is unable to read/write her body beyond the confines of patriarchy. The following exchange between Bodour and her psychiatrist bolsters this argument:

'They stole her from me, doctor.'
'Who is she?'
'The novel, doctor ...'
'I would love to read the novel, Bodour. Bring it next time.'
'I don't have the novel, doctor.'
'Where is it then?'
'Thieves ...'
'What thieves?'
'Those who stole it.'
'Stole what?'
'The baby, doctor.'
'What?'
'I mean the baby novel ...' (73)

Female pain remains undecipherable and misdiagnosed because of the psychiatrist's inability to read Bodour's text/body effectively: 'The doctor was at a loss concerning Bodour's case, for he couldn't get to the source of her pain, and was unable to decide whether it resided in her mind or her body. Her conscious mind was in control of her past memories and stopped them from surfacing' (73). Trivialising female pain, and female oppression as a whole, the psychiatrist fails to recognise that Bodour's illness is conditioned by the rigid societal structures; this malpractice results in misdiagnosis.[4] A perpetrator of patriarchal aggression, the psychiatrist actively contributes to female subjugation, to female pain. His objectification of the female body as a site of desire is a professional breach of duty. Furthermore, the sexual violation he performs on the women constitutes a breach of trust. Attempting to seek answers for Bodour's malaise, the psychiatrist, to quote Patricia Reilly, resorts to 'religious language' (*Be Full of Yourself*: 64). He concludes: '[Bodour's] unconscious mind was a chain of accumulated fears, one layered on top of another, one generation after another, starting from her mother and going back thousands of years to the ancestral grandmothers and the vilification of Eve and the original sin' (73-4). Reilly surmises that religious language is damning because it reinforces our unworthiness, our sinfulness. Eltahawy puts it best when she ascertains that to be 'female is to be the walking embodiment of sin' (*Headscarves and Hymens*: 10). From an early age, young girls are taught that the female body is inherently sinful and unclean, and that bodily pleasures and desires must be suppressed at all costs. Mindful of patriarchal expectations of females: 'Ever since she was a child, Bodour had been mindful of her reputation. She had the responsibility of upholding the family honor' (*Zeina*: 14), and despite her 'yearning for love and the sinful pleasures of the body' (15), Bodour quelled her desire by reading her father's books in which she was 'tempted by the image of Prince Charming, who made love to her until she orgasmed. Her body trembled under the covers with sinful pleasure' (14). The idea of the contaminated female body is reinforced with the onset of puberty, specifically when a girl's menstrual cycle begins. The directive issued reads: 'Menstruation ... is a discomfort; therefore keep aloof from the women during the menstrual discharge and do not go near them until they have become clean' (134). It begs the question: whose discomfort? The response to this body shaming manifests in girls/women viewing their bodies in terms of resentment and hatred. A site of disgust, the body must be sanitised of its impurities: '[Bodour] took a bath warm with water and soap, cleansing her body of its sinfulness' (14). The notion of hereditary sin has had lasting effects on the treatment and expectations of girls and women. Unsurprisingly, Eve bears the 'primary responsibility for humankind's fall into sin; she became the scapegoat for all of humanity and her daughters carry her shame within their bodies, their lives, and destinies' (Reilly: 64). We witness a subversion of the religious doctrine as it is re-interpreted through a feminist lens. Whereas in the original text Eve is portrayed as the consummate seductress, seducing Adam to join her in sin, in this revised text, Naim is the one who seduces Badreya, who 'encouraged her to rebel against God' (*Zeina*: 133).[5] Badreya, unlike Eve is not vilified; instead 'Nessim opened her eyes to injustices on earth and in the heavens, and removed the blindfolds from her mind. He granted her body the forbidden pleasure, and she ate with him from the fruits of the two forbidden trees: the trees of life and knowledge' (136-7). This feminist reading of the narrative rejects the docile, subservient woman, freeing her from male domination and dominion, and reimagines her on an equal footing with her partner.

By the novel's end, Bodour is sexually liberated. 'Her chains [that] were never loosened except during sleep when her mind, soul and body dozed off' are now broken (15). Unshackled from patriarchal expectations of womanhood:

> [She] took off her tight leather shoes with their high pointed heels. She removed the brassiere pressing into her chest and the hairpins and the gold bracelets and the rings studded with stones. She broke the chains that kept her in shackles from head to toe. Her flesh and bones were released from captivity, and the reins restraining her were loosed. She let her body swim freely on the bench ... She heard a whisper in her heart saying, 'I am neither a wife nor widow and I shall not grieve, like Babylon, the whore in the Bible'. (246)

Liberating herself from the reigns/restraint of patriarchal subjugation, Bodour refuses the stigmatisation, the shame accorded to the female body.

Cognisant of not only the contradictions in religious teachings, but also the embodied difference of women that was conveniently used to classify and oppress them, Bodour becomes hesitant about placing her unwavering trust and belief in a 'god that did not address her or mention her by name, and made her subservient to her husband' (133-4). She concedes that religious teachings had one thing in common, the oppression of women:

> God recognized the presence of men in the Qur'an, but not that of women, whose names were completely absent. He didn't mention the name of Eve but referred to her as Adam's wife. Pharaoh's wife who tempted the prophet Joseph had no name, and neither was Khadiga, Prophet Muhammad's first wife, mentioned in the Qur'an by name. In all three books, women were not treated as the equals of men. (133-4)[6]

This pervasive maleness endorses male superiority and contributes to the devaluation of women; in short, it establishes that the feminine is sinful and therefore not divine. Reilly offers a poignant assessment of this politics of exclusivity: 'The use of exclusive male imagery convinces women that they are other than God therefore deficient, flawed, and inferior' (*Be Full of Yourself*: 68). In contrast, the boy-child's resemblance to the divine, to God, 'affords him power and privilege' (68). Reilly's observation that the 'image of a male god who exposed, scrutinised and judged us' bears weight here (68). This 'invasive male god whose image overshadowed even our most private moments' has engendered a haunting that has manifested into fear (68). Bodour experiences palpable fear 'that God might shower curses on Safi ... that [she] might collapse ... suffering from complete paralysis or that her heretical tongue might become paralyzed' because she gave voice to her waning belief in God: 'The more I learned about God the less I believed' (79).

The birth of Zeina heralds a new era, a new beginning, and new hope. This desire for renewal is articulated by Bodour and Safi who both wished for a daughter like Zeina, equally renowned for her beauty and rebellious spirit as she is for her extraordinary musical talent. From the onset of the novel, Zeina registers defiance by refusing to write her 'full name like the other girls' when instructed to do so by a male teacher: 'Write the names of your father and grandfather, asshole;' instead, Zeina 'held the piece of chalk and wrote: Zeina Bint Zeinat' (*Zeina*: 8). Lacking a full name, Zeina is shamed, made to feel that she is deficient and unworthy (the word 'full' emphasises her lack, her illegitimacy), for '[e]very girl has an identifiable father, whose name she wrote next to hers on the blackboard. Each girl was proud of her father, grandfather, uncle or any well-known male relative ... The girl who carried her mother's name was a child of sin' (8, 9). Men, obviously, are the natural possessors or inheritors of 'full' names; meanwhile women are accorded legitimacy through their alliance with them. Refusing to compromise her identity with this male-female alliance that delegitimises and renders women invisible, Zeina opted for female autonomy. Her strong sense of self serves as an inspiration for Mageeda – 'I wished I was like her even if they called me the child of sin' (88) – and has planted the seeds of hope and change in her fellow female classmates: 'On the walls of the school toilet we wrote her name in chalk: Zeina Bint Zeinat' (88). Whereas other girls expressed resentment and shame towards their mothers:

> We were all ashamed of saying the names of our mothers aloud. We couldn't write them in our copybooks, let alone on the blackboard. My mother was not a housemaid like her mother, for she was a distinguished professor and her name was Bodour al-Damhiri, the wife of the great writer, Zakariah al-Khartiti. I wrote his name next to mine on the blackboard: Mageeda Zakariah al-Khartiti. (88)

Zeina, in turn, proudly and unapologetically pays tribute to her mother, the unsung heroine, by writing her name in the annals of history. At one of her performances, Zeina moved her mother from the back rows with housemaids and illegitimate children and placed her next to ministers, the heads, the men and women of letters, the winner of literature, science and faith prizes. She placed her mother in the front row where her head towered above the rest. (149)

Women are encouraged to be complicit in their own demise and participate in their own oppression.

Zeina's written tribute is succeeded by an oral one: a song, akin to a national hymn that evokes and eulogises her mother: 'I dedicate this song to my precious mother Zeinat. She's more precious to me than the earth and the sky, than this world and the hereafter' (114). Miss Mariam, 'her second mother who taught [her] to love music and singing' also receives a rousing tribute. I quote at length:

> She trained us and took us from the street to the world of art. We called our band the 'Mariam Band' and we had no place except the streets, with their dust, men, women, and children, with their demonstrations and cheers, 'Down with injustice, and long live freedom.' The street inspired our tunes and music and rhythms. We drew music from the streets, from the pavements, and the dust, from people's warm breaths on earth and not from the coldness of the sky. (114)

This praise for her mother, a mere mortal, is deemed as blasphemous by Ahmed al-Damhiri, the cousin of Zakariah (114). Unmistakably, Zeina uses her art as a political platform, a fact that does not go unnoticed by al-Damhiri, who expresses indignation: 'She is dangerous, for she plays with words. What does she mean by the coldness of the sky? This is heretical talk' (115).

Zeina's political activism finds full representation in the first poem she wrote as a child for her mother. The song's simplistic theme of building her mother a house 'Made of red brick, / Not of mud / [With] a ceiling to protect her from summer's heat / And winter's cold / A bathroom with running water / And an electric lamp' is politicised; it is profoundly critical of class stratification, of a society that unapologetically discards and disregards its surplus people (116-17). In other words, those deemed expendable, 'the street children [who] were born of sin ... The girls and boys born on the streets without fathers or mothers, without school, church, or mosque, and without papers carrying the official stamp' (98). Her mother's ownership of a house bears the imprint of self-possession, of an autonomous subjectivity. The daily struggles of the masses starkly contrast the life of affluence and privilege lived by the upper crust of the society. Eltahawy's real-life experience as a student at the American university in Cairo, offers a snapshot of this inequity: 'I would take a public bus form the lower-middle-class neighborhood where I lived and an hour later I would be with people who'd been chauffeured for most of their lives. It was a crash course in Egypt's classist society; many of my classmates acted as if there were no one suffering on the streets their chauffeured cars passed through' (*Headscarves and Hymens*: 21). In documenting the criminalisation of the poor, Zeina challenges this orchestrated and predetermined blindness and, in doing so, she challenges the neat narrative of nationalism and nation-building. She debunks the notion that one's class is a marker of legitimacy and undoes the stigmatisation ascribed to so-called street children. This poem is a political call to action to ameliorate the lives of those disenfranchised: the poor and the homeless.

Notwithstanding the patriarchal culture that devalues and demonises mothers as second-class citizens, Zeina refuses to regard her mother, Zeinat, and mothers in general, as an accessory to the patriarchy. Her re-appropriation of the masculinist language and her adoption of the language of female agency and empowerment engenders a calibanesque act. By taking up the proverbial pen (chalk), she topples hierarchal and class structures, engendering an imbalance between the (confluence of) upper class and legitimacy. Notably, Zeina's inspiration and teacher, Miss Mariam, for whom the band is named, is bent on dismantling patriarchal power structures. Her indifference to Mageeda's father's fame and fortune starkly contrasts everyone else's admiration and reverence (88). Instead. Miss Mariam champions female autonomy and empowerment: holding up Zeina's fingers 'for all the girls to see', she pontificates: 'Look, girls, at these fingers! They've been created for music. She's talented and unique, born to be a musician' (88). In challenging female domesticity, women are no longer in the service of patriarchy. Miss Mariam has a personal stake in stripping patriarchy of its power, for her own mother, Fatima, was a victim of patriarchal violence, shot to death by her own father for refusing to agree to an arranged marriage, and later for marrying 'Christian Mikhail without an official marriage contract' (*Zeina*: 44).[7] Furthermore, naming the band after Miss Mariam radiates self-determination that is celebrated further in Zeina's revolutionary and protest lyrics. Zeina's protest manifests in her disdain and disgust for the male-centric school curriculum, resulting in her only attending school two days per week on Tuesdays and Thursdays to attend Miss Mariam music lessons (9). In a case of uncanny coincidence, Zeina's father, Nessim only 'came to university on the days demonstrations were to take place' (19).

Thus, we witness the marriage of music and activism.

In celebrating women, *Zeina* values and re-evaluates women (particularly Zeina under the careful guidance of Miss Mariam) as key political players, and not merely as pawns, in the national discourse. Al-Damhiri acknowledges, albeit grudgingly, that '[Zeina] is not a simpleton' (114-15). Moreover, as articulated earlier, Zeina is to be feared; she must be policed because her politics of subversion poses a severe threat to the existing power structures. The book's title speaks of self-possession, of an autonomous subjectivity. Being named after her mother, Zeina Bint Zeinat subverts the patriarchal custom where boys inherit their fathers' name as a rite of passage, as a continuation of the patrilineage. Challenging this age-old custom and positioning matrilineality as a feasible alternative, the mother (her name) is absolved of shame and ridicule. Celebrated, her name is engraved into the national consciousness; a much-deserved space is reserved for her in the annals of the nation-state.

Significantly, *Zeina* chronicles Zeina's birth, a birth that has its beginnings in grassroots activism and that coincides with political unrest: protests and demonstrations in Cairo. Her palpable and pervasive presence is felt immediately, on the first two pages of the novel, and serves as a counter-narrative to her illegitimacy, her orchestrated invisibility. A product of the 'streets', Zeina rose above her 'lowly station', challenging and dismantling boundaries and barriers as she performs in state theatres and opera houses, spaces distinguished for their high culture, and once reserved and occupied exclusively by members of the highbrow society. Her politicised lyrics that desecrate the sacred simultaneously force a convergence of high and low culture; this convergence, in turn, engenders a collapse of hierarchal structures. In essence, her music transcends the social-class system of the society. Zeina's birth to an unwed mother and father, the epitome of resistance and a revolutionary act in its own right, disrupts the status quo and interrupts the neat narrative of nationalism.

Zeina's embodied resistance (and resilience) is unmistakable: 'She was tall and thin, and her body was as sturdy as if it had been made of more than flesh and blood alone. When she walked, her figure was like a *spear cutting through the air*. She stood proudly erect … *She held the piece of chalk between her long, pointed fingers* … We saw her straight back' (7, 8, emphasis added). Zeina fully inhabits her body that is 'more than flesh'. Dismissing the fleshly attributes of the female body, i.e. its sexualisation, Zeina transcends the flesh. This transcendence finds further representation in Zeina's non-conformity to the traditional ideals of femininity: 'Her frizzy hair ... *stood like black wires*. A girl with this kind of hair was the object of people's scorn, for good girls from good families had long smooth hair *falling softly down their backs*. Their *hair submitted easily* to the movement of the gentle breeze and the *fingers of their husbands* after marriage' (48, emphasis added). Operating within the implied definition of a 'street girl', namely as someone who embodies wanton and unbridled sexuality, Zeina is deemed as intractable and ungovernable. Decent (home) girls are expected to subscribe to the tenets of white femininity; thus, submissiveness is regarded as an inherent female trait. Whereas Zeina lacks feminine decency and decorum, good, respectable girls are rewarded with husbands for exhibiting good behaviour. Furthermore, their long hair (contrasted with Zeina's brittle, frizzy hair) is a symbol of female beauty and desirability, untouched yet touchable. In their subjugated roles, good girls also experience disembodiment, their hair (and indisputably their bodies) that calls attention to their objectification, 'submit easily' to being touched, albeit exclusively by their husbands. Contrarily, Zeina's frizzy, unruly hair connotes looseness, her inability to be tamed. Moreover, her unruliness and waywardness is attributed to her lack of family; but more pointedly to the absence of her father: 'Zeina Bint Zeinat had no family. Her father died while she was still in the womb' (152). Despite his absence through death, Nezzim's paternity remains intact: '[Zeina] inherited from him the stuff stubborn "gene," the upright gait and the robust head. She inherited the hair which stood like *iron spikes* protecting the head from blows' (48, emphasis added), meanwhile, Zeinat's 'intimate connection with the origins of life' is rendered insignificant (Reilly: 70). Her palpable and orchestrated absence heightens her irrelevance. Reilly explains it best: 'In a society that worships a male God, the father's life is more valuable than the mother's' (70). While resistance is a cherished character trait in a man, it is not admired in a woman. Rather, female subjugation is preferred. Furthermore, Zeinat becomes synonymous with her body part, her womb. Puzzled by what she sees as a conundrum, Bodour questions: 'Why did you create me, oh God, as a woman with a hymen and a womb that can carry the seed of sin, and make the male body free?' (*Zeinat*: 127). Furthermore, the womb reflects the value placed on women's reproductive capability. In this masculinist culture, women/mothers are treated as second-class citizens and therefore they remain nameless and faceless.

The stripping of Zeinat's maternal rights is akin to denying her custodial rights to her child; consequently, her mothering ability, or lack thereof, is placed under intense scrutiny. She is deemed an unfit and irresponsible mother: 'At school Zeina Bint Zeinat wore a uniform of *cheap cotton* with *irregular collars* and a *loose belt*. Her *hair was dishevelled* and her *shoelaces untied*. Zeina Bint Zeinat never looked at herself in the mirror, for she didn't have a mirror at home. She didn't in fact have a home' (152, emphasis added). Zeina's uniform made of cheap cotton, her loose belt and untied shoelaces connote a vulgar and wanton sexuality. The cheap cotton from which her uniform is made signals her commodification. Resisting female commodification and subjugation to which both her mother and her are subjected, Zeina seeks vengeance for those marginalised, the nameless/faceless mothers: 'Through the wall of the womb she heard her mother shouting against injustice and hailing freedom' (49). Inheriting the 'masculine' traits of her father and the strong-will and steely resistance and resilience of her mother, Zeina is equipped to engage in battle on the proverbial masculinist battlefield. Consequently, an alternative reading of the female body is necessary, one in which women are not portrayed as commodity, but as speaking subjects. Thus, the 'irregular collars' and 'loose belt' of Zeina's uniform, her dishevelled hair and untied shoelaces are symbolic of her articulating resistance; these symbols exemplify her non-conformity to the patriarchal culture. While the cheap cotton from which her uniform is made a marker of her socio-economic condition; more importantly, it speaks of her repudiation of the regimented colonial education. As noted earlier, Zeina only attended school on the days Miss Mariam taught music. The uniform, a proverbial straitjacket, lends itself to a form of body policing that stifles individuality and creativity. For the same reason, not owning a mirror at home is less reflective of Zeina's poverty and more directive of her self-possession:

> In comparison, women around her seemed like dolls made of wax or clay, painted white, red, green or what have you, and decorated with rings, bracelets, and gold necklaces. They looked like marionettes whose strings were manipulated by other people holding them by the neck, the arm or the leg, and moving them in any direction they pleased. (178-9)

Female bodies are constructed as economies of pleasure to be consumed by men at will. Nevertheless, Zeina resists consumption and commodification of the female body. Unlike other girls, she is not subjected to the tyranny of beauty.[8]

Thus, Zeina's entrance into the world is marked by her insatiable thirst for independence that requires her embarking on a mission that challenges patriarchal dominance. Using her body as a site of resistance, she engenders the spirit and will of the Amazonian women warriors, epitomised in the 'spear cutting through the air', her 'long, pointed fingers', and 'straight back' (7, 8). In true Amazonian spirit, her proverbial battlefield is the mean streets of Cairo. As referenced earlier, Zeina's body (her body of music) is her weapon of choice: 'Zeina Bint Zeinat was unique in that she was fortified against molestation and rape. No man could touch her, even when she was fast asleep. Her long pointed fingers would stick like nails into the neck of any man, and her strong sharp teeth would cut into any part of his flesh like knives and would tear it out' (45). In addition to functioning as armour, Zeina's body is sacred; and as a result, she is untouchable. In the following scene, Zakariah attempts to break with protocol through his attempted rape of Zeina; consequently, we witness how Zeina's 'training in self-defense gained from living on the streets' has fortified her against sexual violence:

> He tore off her white dress and her petticoat made of Egyptian cotton. He removed her little white panties and pulled one leg away from the other, forcing his male organ between her thighs. But he couldn't enter her. His erect phallus couldn't find its way through the folds of flesh. The route inside was completely blocked, as though there was no aperture there and no vagina. She wasn't like other females ... With teeth as hard as nails, she dug into the flesh of his shoulder, neck, belly, and into the tip of his penis, which she tore off. (60-61, 62)

Ready to engage in battle, Zeina adopts a full militarised stance in which her strength, ruthlessness, and ability to withstand great pain comes to the fore. Women, for the most part, are constructed as always sexually available; Zakariah endorses this belief when he surmises that a woman's tears and withholding herself constitute 'part of the game' (62).[9] Zeina, however, resists the oversexualisation of women's bodies; in so doing, she subverts the concept that the female body functions as a receptacle for male sexual gratification. She rejects culturally normalised and tenuous expectations of female sexuality. Moreover, Zeina's perceived anatomical difference has less to do with biology and more to do with societal illness. The desexualised body serves as counter discourse to the hypersexualised female body.

In a similar vein, Zeina is free of the burden of the cult of virginity, as virginity is stripped of its (bodily) significance, is disassociated from the body: '[Zeina] had lost her virginity long ago, when her mother left her on the pavement' (60).[10] Owing to the fact that women's bodies bear the weight of childbearing, of domesticity, and the stamp of virginity, Zeina's bodily distortion – her body turn inside out – meant to deflect the male sexual gaze, is a denouncement of the humiliating virginity test. Divested of its power, this demoralising cult of purity is juxtaposed with real moral issues: the forced abandonment and attendant sexual assault of Zeina and of street children in general, resulting in a premature loss of innocence.[11] Zeina's loss of innocence is rendered most palpable in the following scene:

> As a child, she saw men's naked flesh. Now she was beyond pain and rape, because no man could ever destroy her. She had no father, elder brother, uncle, grandfather, lover, or husband. Only music was her love. She loved those who loved music and loathed those who hated it, even if they were kings and princes. (116)

The absence of male guardians calls attention to (even celebrates) the importance of female kinship and community that is akin to the society that the amazon women warriors inhabited.[12] Further, this absence debunks the myth that a girl's worth is determined by her association with an 'identifiable' father or male figure. In essence, male guardianship and the attendant approval is negated. A warrior in both body and spirit, Zeina is superior to other women (and arguably men) in effectiveness and bravery:[13] 'How could the child of sin be superior to all of us in music? ... But who is she? Why did God give her these self-confident eyes when all the other women's eyes radiate humbleness and timidity?' (79, 116). Escaping a life of forced domestic drudgery, Zeina uses music as a platform for her political activism: 'No man ever possessed her and never could. Even music didn't possess her, but she possessed it and was therefore free from poverty, fear, and bondage' (116). Amazonian women are known to practice celibacy and to reject the tradition of marriage. It is no coincidence that Zakariah presented Zeina with a statuette of Nefertiti's head before his attempted rape of her. Zeina's life parallels Nefertiti's in her defiance of customs that changed the ways of religion within Egypt. A queen in her own right, Zeina challenges the prevailing perception of so-called street children and the way women were treated as commodity. Importantly, she unearths the street children from oblivion, admitting them into 'the theatre without tickets', and issuing each one of them a 'card with his name and photograph ... She registered their names in Mariam's band' (176). Mothers were accorded equal respect and admiration for the children 'could write their mothers' names on the card' on which there was no space 'for the unknown father' (176).[14]

The constant references to Zeina's sturdy, wiry body not only constructs her as dignified and worthy of respect, but also it attests to her inaccessibility, an imagery that contradicts her portrayal as a 'street girl', sexually free and easily accessible to men. Zeina does not subscribe to the patriarchal mandates of female respectability; unlike other girls, she does not aspire to be married, to be a wife and, subsequently, to be a mother. Offering a searing critique of how girls are socialised to support patriarchy, Adichie pontificates: 'Because I am female, I'm expected to aspire to marriage. I am expected to make my life choices always keeping in mind that marriage is the most important' (*We Should All Be Feminists*: 28-9). In other words, young women are taught from an early age that their bodies are commodities to be maintained, to enable them to entice men into matrimony. Appalled by the normalisation of female subjugation, by the disservice done to girls who are raised 'to cater to the fragile ego of males', and who we teach 'to shrink themselves, to make themselves smaller', Adichie calls attention to the insanity in promoting and maintaining patriarchal codes of conduct (27). Cecilia Hartley shares a similar view on the absurdity of normative femininity as she reminds us that 'a woman is taught early to contain herself, to keep arms and legs close to her body and take up as little space as possible' ('Letting Ourselves Go': 61). Bodour's anxiety of taking up too much space manifests bodily:

> Bodour wished to be free of the weight of her body the load of plump flesh she carried each and every day on her arms, chest, belly, legs, and the soles of her feet. She dreamed of a force that would lift this weight off her shoulders. She dreamed of two strong arms reaching down from heaven to crush her body until the flesh dissolved and vanished completely. (*Zeina*: 20)

The weight is not only ascribed to the body but it also attests to the weight of the burden of womanhood. This gendered difference is noticeable as Nessim carried his body that 'seemed to be made of something other than flesh' as though it were weightless (20). It is accepted – and even expected – for men to take up space, whether that means being large in terms of muscularity or simply taking a wide stance when sitting or standing. Furthering the argument, Hartley notes that part of this desire to be small and take up as little space as possible stems from the fact that 'women themselves are seen as somehow less than men [so] their body must demonstrate that inferiority' (Hartley: 62). Zeina, on the other hand, fiercely interrogates female bodily restrictions as 'She moved her arms and legs freely in the air, jumping, bending like a soft blossoming twig. Her voice rose high without barriers or restrictions from earth or sky, and her large blue-black pupils gave forth a dark bluish flame that was unafraid of hell fires' (*Zeina*: 105). Her undisciplined body is 'in rebellion, not only against male power structures but against all that is feminine' (Hartley: 65).

Hartley goes on to argue that those women 'who claim more than their fair share of territory are regarded with suspicion' (61). In this instance, Hartley specifically discusses fat women; notwithstanding, her argument informs my analysis of female subordination and marginalisation. Zeina is the consummate transgressor having committed the ultimate sin of trespassing into the masculine domain. In essence, she enacts a (bodily) transgression by inhabiting the public (performative) space that is reserved for men; hence, she defies the code of conduct that stipulates that women should not be seen or heard. Accordingly, women are expected to inhabit the private domestic space. In choosing the occupation of a musician, or more pointedly, of a 'street' musician, Zeina has not submitted to the rules that society has established for feminine behaviour. By her not being anchored to the home, she interrogates the politics of domesticity. This interrogation finds representation in her music that is a conscious rejection of societal and cultural norms and cultural expectations of femininity.

Rejecting female predestination as the bearer of respectability, Zeina avoids being trapped within the cult of respectability politics. Jean Besson surmises: 'women's concern with respectability is especially underlined by the custom of shaming' ('Reputation and Respectability Reconsidered': 17). Zeina is demonised and belittled for her non-conventional (read subversive) choice of profession: 'Music, like dancing and singing is the work of the Devil. Singing is the job of whores and prostitutes, and not our girls from good families (*Zeina*: 88). Zeina's public persona is just cause for derision; she is linked to whores and prostitutes whose sexual deviance and promiscuity is a given. No stranger to female demonisation, Zeina is 'familiar with this type of man. They thought they could possess her, that she was a whore, a slave girl or a concubine' (178). Unlike street 'workers' who epitomise vulgarity, 'girls from good families' are expected to be paragons of virtue and are accordingly socialised to achieve this ideal. The street is imagined as a space of corruption and contamination, and as such, Mageeda is issued a directive that the streets must be avoided at all costs:

My father warned me against *going out on* the streets [because] good girls from good families didn't play with street children ... The windows of our home were always secured with double glazing and curtains, to prevent the street dust from coming through, and to keep out the escalating noise from the loudspeakers hung on the minarets, the drumbeats and cheery sounds of weddings, nightclubs and discos, and the sirens of police cars and fire engines. (11, emphasis added)

Ahmed al-Damhiri cautions that Zeina has ventured into prohibited territory when he advised Mageeda that Zeina should 'go back to God', to redeem herself from sin, to which Mageeda rebutted: 'My friend Zeina is a decent young woman, Uncle. Her life is given completely to art, music, and sing...' (112). In al-Damhiri's estimation, Zeina has descended into the abyss of female indecency for we are duly reminded that not only were women 'the Devil's allies [but also that] cleanliness was godly while dirtiness was womanly' (174). Zakariah reinforces ideal womanhood by issuing Mageeda a cautionary message: 'A girl's honor is like a match. It can only light once' (98). This desire to control female sexuality is built into the masculinist language. A girl's honour rests on shaky grounds. Moreover, likening a girl's honour to a match intimates her looseness, her sexual proclivity. Similar to a match that can be easily ignited, a girl is unable to keep in check her sexual impulse and therefore is easily sexually aroused: 'A woman like any other, [she is] deficient in mind and religion, weak before her lusts' (179). Her chances of avoiding the pitfalls of degeneracy are frighteningly slim: 'it can only light once'. Shame and immorality are etched onto the female body. Notwithstanding, Zeina challenges rigidly feminised roles, as she refuses to be 'the plaything of anybody or anything else, a woman who was free of fate and destiny, a woman who stood outside earth and sky, outside time and space' (177).

Zeina's challenge to prescribed femininity and respectability manifests in her attire: by donning a white dress, the colour of purity, she mocks the cult of female chastity and purity: 'In her there was a touch of overwhelming masculinity merged with soft femininity. Her breasts, which were as firm as rubber, moved underneath the white cotton dress with the rhythm and cadence of the music. She was like a wild, unruly mare that not one could possess' (105). Zeina's self-possession is exemplified further in her powerful voice, having a 'laugh of a woman who was in full possession of herself' (177).[15] Thus, she transcends the lamentation of the female character of Alifa Rifaat's 'Bahiyya's Eyes' by living the life she wanted and for which she was destined.[16] Later on, likening Zeina to a white butterfly and defining her body as light and agile speaks of her transformative, transcendental powers, her ability to effect change. The colour white furthermore becomes a symbol of revolution, of change, of revolutionising female desire and power.[17] In denouncing the sexualisation and commodification of female bodies, Zeina not only challenges women's construction within the framework of masculine desire, but also male control of female sexuality. In essence, she challenges the nation's rigid definitions of sexuality, morality, and propriety, while wresting back female power from patriarchal discourse.

Zeina's disgust with female subjugation is exemplified in her violation of the sexual roles that place her in subordination to the man (Hartley: 62). Female subordination is achieved through the constant belittling of women, through marginalisation, and relegating women to inferiority as second-class citizens. This concept of female inferiority plays out even in the conjugal space: Zakariah

> believed that a wife's proper place was underneath him in bed. Even if she moved up in the world and became a professor, a doctor, a minister, a prime minister or a president, her natural place would still be beneath her husband in bed and never on top of him. Should she climb momentarily to the top, she must be returned to her place again. (144)

Women must be controlled, lest they descend into the pit of whoredom, being 'just a few degrees short of sexual insatiability' (Eltahawy: 12). Zeina is no exception; and is not spared the rod of correction: '[Ahmed al-Damhiri] wanted to hold her head in his hands and smash it, break the insolent eyes, and *tame the unruly shrew* in bed. He wanted her to lie beneath him so that he could penetrate her with his iron rod and gouge her eyes with his finger. He wanted to make her moan endlessly underneath him, pleading for forgiveness like a worshipper praying to God for His mercy' (*Zeina*: 117, emphasis added).[18] Al-Damhiri wishes to subjugate Zeina, to punish her for her insubordinate female behaviour, to transform her into a sex slave, rendering her obedient, desirable and compliant. Al-Damhiri's sexual objectification of Zeina is designed to restrict her mobility; his threat to sexually assault her is to 'remind women that public space is a male prerogative' (Eltahawy: 18). Al-Damhiri engenders a proverbial veiling of Zeina in his attempt to silence and to render her invisible. Furthermore, her public performance is viewed as analogous to being exposed, being unveiled, resulting in her devaluation. After all 'a woman's voice, like her naked body, is forbidden and must be concealed' (*Zeina*: 168).

Zeina's path 'from the street to the world of art' captures the transcendence of the local to the global, of the public to the private, from the streets to the state theatres and auditoriums of operas houses, from grassroots activism to state-sponsored political campaigns (114). Furthermore, Zeina's unrelenting political activism lends voice to the cliché that women's rights are human rights and exemplifies that women's struggle is transnational. Zeina/Al-Saadawi constructs an alternative vision for women, one that accords them agency and frees them from patriarchal reign. Women are unshackled from the chains of patriarchal oppression and female subjugation. To echo Kuppers, Zeina 'transforms a potential narrative of victimisation into one of power' ('Fatties on Stage': 279). Nessim's prophetic words to his 'partner in crime,' Bodour/Badreya: 'We'll have a baby who will change the world' (74) came to fruition. Zeina Bint Zeinat is her name.

NOTES

1 Bodour intimates that her husband, Zakariah al-Khartiti stole the novel. Still enamoured of her first love, Nessim, she unequivocally and unapologetically articulates that Zakariah 'was not her Prince Charming' (41).
2 An advocate of originality, of women as forerunners, Bodour envisioned her role as a literary critic as parasitic, referring to herself and those professionals as 'failed creative writers [who] make up for our failure by criticizing the works of others' (32). Her double, Badreya, is therefore imagined as the courageous heroine of *The Stolen Novel*, of 'real literature and art' (32). In like manner, her 'illegitimate' daughter, Zeina Bint Zeinat is revered for her (in)difference, her originality. A consummate performer, 'she writes her lyrics and her music herself. A truly talented artist!' she is a 'real' artist, an original (83). Further, Zeina's portrayal as originator destabilises the masculinist narrative that constructs woman as evil, as sinful, having committed the original sin, and reinstates her as the creator. Whereas, the established and renowned male musician 'Umm Kulthum used lyrics and music of others ... Zeina Bint Zeinat is a musician and a poet, and has a lovely voice' (83).
3 Although only a character in *The Stolen Novel*, Badreya 'lived in Bodour al-Damhiri's world as though she were a woman of flesh and blood' (34). Bodour confesses that not only did Badreya aid in the writing of the novel, but she also urged her to rebel; 'it was Badreya who wanted to have [Nessim's] child' (34, 40). The names Badreya and Bodour are used interchangeably in this article.

4   My use of the word 'malpractice' is deliberate. The psychiatrist has violated medical ethics in his routine sexual abuse of both Safi and Bodour. He sedates them prior to violating them.
5   Similar to Bodour, Nessim has a double, Naim.
6   Identifying additional variations in the religious texts, Bodour points out that 'God had children in the Torah, His first book and [had] no children in His third book', the Qur'an. In the Bible, 'God also preferred males, for the Virgin Mary gave birth to Christ from the spirit of God that was male and not female. Christ was God's son and God warned people against adulterous women' (130).
7   Mikhail and Fatima committed two infractions: 'Both Shari'a and civil law forbade the union of a Muslim woman and a non-Muslim man' (44). As runaways – Fatima ran away from her family in Upper Egypt and Mikhail ran away from his in al-Beheira province – Fatima and Mikhail qualify as 'street children'. They share a similar history with Badreya and Naim, having 'met in Cairo during one of the anti-government demonstrations' (44).
8   Zeina's short hair, ascribed to the masculine, registers resistance and subsequent liberation from the cult of beauty.
9   El Saadawi writes that the one type of femininity with which Zakariah is familiar is that of women raised in submissiveness (61).
10 This disassociation is portrayed in the desexualised body, that is, Zeina's body turned inside out, the body that has no aperture. Here, desexualisation functions as a form of empowerment.
11 Not only are young girls the subject of male sexual assault, but young boys are as well. At the age of 8, Bodour witnessed her own father sexually assaulting a young boy the same age as her. It is routine for male adults to rape 'young boys in the silence of the night' (176).
12 In keeping with this theory of the women warriors, arguably Miss Mariam recruited Zeina and gave her music as a weapon.
13 Zakariah is brought to his knees literally, for he '[c]ouldn't triumph over a nine year old girl who tore his flesh with her teeth and locked him in the room'. Helpless, he then wreaks revenge on his wife and daughter (63).
14 So as not to enact religious discrimination, the religion field was also omitted from the card.
15 Ironically, the emir had issued a ruling that women's voices were a source of shame (174).
16 The mother-protagonist of Alifa Rifaat's poem laments to her daughter about being unable to live 'my life and my youth that have come and gone without my knowing how to live them really and truly as a woman' (*Distant View of a Minaret*: 11). The mother writes an open letter (that resonates with Bodour writing a novel) to her daughter in which she chronicles her experiences, which includes being a victim of female genital mutilation, as a young girl and later as a woman under a totalitarian regime. Zeina escapes this wounding of the flesh, in the form of female genital mutilation

and rape, through her bodily rejection of male penetration and sexual violence as a whole.
17 Zeina, Bodour and Nessim routinely wear white. Several references are made to Nessim's white shirt, his white collar, his white vest and his white Egyptian cotton pants. His blood-stained pants, the result of his being attacked during the on the day of the demonstration, further register resistance. Bodour carried her white cotton dress 'with the dry blood stain and the tears and the sweat that had never dried' in her suitcase (246). The bloodstain was from her 'brief moment of love, the fleeting moment that was worth her whole life' and from Nessim's bleeding arm (230). She wears this dress once again at the close of the novel when she walks away her oppressive marriage. Zeina 'wore her white dress made of cotton' the day she was executed: 'Blood-red lines started leaking from her chest' (245). Added to the death list for violating religious principles and threatening public order, Zeina died doing what she wanted to do: 'To play and sing and dance until she died on stage' (178). Red, the colour of blood, signals resistance and passion.
18 One cannot help but notice the not-so-subtle reference to Shakespeare's *The Taming of the Shrew* in which the headstrong, obdurate shrew Katherine, initially an unwilling participant in the relationship, is 'tamed' by Petruchio.

WORKS CITED

Adichie, Chimamanda Ngozi. *We Should All Be Feminists*. New York: Anchor Books, 2015.

Ahmed, Leila. *Women and Gender in Islam*. New Haven: Yale University Press, 1992.

Besson, Jean. 'Reputation and Respectability Reconsidered: A New Perspective of Afro-Caribbean Peasant Women'. In *Women and Change in the Caribbean*, Janet H. Momsen (ed.). Kingston, Jamaica: Ian Randle Publishers, 1993: 15-37.

Braziel, Jana Evans and Kathleen LeBesco (eds). *Bodies Out of Bound: Fatness and Transgression*. Berkeley, CA: University of California Press, 2001.

El Saadawi, Nawal. *Zeina*. London: Saqi Books, 2011.

Eltahawy, Mona. *Headscarves and Hymens: Why the Middle East Needs a Sexual Revolution*. New York: Farrar, Straus & Giroux, 2016.

Guéye, Khadidiatou. '"Tyrannical Femininity" in Nawal El Saadawi's *Memoirs of a Woman Doctor*'. *Research in African Literatures*, Vol. 41, No. 2 (2010): 160-72.

Hartley, Cecilia. 'Letting Ourselves Go: Making Room for the Fat Body in Feminist Scholarship'. In *Bodies Out of Bound: Fatness and Transgression*, Jana Evans Braziel and Kathleen LeBesco (eds). Berkeley, CA: University of

California Press, 2001: 60-73.
Kuppers, Petra. 'Fatties on Stage: Feminist Performances'. In *Bodies Out of Bound: Fatness and Transgression*, Jana Evans Braziel and Kathleen LeBesco (eds). Berkeley: University of California Press, 2001: 277-91.
Reilly, Patricia Lynn. *Be Full of Yourself: The Journey from Self-Criticism to Self-Celebration*. New York: Open Creations, 1998.
Rifaat, Alifa. *Distant View of a Minaret*. London: Quartet, 1986.

Literary Supplement

Pregnancy in the Time of Ebola

Short Story

M'BHA KAMARA

Mariatu felt a sharp and sudden pain on the bottom left side of her belly. She turned on her other side, careful not to awake her husband sleeping beside her. This must have been a good decision for she soon fell asleep. She was startled from her slumber a few hours later, not sure whether it was by the call to prayer or by the pain, this time in her lower back. She got up all the same.

She wrapped a towel around her waist and breasts as she tip-toed out of the room. With the aid of the light from her cellphone, she filled a bucket with water from the large metal drum in a corner of the parlor. Outside, in the detached pebble-floored washroom, as the first lights of day prepare to peek through the predawn veil, Mariatu cleansed herself in preparation for the *fajr* prayer. Back in the room she draped herself in a silken *mulafa*. She then oriented herself on the crimson prayer rug in the direction of the *qibla*, adjacent to the wall decorated with pictures of the Via Dolorosa, the Madonna and Child, and of her husband receiving his First Communion. Mariatu performed two *sunnah rakats*, then the obligatory two. 'As Salam Alaykum wa Rahmatullahi wa Barakatuhu' to the right; 'As Salam Alaykum wa Rahmatullahi wa Barakatuhu' to the left. 'Peace be unto you and so may the mercy of Allah and His blessings!'

Of late, this required act of her faith has become somewhat of a travail for Mariatu, though she still finds genuine pleasure in it. Very soon, she thought to herself as she got up and folded the rug, she would no longer be able to do the bowings and prostrations of the five daily prayers. She found solace in the knowledge that other options were available to the pregnant believer. God is merciful!

She removed her *mulafa* and donned a light flowery cotton kaftan. She returned to bed, as has been her custom of late.

'Going back to bed after praying? You are becoming too lazy, Mariatu. Whatever happened to your motto "the early bird communes with the worm"?' Her husband chided her playfully, making more room for her in the bed as he did so.

'Did you hear about the 32 year-old woman infected with Ebola?'

'No! What about her?' Mariatu looked at him, curious.

'Well, her family clandestinely removed her out of Connaught Hospital yesterday. Now the government is warning everyone to be on alert and promises severe punishment for the guilty family members.'

'Why did they take her away?'

'I guess they are afraid of what might happen to her if she doesn't get cured.'

'Poor woman! It is hard to blame them. Would you?' A cloud of sorrow crawled over Mariatu's face. 'You have seen the way the Ebola dead are wrapped in plastic and tossed into hurriedly dug mass graves. It makes the heart cry! No wonder people are reluctant to report their loved-ones infected with the virus.'

'Can we talk about something positive?' Jacobson said, sensing the effect the Ebola conversation was having on his wife.

'What do you have in mind?'

'Let's talk about the child,' Jacobson said excitedly.

Mariatu nestled closer to him and smiled. Jacobson rubbed her belly and, gently, rested his head on it.

'So what shall we call the child?' Mariatu asked.

'The child shall be called Emmanuel,' Jacobson said without even thinking.

'Emmanuel! What makes you think it is a boy? What if it is a girl?' Mariatu chuckled.

'That's easy. We will call her Manuela.'

'So you are going to have your Emmanuel, whatever form or shape he comes in, aren't you?' Mariatu smiled broadly. 'Ok. Enough of this talk about the child's name. My mother used to say that talking about such things before the child is born is no good.' Her smile narrowed.

'Why so?' Jacobson got up and out of bed.

'You never know who or what is listening. We are surrounded by people and jinn, and not all of them mean us well.'

'Superstition! Superstition! Has going to school not taught you anything?' Jacobson asked in mock seriousness.

'As a matter of fact it has. It has taught me that you are a fool to dismiss such things as superstition,' Mariatu retorted.

'You know how much I love you, smart woman,' Jacobson said. 'But I need to get to work before the jinn stop me,' Jacobson kissed her on the forehead and ran out of the room.

The spartan room she shared with her husband is one of two in a small wooden shack belonging to Jacobson's parents. Apart from the pictures already mentioned, there is a double bed, a small book shelf, a table, and a chair. Standing against the wall opposite the bed, is a clothing rack large enough for up to ten hangers. A large suitcase is ensconced between its spindly legs. The ceiling comprises two large woven straw mats held precariously in place by flimsy-looking strings nailed into the four corners of the interior walls.

As she lay in bed, a light breeze from the outside animated the bluish lace window blind into a dance of marionettes. Mariatu's attention clung to a ray of light fluttering back and forth with the window blind and wandered out through the open window into the yard where a bird was chirping rather insistently.

***

Mariatu finally left her room and stepped into the full light of the rising sun. She went about her usual morning chores, without saying a word to her mother-in-law about the pains that visited her the night before and early that morning. Even when the observant mother-in-law asked her if she was ok, she replied she was fine; that it was nothing to worry about. The older woman did not insist. She just threw, every now and then, surreptitious glances the young woman's way. The progress of the day, from dawn to sundown, brought Mariatu little, if any relief. As a matter of fact, she spent a good part of the day trying to convince herself that the backaches, the painful cramps in her belly, the intermittent fevers, and the light but frequent pelvic pressures were less severe than they really were.

Night fell upon Mariatu like a thick blanket of angry fire ants. She took a cool bath, bade her mother-in-law goodnight, and went to bed earlier than usual. She tossed and turned, and cajoled sleep anyway she could. When sleep finally came to her, it was quarter till 3 in the morning. And before long she was snoring lightly. For the first time in a long time she slept past 7 a.m.

Mariatu woke up with a start, groaning. Jacobson, who had also managed to doze off after Mariatu, was aroused from his restive sleep. He ran to fetch his mother. Upon noticing that Mariatu had spotty bleeding and a light fever, the older woman advised that her daughter-in-law be taken right away to the clinic.

When they arrived at the Community Health Center, they were greeted by a poster encouraging pregnant women to get tested for HIV.

A row of pregnant women and nursing mothers waited for their free care. Mariatu and Jacobson joined them in the wait.

An hour or so later, it was Mariatu's turn to be seen. The only nurse on duty, aided by a timid assistant, examined Mariatu. 'Our surgeon and senior nurse are not here today,' she said with concern as she listened to her heartbeat. 'They left for Connaught Hospital this morning to help there with personnel shortages caused by the Ebola outbreak. I am sorry, but there is nothing we can do for you here. I would advise you to go to Freetown right away,' she added as she let the stethoscope diaphragm drop gently onto her blouse.

She gave Mariatu two codeine tablets. 'Take one now. If after four hours you are still in pain, take the other one.'

'Thank you,' Mariatu and Jacobson said in unison.

By the time they left the clinic, it was nearly 2 p.m. The 90 degree heat from the sun was tentatively mitigated by low-hanging clouds. The smell of imminent rain hung in the air. Mariatu could only walk by leaning on Jacobson. About twenty people were already gathered at the *poda-poda* junction. The crowd heaved forward as the empty minibus came to a screeching halt, its door swinging back and forth on its hinges. On the front of the vehicle, just beneath the wiper blades, are emblazoned the slogans 'Quick Service' and 'Bodyguard for life.'

'Everybody pay before we take off,' the driver's apprentice, reeking of sweat and rudeness, screamed at the passengers. 'Tu touzin for Pee-Zed, wan touzin for all oda stops.'

Mariatu and Jacobson took their seats, squished against the other eighteen-odd passengers. Music blasted from the radio in front. The rolling green hills bordering the left flank of the Freetown–Waterloo highway puttered by nonchalantly, mimicking the speed of the *poda-poda*. The vehicle passed through the towns of Devil Hole, Rokel, Kosso Town, Grafton, Lower Allen Town, stopping frequently to allow passengers to alight or embark.

'Unu kaboh, mi fambul dem!' a voice came on right as the music on the radio faded. 'This nar unu favorite dj Daddy Cool from FM 89.5. Ar get big nyus for unu.' The World Health Organization just announced they finally found patient zero. You know, the first person to be infected with the Ebola virus now ravaging our countries. Mi fambul dem, do you know who that patient is? Well, mek ar tell unu. He is a two year old boy from Guinea. His name is Emile.'

'Well, ar get question for world health organization,' a passenger from the rear interrupted dj Daddy Cool.

'How can they be sure it's the child?' he continued, surveying his fellow passengers. 'Let them tell me how the two year-old Emile got Ebola and spread it? Did he wake up one morning and tell his parents: 'mommy en daddy, don't worry. Today is the day. I will go to the bush and hunt bush meat.' Trust White people to come up with outlandish ideas. Poor Emile! I wish he were still alive to tell his own side of the story.'

'But they may be right,' chimed in another passenger, as timidly as the 'may' in his utterance.

'I am not saying they are not right. All I am doing is asking questions.'

'Kissy, Kissy,' the apprentice cut the debate short as the bus came to a jolting stop.

When it was time to resume the journey, the *poda poda* refused to start. Nothing the driver and his apprentice did could appease the vehicle.

As they sat on the ground under the vertical shade of a semitrailer, awaiting their next transport, Mariatu's temperature rose and her abdominal pain intensified. She nibbled on her share of the *bottombele* Jacobson bought from a nearby vendor. She took the remaining codeine the nurse had given her at the clinic. And noticing a thin outline of blood on her skirt, she removed her head-kerchief and wrapped it around her waist.

'Jacobson, we need to get to the hospital any way we can, even if it means taking an *okada*.'

Jacobson, though not convinced this was a good idea, realized it could be their only means of getting to their destination. So he hailed an *okada*.

'Where to?' Asked the motor-cycle operator.

'Connaught Hospital,'

'I can drop you off at FZ. That's the best I can do for you. Even that I will be going out of my way. And you must pay before we leave.'

'Ok,' Mariatu arose from the ground.

Jacobson sat in front facing the driver, with his head resting on the latter's left shoulder. Mariatu took the rear seat, facing Jacobson, with her head on the driver's other shoulder. Husband and wife held hands firmly, sandwiching the driver in their embrace.

The *okada* entered Freetown via Kissy Road. A huge banner floated in the humid breeze with the advice: 'Ebola is for real: Protect yourself, your family and your community.' Underneath the banner, a small crowd of people was listening to a young woman talking into a loudspeaker: 'Listen, my people,' she said rather evangelically. 'Ebola is real, and like the devil, it is now amongst us. That is the bad news. The good news is, it can be prevented. And prevention is better than cure... There are five ways to stop Ebola: One, wash your hands with soap and clean water, or with chlorinated water; two, don't touch someone who looks sick or who may have died of Ebola; three, avoid bush meat; four, don't spread false rumors about Ebola; five...'

A few blocks away, a large billboard sign read: *Sierra Leone Vision 2025. Sweet Salone. United People, Progressive Nation, Attractive country.* This uplifting message was printed against a painted background of fading lush mountains, blue seas, and sand beaches.

'Thank God we are getting close.' Mariatu sighed. Jacobson gently squeezed her hands in agreement. 'Now we have to make it through this traffic,' he vocalized her thought.

As they approached Clock Tower, at the end of Kissy Road and the start of Sani Abacha Street, Ebola became increasingly visible. It is everywhere. Like a black hole, it sought to pull everything around it into its insatiable orbit.

People milled around, some wearing cheap plastic gloves and face masks. Women used their colorful kerchiefs to cover their noses and mouths. The majority of people had no form of protection whatsoever. Bright plastic buckets purportedly containing chlorinated water decorated store fronts.

The clock Tower chimed 6 p.m. Across from it, in front of the erstwhile Annie Walsh Memorial school, a crowd congregated to watch a prostrate man twitching spasmodically as another man sprayed him with some kind of pungent liquid. Just a few feet away, a young girl was manning a table covered with mangoes, bananas, akara, and slices of breadfruit. Up in the hazy sky, the sun seemed to move faster in its descent toward the west.

Meanwhile, in the midst of the cacophonic symphony of the Freetown street, the *okada* inched its way through the crawling traffic, negotiating with *poda-podas*, taxis, other *okadas* and all manner of pedestrians and *omolankes*.

As they arrived at PZ, Jacobson noticed his wife's eyes closing and her head slumping deeper into the shoulder of the *okada* driver. He also noticed that the head kerchief around Mariatu's waist was now wet with blood. He instinctively tightened his grip on her hands.

'My wife is sick,' he spoke to the *okada* operator 'and we really need to get to the hospital fast. I will pay you double if you take us there.' He pleaded.

The *okada* driver noticed Mariatu's bloodstained clothes and stepped abruptly on the brake. Were it not for Jacobson's vice grip, his wife would have been thrown off the bike.

'No, I won't even if you give me one million,' he said as he wiggled his body from underneath husband and wife. 'You want me to catch Ebola and take it home to my wife and children?' He zoomed away as soon as the couple liberated his bike.

Jacobson carried his blood-soaked wife and laid her in a shaded area in front of a photo-printing store.

'Ebola. She has Ebola.' One person screamed. People instinctively ran helter-skelter, knocking over stalls and other people as they did so.

'My wife doesn't have Ebola. She is pregnant and she is bleeding. That is all!'

'Yes, she is pregnant, but will that stop her from getting Ebola?' another person retorted, with an air of wisdom.

All the taxis Jacobson hailed drove off as soon as the drivers saw the blood on Mariatu. By this time, Mariatu had fallen unconscious. He realized he would have to carry his wife. He picked her up and commenced the ten or so block trek to Connaught Hospital.

'Where are you going?' Asked a tall and lanky man pulling an *omolanke*.

'Connaught Hospital,' Jacobson replied, not stopping or looking at the source of the voice.

'I will help you take her there.'

Mariatu was hoisted onto the floor of the hard cart. Jacobson pushed as the *omolanke* owner pulled.

Twenty minutes later, after traversing streets with names reminiscent of the halcyon days of the British Empire, the *omolanke* pulled up at the entrance of the country's main referral and teaching hospital. The entrance is flanked on either side by a makeshift Ebola screening tent. A man in Tyvek coveralls, rubber gloves, and a face mask walked out of one of the tents, spraying his boots with a chlorine solution. A large crowd of people gathered outside the hospital, probably waiting for news of their loved ones undergoing treatment in the Ebola isolation wards within the hospital. A rainbow of wellington boots was drying out on stakes buried into the ground, soles watching God, as if in supplication on behalf of all the unfortunate souls, dead or alive, who could no longer trust their governors and trustees with their wellbeing. The heavy effluvia from the hospital, after joining in a dance macabre with other emanations from the nearby Kroo Bay, wafted in the air before becoming a whirlwind engulfing body and spirit on its path. Beyond, one of the tents could be seen the morgue. The sun hurriedly disappeared into the horizon as heavy drops of rain announced a premature thunderstorm.

Jacobson and the *omolanke* owner helped Mariatu out of the vehicle and carried her into the hospital, squeezing through the chaotic stream of people weaving in and out of the hospital. The woman at the registration window told them to wait. The two benches in the waiting room were already full, and there was not even room for standing. So Jacobson and Mariatu went back out to wait in the main reception area, as close to the waiting room entrance as possible.

Jacobson gave the *omolanke* driver two thousand leones, which the man refused.

'You don't owe me anything,' he said. 'I hope your wife gets better.'

Jacobson thanked him as the man walked away.

Mariatu sat on the floor, resting her entire weight on Jacobson who put his arm around her shoulder, rocking her gently. A mosquito noisily buzzed past them, then returned to land on Mariatu's exposed arm. Jacobson deftly scooped it away in his cupped hand. An hour went by, the crowd in the reception area and waiting room showed no sign of depleting. Mariatu's fever rose as she fell in and out of consciousness, groaning intermittently.

Jacobson explained her wife's worsening condition to the woman at the registration window and asked her if anything could be done about it.

'There is nothing I can do. You have to be patient. She will be seen eventually.' The jadedness of the response brought no solace to Jacobson.

Close to around midnight, a nurse and a doctor entered the hospital boisterously. Jacobson approached them.

'Please help my wife...' he said, pointing to Mariatu.

The nurse slowed down and glanced in the direction of Mariatu who was now curled up on the floor.

'Nurse Florence, you need to hurry,' the doctor instructed. She sped up to the doctor.

'The woman is pregnant and in terrible shape, doctor. There is blood all over her, and she seems to be unconscious.'

'I can see that, but that is not why we are here.'

'I know, doctor. But what makes one life better than another. This woman and her child need our help as much as the Ebola patients we are here to see need our help. It is a sad thing we have to choose between one patient and another.'

'Please doctor,' Jacobson pleaded, with tears in his eyes.

'Ok, wait here. Follow me, nurse Florence,' the doctor said as he walked away.

Nurse Florence returned twenty minutes later with a stretcher. She and Jacobson carried Mariatu into a makeshift operating room.

'Your wife needed surgery at least ten hours ago. I won't hide it from you, her condition is critical. It will be a miracle if the child is still alive. To avoid irreversible complications for the mother, the child has to be brought out. At this point, nothing is guaranteed. We will do our best.'

When Mariatu woke up the next morning, her husband and mother-in-law were standing at her bedside. Jacobson explained to her everything that had transpired. Thirty minutes later, she was presented her still-born child swaddled in simple white cotton cerements.

'Hello Manuela,' Mariatu said, her eyes drenched in liquid sorrow.

She cradled the baby in her arms as she hummed a lullaby to her. A solitary teardrop left her right eye and landed in the middle of Manuela's forehead. It spread into ripples, anointing the rest of the child's face. Jacobson took Mariatu's hands. The couple looked into each other's eyes and exchanged a smile. Outside the sun and the people of Freetown went about their business as usual.

Okonkwo's Revenge

Short Story

PEDE HOLLIST

Reverend Jeremiah Smith clenched his jaw, inhaled, and patted the bulge in the right pocket of his trousers, as one would do to assure a wallet of crisp dollar bills had not been stolen. If the commissioner of Bible Technologies for the Global South project had been less agitated, he would have realized that the odds of his wallet being stolen were zero because his right leg was jammed next to the external wall of the medical office waiting room. He would also have realized that the other patients with faraway looks, bowed, or nodding heads had more sublime concerns than money.

Like them, Reverend Smith had been waiting for over an hour to see Dr. Ezinma Okonkwo, the internationally renowned New York psychiatrist. Her waiting room overflowed with patients. They had heard that she overbooked. But that she took whatever time was necessary with each patient. So few complained. Instead, they resolved to make up for the long wait by unburdening themselves when their turn came to talk to her. Such was Reverend Smith's resolve as he shifted his buttocks to ease the pain hammering his lower back. A transplant to the United States from a British missionary family, Reverend Smith saw the world in ones and zeros, and digital technologies were his weapons to slay the children of Baal. Until they beguiled and sent him on a downward spiral – a falling apart he hoped Dr. Okonkwo would arrest.

After shimmying his buttocks in an effort to relieve his back pain, Reverend Smith picked up *Scientific American* from the oversized coffee table and fanned the stale, hot air. The makeshift fan brought little relief, so he opened the magazine and began reading an article on the brain, about its plasticity, its capacity to create neural networks that enable people to learn new things. Dedicated to spreading God's Word through technology, Reverend Smith became entranced in a future world in which ignorant, lost, and dammed souls would be redeemed if he could use technology to saturate their brains with His Word.

'Do you think he hanged himself?' Reverend Smith said, surprised to hear his own voice questioning Dr. Okonkwo when she walked into the consulting room.

'Good morning to you too,' Dr. Okonkwo said. Born in the US, single, with three daughters, and specializing in suicidality, she had earned the respect of some of her peers for developing the breakthrough non-linear model to diagnose and treat patients. But her unorthodox methods had also incurred the wrath of other colleagues. 'Bush psychology,' an older, Harvard-Medical-School educated male critic had said and stormed off after he and other hospital workers had watched live TV coverage of Dr. Okonkwo talking, some said wrestling, down an elderly woman about to jump off a sixth-story balcony. The video of the rescue had gone viral and, overnight, Dr. Okonkwo became an international celebrity: 'US-based Nigerian Doctor Wrestles Mad American Woman from Death,' an Enugu-Nigeria TV anchor had headlined her 'Only in America' segment. 'Extreme Psychiatry: When Doctors Attack – to Save Lives' the nationally renowned *America Today* had quipped. 'Dr. Life, the woman who could talk youth back into a centenarian,' a New York tabloid had proclaimed. Business at her clinic had picked up.

'Tut-tut, a sister with an attitude?' Reverend Smith countered, his back toward Dr.

Okonkwo, like a prize fighter too confident of his skills to even bother to look at his opponent.

Dr. Okonkwo ignored Reverend Smith.

'I said, did he hang himself?'

Reverend Smith spoke at full throttle, powered by a decade of zeal as commissioner of the project to spread the word of God through digital technologies. 'The Pacification of the Global South,' was the title of his proposed memoir.

Dr. Okonkwo stood and sized up Reverend Smith. He did not look at her, but he crouched slightly as he surveyed the tall bookcases, sentinels of knowledge, which lined three of the four walls of the consulting room the nurse attendants dubbed the ring. Many times they had heard shuffles, grunts, and thuds coming from within it. After, patients emerged looking ruffled or beaten up.

Ceiling track lights illuminated the thin, silver-coated metal carvings of double-leg take downs, Fireman's Carry, butt drags, ankle picks, leg laces and other wrestling moves that sat on top of the bookcases. Between them stood zebra-hide floor lamps, their bulbs angled to highlight Dr. Okonkwo's framed certificates, licenses, and awards. The fourth wall was, in fact, not a wall but two oversized frosted sliding doors. A red valance and theater-grand drapes that swooped down to the floor framed the doors.

*****

Normally, when Dr. Okonkwo walked into a session, patients would already be seated in one of two faux-leather armchairs facing each other. She had specifically chosen the types with wing-back shoulders, thick padded arms, and soft cushions. Patients sank into them and babbled like well-fed babies. Not Reverend Smith. His fingers traipsed across the spines of the books to the tapping of his shoes on the shiny wooden floors.

'Perhaps you ought to sit down, Mr. Smith,' Dr. Okonkwo said, the nerve pathways of her body firing up as they always did in response to non-compliant patients.

'Reverend!'

'Reverend?'

'Is there an echo in here?' Reverend Smith said and continued his anti-clockwise prowl around the room, his eyes askance as if anticipating Dr. Okonkwo would pounce on him.

She ignored his question, recognizing she had to restrain a rising irritation. Her medical school career had been one long battle against the orthodoxies of entitled men like the one in the room with her. She took a deep breath, closed the door, walked between the armchairs to the desk behind them, and sat on its front edge, half eyeing his medical chart – elevated cholesterol, basal cell carcinoma (in remission), slipped disk, renal insufficiency, no prior mental health issues – and half observing his movements. The 60-year-old, weather-beaten project commissioner stopped in front of the sliding doors.

'What's behind them?' he said but did not look at Dr. Okonkwo.

'Freedom!'

'Freedom?'

'There's definitely an echo in here.'

Reverend Smith pushed his lower lip outward, nodded, and smiled. 'Freedom from what?'

'This room. This stage and the stories that are told in them. Freedom from limitations and control by others. I call it the door of no return. No patient who has walked out through it has ever come back to tell me what's on the other side. You should know a thing or two about the other side, right?'

Reverend Smith turned to face Dr. Okonkwo, but his eyes settled on her chest – that seemed to huff and puff beneath her white coat. He licked his lips. His pupils dilated. He inhaled and exhaled, raised his head, and looked Dr. Okonkwo in the eyes. She recognized the look that flattered but objectified, that lifted in adoration only to bring down in subjugation. She had a countermove for it the one she had used on her daughters' three fathers: she had watched their eyes land on her chest and linger. She had remained still, allowing them to forage. Then as each man raised his head, she had struck: in one swift, wordless motion she ripped off her blouse and let her breasts with the kola-nut size nipples tumble out, heavily, purposefully, a mother lode from a treasure chest. After, she had held out her hand and had led them into fatherhood.

'And that door? Reverend Smith pointed to the one Dr. Okonkwo had walked through.

'Revolving.'

'Revolving?'

'For patients who come back. Their problems remain. If they remove the veil, they become free from self-delusion and embrace self-knowledge.'

'I have that already. That's why I want to kill myself. To solve my problem.'

'Tell me about your problem. Maybe *you* can walk through the door –'

'Don't think so.'

'Why?'

'*They* will be waiting for me behind the door.'

'They?'

'Do you have to repeat everything?'

'Make God's glory resound; echo his praises. Isn't that what your Bible says?'

'*My* Bible?' A glint of admiration wiped across Reverend Smith's face and disappeared as quickly as it had appeared. 'Of course, many of *your* people don't know the Word.' He smiled. 'Not to worry.' Reverend Smith reached into his jacket pocket, pulled out an iPhone, and shook it from side to side.

Dr. Okonkwo raised her eyebrows.

'The weapon to wipe out ignorance. Contains the Bible, with pictures and commentary from the best minds. Knowledge in the palm, not palm wine, of every hand in the world. Reverend Smith

smiled. The muscles in Dr. Okonkwo's shoulders tightened.
'Who are the ones waiting behind the door?' she said.
'The line cutters.'
'Who?'
'People like you who cut the line instead of taking your place in it.'
'*My* place at the back, huh?'
'Yes – '
'Of a line going in the wrong direction?'
'Form a new line then.'
'But I prefer a circle, not a line.'
'Then form a circle.'
'That's the problem?'
'What?'
'Those in the line don't want a circle because they will lose their place.'
'Well that's why *you people* should learn to be on time so you can be ahead in the line.' The tightness across Dr. Okonkwo's shoulders coiled down into her arms.
'Maybe *your people* should learn to appreciate new shapes.'
The canvas of silence stretched out between the Reverend standing by the bookcase and the doctor half sitting on the desk across the room. They eyed each other.
'Why don't we sit down?' Doctor Okonkwo broke the tension.
Reverend Smith crouched forward and sideways, as if he was ready to fend off Dr. Okonkwo if she tried to wrestle him into the armchair. Noticing his defensiveness, Dr. Okonkwo stood up from the desk, circled around the right armchair and sat in it. Satisfaction coursed through Reverend Smith, the way it always did after he had extinguished opposition from a doubting parishioner at Bible study. Her capitulation over, he raised himself into a full stand, nodding as he swaggered over to the back of the other armchair, flicked off an imagined mite from the top edge, once, twice, three times. Then he sidled into it.

*****

'Tell me about these judges,' Dr. Okonkwo said.
'They want to see me dead. It will make them happy.'
'Why will they be happy?'
'As much as possible use the patient's own words to frame your questions. Look, I studied counselling as part of divinity school. I get

what you have to do, but I'm desperate.'

'Desperate?'

'Yes, damn it, I want to kill myself! Your job is to figure out how to stop me. I could have gone to a million other doctors but I chose you.'

'Thank you.'

'Don't thank me. Thank your name.'

'My name?'

Reverend Smith rolled his eyes. 'A quota child that stumbled upon some good publicity?'

'Quota child?'

'That's how you got into medical school, right? I did my homework. I know your test scores the names of your daughters, their fathers, and even some of your cases. Blame it on this,' Reverend Smith shook the hand which held his iPhone and put the device back in his pocket. The coil graduated into Dr. Okonkwo's torso.

'Did you say you wanted to kill yourself or be murdered?'

'You can't say that.'

'Why not?'

'It's unprofessional.'

'Here, it's just you, me, and our consciences.'

'Not true. The judges are always behind the fourth wall,' Reverend Smith pointed to the slicing doors.'

'The judges?'

'This repeating has to stop.' Reverend Smith reached for the bulge in his pocket and took out a silver .22. After several tries, he balanced the gun on the armrest, the muzzle pointing directly at Dr. Okonkwo. Coils spiraled into her thighs and calves. Her chest huffed and puffed. Her eyes popped.

'Here,' Reverend Smith handed her a white handkerchief. 'Now, stop this repetition nonsense and answer my questions? Why did he kill himself?

'He?'

'Your idiot great-great-great grandpapa.'

'Who?'

'Okonkwo!'

'Okonkwo?'

*****

'Here,' Ezinma had answered roll call on the first day of her 12th grade class studying world literature.

'Any relation to him?' Mrs. Faraday her teacher had smiled and had held up a copy of Chinua Achebe's classic *Things Fall Apart*. Heads that had been bowed in obeisance to smart phones and tablets lifted and stared at the primitive communication form, which Mrs. Faraday then pointed at Ezinma – slouched in her chair, indigo-blue skin, flat nose, cornrows, Jaws-like metallic braces, and a black do-rag clutching her skull. 'She has the same last name as Africa's most famous warrior,' Mrs. Faraday beamed multicultural awareness to the classroom. Ezinma sneered at the revelation with high-school disdain.

'Kunte Kinte!' a voice broke from the back corner of the classroom. Chuckles rippled through the air.

'Doctor, are you even listening?' Reverend Smith said, his right palm now over the gun. 'Your relative Okonkwo hanged himself because of my great-great-great grandpapa.'

'What?' Dr. Okonkwo blinked back to the ring.

'See, I come from a long line of Anglican missionaries. My great-great-great grandpa, The Right Reverend James Smith Snr., actually lived and worked in eastern Nigeria. The story of your ancestor who killed himself is lore in my family.'

Dr. Okonkwo squinted, trying to understand, to remember...

'Ma, are we related to Okonkwo in *Things Fall Apart*?' Ezinma had asked her mother the evening of Mrs. Faraday's revelation. Her mother was sitting in a Lazy-Boy reading Toni Morrison's *Song of Solomon* in their cluttered apartment in Amherst, Massachusetts. The mother put down the novel on an end table, stood up, walked over to a three-shelf bookcase, and pulled out a faded edition of *Things Fall Apart*. She placed it on her heart as if she were about to sing the national anthem.

'Your dad gave this to me when we first met. "You are a direct descendant of the chief priestess of Umudioka," he said, "and the world will never be right until I take you back to where you rightfully belong."' Nostalgia graced the mother's face.

'Are we related to Okonkwo or not?' Ezinma said.

'You belong to the Okonkwos of Umudioka. This one,' the mother thrust the novel at her daughter,' is not real.

Ezinma snatched it, marched into her bedroom, opened the first page, and entered the forests of Umuofia. She saw the young agile wrestler Okonkwo slam his opponent Amalinze the Cat flat on his back. She listened to Okonkwo's father, Unoka, play the flute and watched him drink himself to his grave. She cried when the village banished Okonkwo from Umuofia and sobbed when the white men wiped out the village of Abame from the face of the earth. She understood the anger which made Okonkwo kill the messenger and the betrayal which made him hang himself.

Ezinma emerged from the forests of Umuofia the next morning determined never to be either like the father-character Unoka or her real-life father. At school later that day, Ezinma walked into the wrestling tryouts, routed her way onto the team, and became known throughout the 62 counties of New York for her stealth and risky takedown moves. At the University of Iowa, she became an All American wrestler. Only an unfortunate knee injury, which left her with a limp, prevented her from going on to earn a gold medal for the U.S. at the Olympic Games.

*****

'I am American,' Dr. Okonkwo jerked herself back to the present.

'With a name like Okonkwo?' Reverend Smith doubled over in laughter.

Dr. Okonkwo sprang to her feet, a coiled mass of anger. The bookcases, the carvings, the lamps, the judges merged into a mute backcloth.

'The people you call my relatives are characters in a story,' she said.

'Pssh, doctor, tell me something insightful. Aren't we all characters in other people's stories?' Reverend Smith tapped on the gun. Dr. Okonkwo recoiled into the armchair.

'I want to know if you think your great-great-great grandpa killed himself,' Reverend Smith said.

'Am I supposed to know his motives?'

'Yes! One, because *you are* a relative –

'I am not – '

'And two, your job is to use your imagination to figure things out.'

'Tell that to my colleagues who think we must only use rating scales.'

'I don't care about your professional disagreements. You weren't holding a checklist when you tackled that woman on the balcony.'

Church bells sounded, taking them both by surprise. Reverend Smith recovered first. He reached into the same jacket pocket from which he had pulled out the white handkerchief and whipped out his iPhone, glanced at the screen, grimaced, swiped right, and tapped. 'A call,' he said.

'From Him?'

'Him?'

Dr. Okonkwo pointed to the ceiling.

'I wish.' Reverend Smith knotted his face and stared at the sliding doors.

'Parishioners?' Dr. Okonkwo said.

'In a manner of speaking.'

'Technology has its downsides.'

'Yes, but you are deflecting. Maybe you can't handle patients you don't have to wrestle?'

Dr. Okonkwo interlocked her fingers, stretched out her arms and moved to the front of her chair. 'Let's start with *your* imagination. Tell me why Okonkwo hanged himself?'

'Aha, but he never did,' Reverend Smith smiled.

'How so, his best friend saw him hanging and supervised his burial?'

'Not true. See, Okonkwo had his escape planned all along. After he killed the messenger, he walked to the market, killed a stranger about his height and weight, and stuffed his face into an anthill. After the ants bit into the face until it became unrecognizable, he hung the body. That was the one his friends and the commissioner buried. Okonkwo's revenge, I call it.'

'Revenge? On who, for what?'

'My ancestors. They thought they had won. The judges. They think they know the real story, but Okonkwo lives. He comes alive every time people open *Things Fall Apart*.'

'Like Him?'

'Who?'

'Christ, for Christ sake! Does he not come alive every time *your people* open up *your* Bible?'

Reverend Smith paused. The gears in his brain engaged. 'I guess so, but are you comparing Okonkwo to Christ?'

'And why not? Do they both not come alive when you open a book?'

'No, Christ is the living – '

'Living-dead, dead-living. Point is you want immortality, right?'

'More though.' Reverend Smith leaned forward, his arm nudging the gun which almost fell off the armrest. 'I want to make sure your Okonkwo knows I am his nemesis. Then, now, forever.'

'Let's be clear. You're definitely not Christ. He had the ability to rise from the dead. Blow out your brains and all you will end up doing is messing up my floor and furniture. There's no returning for you.'

'Ha, but in *this* story I will always be able to return.'

'See those over there?' Dr. Okonkwo pointed to a section of books. 'Not all stories get retold you know. Many characters are trapped in story purgatory.'

'Maybe, but this story has your name. I will be immortalized next to you.'

'You're – '

'Nuts?'

Dr. Okonkwo did not reply. She bowed her head for a few moments then raised it.

'Do it,' she said.

'What?'

'You heard me.'

'Shoot myself?'

'Yes.'

'You're crazy. Professional misconduct.'

'What do you care? I will live forever in infamy. The doctor who threw away all standards. But you? You will live forever with every retelling of this story.'

Reverend Smith smiled, picked up the gun. 'Wait a minute. Okonkwo gets to live in my story. I came here so you could rescue me, make me live in real life but appear to die.'

'You mean, I have to find some clinical way to explain your misdeeds so you can get away with them?'

'I guess you are a deserving quota child after all.'

'I won't do it.'

'What?'

The church bells chimed and distracted Reverend Smith. He whipped out his iPhone, glanced at the screen, grimaced, swiped right, and tapped. 'Another parishioner,' he sighed.

'Here,' she handed him the handkerchief he had given to her earlier. He dabbed his forehead several times and then with the dampened part of the cloth covering his pointer finger, he swabbed between his collar and neck. First one way, then the other. A grey-black soot showed on the cloth around his finger. At the sight, Dr. Okonkwo reached over to her desk, grabbed the box of tissue which she kept for patients, and placed it on top of the chart on her lap.

'I am guessing whatever brought you here has to do with them,' she said.

'Who?'

'Your parishioners, damn it! You can't have it both ways. Those who read your story will want to know your motive. That's all they ever want to know. Either tell me your story so I can make you walk through those sliding doors or shoot yourself. I have other patients waiting.'

'No, there's a third option. I can shoot both of us,' Reverend Smith flicked the gun's muzzle at Dr. Okonkwo and then at himself.

'Like I said. No motive, no interest, zero chance of immortality. Christ died to save our sins. His disciples lived to tell his story. That's the way it works.'

'I am beginning to think you want me to kill myself.'

'Guess *you* got into seminary school on a quota too?'

'Well, I'll pull the trigger right now.'

'And your work of pacifying the world stops. You just get to be a character in a story that never gets retold.'

So what's your solution?'

'Tell me what brought you here. I need to understand your motivation. Then I can figure how to tell your story and you can continue your work pacifying the dammed.'

Reverend Smith smiled. 'I touched them.'

'What?'

Had she winked, Dr. Okonkwo would have missed the flick of his pointer finger, like the twitch of an unconsciousness patient, toward his crotch.

'There?'

He nodded.

'Who, when?'

'It began on my mission trips selling e-readers.'

'Carry on.'

'But they never complained.'

'They chose to stay in the line. But the ones here refused and are cutting the line eh?'

He nodded.

'And now?'

Reverend Smith's iPhone Church bells sounded again. He pulled it out, pressed the off button, slide his finger to the right on the screen, and stuffed it back in his pocket.

'They found out about each other and want to go public,' he said, his voice subdued. He stood up, paced around, tapping the muzzle of the gun first on his palm and then on his nose.

'And so you want to kill yourself because you are about to be exposed?'

'See, I knew you were not too bright.'

'But what about all the good you have done?'

'Exactly. How do I convince people of all the good things I have done?'

'You'll need me to tell your story. Without me, you won't exist.'
'Will you really?'
'Yes.'
'Why should I trust you? How will I know my story lives on?'
'Because my name sells.'
'And the judges?'
'*They* know enough now to partly understand you.' Dr. Okonkwo sprang to her feet. The box of tissues and chart that had been on her lap tumbled to the floor, a footstep in front of her. 'We can do it.'
'Yes, yes!' Reverend Smith said and stood up.
'And they will not be sure because your story will seem implausible, incomplete. This will force them to read it again and again and again...'
'Yes, yes.'
'And through story you will achieve immortality?'
'Exactly!' Gun in hand, satisfaction coursing through his veins, Reverend Smith lunged at Dr. Okonkwo, as if to hug her. That was the moment Dr. Okonkwo had been waiting for, to see Reverend Smith relax, like all the opponents she defeated in high school and college. She stepped forward, except it was into the open box of tissues, which slid on the shiny wooden floor. She lost her balance and stumbled into Reverend Smith: shuffle, groans, thud, and thud!

The noise alerted the nurse attendant the interview session had neared its end.

*****

Dr. Okonkwo, wide-eyed and ruffled, walked into the consulting room.

'Do you think he hanged himself?' the patient asked, surprised to hear his own voice.

The End

Guilt

Short Story

CHIOMA DURUAKU

Dear Mukaosolu,

I write to admit that I am guilty of a heinous crime and hope that you would find it in your heart to forgive me. I didn't ask for this, yet I found myself living with this deep guilt that I cannot shake off. Really, I wish I could turn back the hands of time but...

My heart is shattered, but I shall always tell our story. When matters of the heart are involved, people would believe what they want. They blame you here or there for sharing your problems with them oblivious of the facts, or the thought that they too, could be in a bigger mess, faced with the same scenarios. They all come to judgment. But they do not always know the story. Everyone now blames me about Okwuchi, my childhood friend. It all began when we both attended a Multidisciplinary Conference at the University of Nevada Las Vegas, USA ten years ago? Mmh ... I recall that it was her first time of leaving the shores of Nigeria. She was so nervous that almost everyone in attendance, noticed. I was like her guardian angel, always at hand to rescue her.

Hey! Did you just laugh? '*Bia, enyi*, this ain't funny – like the Americans would say. Now you know, in those two weeks of our sojourn in America, I was able to pick up that expression – 'this ain't funny.' It has since stuck in my head. These days I blurt it out with the heaviness of my Igbo accent. Lol! But I was telling about Okwy. After a few days in Nevada, she finally was able to relax. That was when she caught the attention of this very tall handsome young man, who had also come for the same Conference from Nigeria. We had all been aboard the same Delta flight from the Nnamdi Azikiwe International Airport in Abuja, en route to the Maynard Hartsfield Jackson's International Airport, Atlanta. That was our first port of arrival before boarding the domestic flight for Las Vegas. But we didn't notice one another till our arrival two days later, at the Conference registration venue and what followed, felt like the usual chit chat one sees in Nollywood movies. I remember the first time he came over to us, and introduced himself, all full of the Nigerian male agro.

'Hello beautiful, I am Nnalota. What is your name?' Truth is, I prayed silently, fervently that Okwuchi's 'shakingmania' as we always referred to her discomfort amidst the opposite sex, would not erupt like a volcano. But that was not to be. She stumbled on the chair in front of her and tripped over. Nnalota was alert; quickly he dashed to her before she could reach the floor. It felt all awkward. For me, that was really the height of the embarrassment! What flew into my head was 'Chai! Upon the many miles we flew from Nigeria to '*obodo oyibo!*' But one look at the concerned face of this guy, who caught her before the crash, made me swallow the words.

Looks were not the only interesting and adorable thing about Nnalota. When his eyes full of care and his mouth uttered the words 'are you okay?' with his deep baritone voice, those were enough reasons for any girl to jettison good home training and follow him home. Okwy and I, melted away like butter in contact with a hot knife, but quickly regained our composure. We sat down soon afterwards, and he ordered coffee and croissants. I am not a coffee person, so asked for tea. The dude serving at the Starbucks asked, 'Green or black?' I did not know what he meant, Nnalota again came to the rescue. 'Black tea, I think…' he said, 'make it Earl Grey.'

'Decaf…'

He turned to me and said, 'I think you must like it strong.'

'Yes, strong,' I said, 'decaf…'

We all laughed at that moment. We shattered the glass of difference and estrangement, and soon sat to easy conversation. There was a quick bond, the sort that happens when Nigerians meet themselves in strange countries and felt alone, and have to depend on each other for social contact. In that mood, Okwuchi rose from her shell.

'My name is Okwuchi Dimezue, but I can allow you call me Okwy, like my friends do … Just because you didn't let me hit the floor.' The three of us again burst into a hearty laughter.

I had never seen Okwy that free with a man. From our teenage to adult lives, she was always a little shy with men. Which was always surprising because Okwuchi sometimes was the boldest and most rebellious of all of us her friends – at other times. Soon, we were all beginning to feel a little adventurous. In one instant, all that intrinsic rebellion she would ordinarily exude in the face of such challenges, gradually came to fore. She seemed to have found her voice. That was the beginning of her romantic escapades with Nnalota. Truth be told, I was a little jealous, even then. But it seemed to be an answer to Okwuchi's many years of prayers for a life partner. We were all at that time twenty-nine years. She had never had a serious relationship. She promised herself that nothing, and no one would come between her and this bliss. It was quick. We thought love at first sight.

It is now many years since that acquaintance was made. Her heartthrob – Nnalota, whom she came to call 'Lota Nke M' (my own Lota) in endearment, had been true to their union. His heart, body and soul was completely bequeathed to Okwy. No day passed without his reassuring her of his faithfulness. They had their two children Afamefuna and Nmasinachi, who lacked neither for love nor for store. Their Daddy made sure their needs were met. Okwy's beauty radiated so much so that she became the envy of her friends and other women in her work place.

But the saying 'they whom the gods want to destroy, they first make mad' best describes what happened to Okwy – my friend; the mess she made of her life and marriage. She has refused to see things from any other person's perspective. But Okwy was always a drifter. That's her great flaw: restlessness. While we were at university she drifted from one fellowship center to another. She was always searching for something. She was a regular face in every campus fellowship and if one ever admonished her for that, her readymade answer 'the scriptures says, test every spirit...' I am very sure your eyes lit up in reminiscence of her favourite reply. I can almost hear you chuckle now.

The way she now lives, is as if she has been placed on a self-destruct button. It began not too long after her second child. For a while, we thought it was a long postnatal fog. Okwy just simply changed. She began to nag her husband at every point. She became suspicious of his every move; she monitored his mobile phone daily, looking to find texts a woman may have sent him, or whose name is on his call log. It was all so messy. Onetime, she sent a long trail of abusive texts to Nnalota's new partner, Ogechi Ekpo, who Okwy taught was a woman. It was the year Nnalota moved from the firm where he worked, to the new Architectural firm where he had been made partner, and where he was involved in the design of the new offices of the Regional Board of the Securities and Exchanges Commission. His very first week of orientation. That evening he returned from work, and not long after got a text, saying, 'Nna, you must come back to look this thing over again. I'm waiting in the office, Ogechi.' Okwy saw the text message, and flew into a rage, and rushed off a broadside, and then a series of abusive texts, even when Nnalota kept trying to tell her that the Ogechi was a man that he was not in a same-sex relationship, and that it was his new partner asking him to correct or verify some numbers on a file they'd been working on together for a client's meeting the next morning. I was there visiting them, and it was all so embarrassing. I felt deep sympathy for Nnalota that moment.

I have warned Okwy many times that fighting for a man's love, is the easiest way of losing it. She should ask no questions so she would be told no hurting lies. But not Okwy. All she heeds is that first idea that ignites in her spirit, be it true or false. Then, not long after, she found common cause with a group of '*Oku-enu*' women – by day self-righteous and deeply religious, and by night, fire. They would always go with their Bibles in hand for their fellowships. Every other person, not a member of their insider group, they looked on with the fierce disdain of the zealot. This went on for about a year, but no one realized at that time that under this Christian fellowship, were women, who proclaimed their 'holiness' but it was all a mask for all kinds of perversion. The Priests have become an endangered species to Okwy and her group. The young girls in the various Secondary and Tertiary institutions where they work were not spared either.

I do not know exactly what it was with Okwy. It may have been an early onset of midlife crisis, or a sudden awareness of mortality, and the futility of it all, she grew suddenly, a wild sexual appetite that I never knew she had! She was completely ensnared by this raging wild fire. She was sleeping around with fellow women – some of her 'sisters' in the cover of their Christian fellowship. She slept with men too, some of whom she met online. She had no boundaries. Her marriage was by this time in a spin. I really wonder how she was able to pull this off. She upped her nagging at home. She would not allow poor Nnalota peace in their home. Yet, she was the one who bore the looks of a much-suffering wife. You know how it is with our society – the men are always believed to be the ones cheating on the women yet women are busy fucking whoever they want. We, women, believe now it is our time. We put on our holy front. It is a question of the more you look…

But back to my story. Some have asked, how did I get involved in all these? Well, it all started about a year ago. Okwy had received a text message, and she called me thereafter. Nnalota she said was out of town in Lagos for the SEC client's meeting, and he would be back by the earliest flight the next day. But she wanted me, since I was on my annual leave, to come stay with their kids. I was their 'auntie' and they'd be more comfortable with me there than their nanny until their father returned. She just needed to go to Port Harcourt urgently for her Christian fellowship billed early that Friday of the same week.

'Fellowship *ke*?' I was skeptical.

'Yes now...'

We bantered for a little while, but I agreed. Okwy was my oldest friend, and always knew how to make me do things. She left for Port Harcourt that day. I drove to her kids to school, and brought them home at the end of school. I made dinner with their nanny and they ate, and I read to them before they went to bed. Nnalota returned from Lagos the next day, and drove in straight from the airport. He was surprised that Okwuchi was in Port Harcourt for her Christian fellowship. They'd not discussed it, and he had pretty little idea what her plans were. That night, we spent it together, after the children had gone to bed, talking about his troubles at home; his frustrations about the changes that Okwy was going through, and its effect on their children, and their relationship. 'I often think about the children. What would happen to them if we divorce? Children are always the victims in these...' Nnalota seemed very downcast. The more he talked, and reflected on their troubles, some so intimate, I did not know it was that bad, or what to say, the more I felt his quiet rage. But he was glad for a listening ear. I held his hands to stop them from shaking from his sudden, and powerful sobs. It is heart-rending to see a man weep. It releases something very maternal and primitive in a woman, and that was when, from pure instinct I kissed him. First it was reluctant, then tentative; we groped for certainty, but we soon found ourselves surrendering; making love on the floor...

I was shocked by what grew between us. And it grew stronger in the course of days. Meanwhile, Okwy became more absorbed with her Christian fellowships – it provided coverage for her frequent travels, and my frequent stand-ins for her at home. I tried to talk with; to get her to reason, or even to see the growing thing between her husband and me. I felt both the thrill of pleasure and the gnawing pain of guilt at the same time. I am by no means a perfect woman, I have my flaws, but one of the most important things for me is loyalty – I have fierce loyalties – and Okwy was my oldest friend, and now, I was having an affair with her husband. Nnalota and I often talked about this after each lovemaking; about whether we should stop, take a deep breath, and reorder things; let things cool off a bit. But events spiraled, shaped I think by the hand of fate, out of my hands. Two weeks ago, Okwy came home, and told Nnalota that she was billed to go to her Christian fellowship in Port Harcourt for that weekend.

Lota's plea for her to rest since they would soon travel fell on deaf ears. I sat down with my friend Okwy, and tried to warn about the dangerous game she was playing, and the consequence of it. It led to a spat. We did not resolve anything. 'Mind your business!' she snapped at me. 'In short, stay away from my business from now on. You do not think I see the way you look at my husband? Stay away if you know what's good for you!' That was my first real row with Okwy since our years growing up, and meeting in the same boarding school for girls, and becoming friends. I knew what her 'Christian fellowship' in Port Harcourt was. It was an 'all-girls' affair. But it was not in Port Harcourt as things turned out.

Okwy had checked in at hotel *D'Exquisite*, in the New-Found-Land Estate, which was located by her office on a Thursday. The next day, Nnalota sent me a text. Incidentally, that weekend, there had been scheduled a meeting to sign a Memorandum of Understanding between his firm and a group of Architects that arrived from Dubai, who had checked in at *D'Exquisite*. There was a reception planned afterwards and he wanted me to accompany him as stand-in for my friend, since Okwy was away in Port Harcourt. I was both as thrilled as I was overcome with guilt. I could not do it, I said to Lota. 'I'm not sure it is a good idea, Lota'

'Do you have a better idea?' he laughed his throaty laugh, 'everybody will come with their spouse.'

'But they know your wife. I'm not your wife.'

'I'll tell them...'

'*Mba*, Lota! It's not a good idea...'

'Okay then. Join me for a drink.'

'A drink?'

'Just a drink.'

'Where?'

Hotel D'Exquisite. I'm already at the bar...'

'It's just a drink'

'Just a drink.'

To cut it all short, I went to meet him at the bar of the hotel. He was sitting at a slightly removed corner of the bar, which gave him a sweeping look at the reception area. I joined him, and he ordered a martini for me, and a platter of *Escargots a la Bourguignonne* – really, snails in this butter and garlic sauce. We were not too far gone into it; it was in short a little under an hour, when Okwy walked gaily in.

Lota saw her first, and said, 'There is your friend walking in...' He did not seem shocked. I was shocked. 'You knew all along?'

He nodded his head. 'I've known for quite some time.' He was looking into my eyes, 'you did not tell me...'

'I...' I felt suddenly tongue-tied.

Without enquiries from the lady at the reception, Okwy had made her way to the elevator that took her to the fifth floor. I felt sweaty. The air, suddenly, felt thick and intense. Lota stayed calm. He gave his wife close to twenty minutes before we went to the reception and inquired of the pretty receptionist, which room the beautiful dark complexioned lady in a skimpy red gown had gone into. Trust hotel workers to part with innocent details with the right smile and the right weight of some currency notes. He immediately got answers. We went to the fifth floor. My pleas, and pulls, to get Lota to back-off only seemed to fuel his stubborn need to confront his wife that day and settle it all with the man with whom she was frolicking. As desperate fortune would have it, a house steward was rolling a tray of white wine cooling in a bucket, and two dinner plates covered, and was heading to the same room. Okwy waited for him to say, 'Room Service!' and an indistinct voice responded from inside. There we waited for the room service to leave, and just as he was about closing the door, Okwy placed his foot before it snapped shut, and we entered. The unsuspecting occupants of the room, who had ordered the meals and drinks, gladly had one of them go to the door again when Lota knocked and declared 'room service' in a truly pleasant voice.

Okwy was in her lingerie, and in the arm of her own partner. They were engaged in that moment in passionate embrace, kissing, and tonguing each other. And there, stood her husband, staring at her. It was a party alright. A room full of women, and Okwy's face registered the full weight of his disbelief. He stood there transfixed, and just saying, 'I don't understand. I don't understand...'

'What is this?' Okwy said, suddenly aware of him. But her question was directed at me. 'I said what is this? Is that your plan? To take my husband? *Oma nle*! It will not work for you!' The presence of a man in the room had raised a commotion that forced Okwy and her friends, to dress up quickly. Some of the women soon disappeared from the scene. Okwy trained her words of abuse on me and on her husband. That was her first instinct: to be defensive, and to assume the posture of the flared and awakened hen. But her barrel was soon dry. What followed was another act of self-defence: sobs, pleas, remorse.

'Okwuchi,' said Lota, 'I don't understand...'

'I'll explain if you give me a chance...'
'I don't understand'
'Let me explain it then. .'

Without a word, Lota left the room. A weight seemed to fall on his shoulders. It was not clear what shocked him more, and broke him: that his wife was having sex with another woman, one of her 'Christian sisters', or that his plans to settle the matter once and for all with another man whom he thought was at the center of his woes, had ended in a no-contest. He did not understand. He did not even remember that he had come with me. He drove off the hotel premises with unseeing eyes, into the very busy avenue. No one could tell how it all happened but Nnalota ran under a truck...

We buried him yesterday.

Tribute
Ben Obumselu (1930–2017):
Pioneer African Literary Critic

ISIDORE DIALA

'Every man', Ben Obumselu wrote, 'is a lover and follows the Muse'. Prodigiously gifted, extraordinarily learned and informed, oracular in his pronouncements in spite of his unassuming mien, Obumselu was himself the fulfilment of every ambitious student's deepest dream of the intellectual Muse. He, moreover, had the patience, the compassion, and the generosity to guide the enthusiastic student on the challenging path to truth. When I and my generation of students at Imo State University, Etiti (now Abia State University, Uturu, Nigeria) first met Obumselu in the classroom in the early 1980s, the experience was nothing short of a revelation of the enthralling delights of the life of the intellect. Our stars could hardly have been more auspicious. Dreams were engendered; careers were born; eternal discipleships were begun.

Discovering Obumselu and his work has been one of the profoundest experiences of my life. A pioneer student in the honours degree programme in English in the University College Ibadan under the headship of Professor Molly Mahood, Obumselu entered the University in 1951 as the winner of the Open Scholarship for the best candidate in the Faculty of Arts. He maintained the scholarship level of performance for the six years he spent as an undergraduate and won the Faculty Prize as the best graduating student in 1957. He achieved these results while holding the office of the President of the Students' Union in 1955/56 and the first President of the National Union of Nigerian Students (NUNS) in 1956/57. Remarkably, he was offered a scholarship for postgraduate studies at Oxford University, England even before he had earned his first degree. On his return from Oxford with a doctorate, Obumselu taught for three years at the University of Ibadan before moving at the onset of the Civil War to the University of Nigeria, Nsukka. Fleeing the country at the end of the War because his roles in Biafra placed him under military surveillance, Obumselu led the life of a wandering scholar and taught in universities in the United

Kingdom, Zambia, Zaire, Botswana and Swaziland. He returned to Nigeria in 1981 to serve as Special Adviser to the then Governor of Anambra State, Jim Nwobodo and, at the collapse of the Second Republic, taught for several years at Abia State University, Uturu. Obumselu left the university in 1986 to begin totally new careers in Lagos.

Obumselu, however, expressed special preference for the vocation of the university teacher. He thought particularly highly of research as a means of generating new insights and saw scholarly publication as a serious gesture aimed at the attainment of immortality. Consequently, beginning from his first essay 'The Background of Modern African Literature', published in Ibadan in 1966, he consistently demonstrated the rigour which responsible scholarly publication demands. He was remarkable for the catholicity of his interests, the thoroughness of his modes of enquiry, and the charm of his formulations. He was also typically tireless in his zeal to trace ideas to their ultimate sources and to follow their varying mutations. Regarding cultures as necessarily alive, dynamic and exogamous, he methodically explored the history of a great diversity of literatures, sculpture, music, languages, religions and other human endeavours to contend that the mystique of national culture is a twentieth-century error. One of the pleasures of reading Obumselu is that every typical piece is an ambitious multidisciplinary *tour de force*, expressed, moreover, in graceful and powerful language. Two publications of his set this in particular relief: his 1980 publication in *Research in African Literatures*, 'The French and Moslem Backgrounds of *The Radiance of the King*' and his 2010 publication also in *Research in African Literature*, 'Cambridge House, Ibadan, 1962-1966: Politics and Poetics in Okigbo's Last Years'.

In the earlier article, refuting the stereotype of Laye as an African writer drawing on privileged African material to exalt a permissive moral outlook, Obumselu locates *The Radiance of the King* in the context of values that derive both from Islam and the twentieth-century intellectual novel in France. If Obumselu's exploration of Islam with its Sufi revivals is astonishing, he equally methodically explores the oeuvres of many influential French writers and thinkers of the twentieth century to foreground Laye's indebtedness to the West with regard to his moral vision. Sartre, Camus, Julian Green, Francois Mauriac, Flaubert, and especially Kafka are studied with breath-taking mastery as writers whose works are instructive for understanding Laye's craft and preoccupation.

'Cambridge House, Ibadan, 1962-1966: Politics and Poetics

in Okigbo's Last Years', like 'Christopher Okigbo: A Poet's Identity' which preceded it, has as its thesis Okigbo's multicultural filiations. Obumselu's contention is that Okigbo observes no cultural frontiers but regards the entire baggage of humankind as his patrimony which his genius subjects to an original and life-enhancing synthesis. Serving his apprenticeship at the feet of T. S. Eliot, Ezra Pound and Stéphane Mallarmé, Okigbo, Obumselu demonstrates, in his pupilage to Leopold Sedar Senghor and oral African (actually primarily Yoruba) literature was equally absolute in his dedication. Examining Okigbo, Obumselu ranges through the poetry of Virgil, Eliot, Pound, Yeats, Lorca, Mallarmé, Shelley, Wordsworth, Coleridge and Senghor, and through the varying genres of indigenous Yoruba poetry as well as the music of Debussy and funeral African drums. In obvious adulation of Okigbo's supreme embodiment of the active and contemplative lives, Obumselu also brings to his study of Okigbo insights that derive from his earlier examination of Tolstoy, André Malraux, Iris Murdoch, André Brink and Ancient Greek tragedy. Reflecting at length on the mystical tradition in Western philosophy which pictures virtue as a kind of dying, Obumselu repeatedly dwelt on the recognition of the temporality of human life as a creative realisation capable of inspiring selflessness and self-transcendent action. Thus, in his reading of Okigbo's 'Elegy of the Wind', he highlights with great admiration and power how the poet's acceptance of his mortality and transience beside the imponderable mystery of life liberated him from the fear of death and released his energy for gallant self-forgetful action. In its ambitious scope, as in its intellectual depth and speculative resonance, 'Cambridge House, Ibadan, 1962-1966: Politics and Poetics in Okigbo's Last Years' is a typical Obumselu offering.

Obumselu spent the last days of his life as an 'Igbo icon' and played an exceptional role quietly, persistently, creatively, selflessly and almost invisibly in Igbo public life in restructuring the community both in politics and cultural formations. He had equally played prominent roles in Biafra as a member of the Briefs Committee that produced drafts of most of the young nation's pivotal documents and especially in setting up 'His Excellency's Special Brigade'. He was reading voraciously too in his final years and was at work on a book on the African novel. As always, the planning was painstaking; the procedures and execution rigorous. Old books were reread and new ones were ordered from different parts of the world; new and old journal articles were consulted, and the writing itself was meticulous and unhurried. But the body was steadily giving in to the exertions of a life that always reached out to new horizons. Obumselu's response though was even greater devotion as he found in scholarly work a refuge from searing pains.

I met Professor Obumselu for the last time on 9 February 2017 at his residence in Lagos, as he was about leaving home for the last time for the hospital. He had been in and out of hospital for quite a while. He certainly felt the need to say much to me but could not on account of his health. His words when they came that afternoon were like haloes, luminous above the grating of rasping coughs and the thundering silence of the intervals. Speech was an act of defiance and he typically persevered. I strained in vain to decipher meanings that had transcended mortal thresholds. He spoke of the state of African literature and scholarship, and of his unfinished book project on the African novel. He was much stronger and his voice firmer when he called me on the phone from the hospital on 26 February. We discussed placing his new article on Soyinka's *The Interpreters*, a part of the book project, in a journal. A perfectionist to the end, even on the hospital bed, he gave instructions on bibliography! That article was accepted posthumously by *Research in African Literatures* and is to be published in 2018.

In his tribute to Obumselu at his passing on 4 March 2017, Professor Wole Soyinka appraised him in veneration as 'a solid academic, one of the pioneers of the distinctive University of Ibadan brand, and one whose personality helped to shape Nigeria's collegial culture before its later debasement'. Soyinka regretted that Obumselu had been 'for far too long a yawning gap in any compendium of African literary criticism, since Obumselu was such a reticent expositor of his own productivity'. In like manner, preeminent literary scholar, Professor Abiola Irele, who himself was sadly to depart this earthly realm of being shortly after Obumselu, eulogised Obumselu's career and remarked especially on 'the acuity of his insights and the elegance of his formulations'. Appraising Obumselu's article on Laye particularly highly, Irele commented that Obumselu's work deserved wider dissemination especially after his death so that his memory could be kept alive 'as part of the institutional heritage of the University of Ibadan and our other academic institutions in Nigeria'.

In this regard, arrangements have virtually been completed for the publication of a compendium of Obumselu's representative works on African literature with the title *The Intellectual Muse: Obumselu on African Literature*. Having some of Obumselu's best work in a volume is bound to be a boon to scholars and students of African literature. Yet

The Intellectual Muse, when it is published, will only be a telling token of the much that Professor Ben Ebelenna Obumselu accomplished in an eventful life of unusual distinction led as scholar, critic, entrepreneur, soldier, statesman, adventurer, counsellor, journalist, speech writer, orator, intellectual muse and much more.

Isidore Diala
Professor of African literature, Department of English
Imo State University, Owerri, Nigeria

Reviews

Ezra Chitando & Adriaan van Klinken (eds).
Christianity and Controversies over Homosexuality in Contemporary Africa.
London and New York: Routledge, 2016, 212 pp, $128
ISBN 97814742444745, hardback

Adriaan van Klinken & Ezra Chitando (eds).
Public Religion and the Politics of Homosexuality in Africa.
London and New York: Routledge, 2016, 278 pp, $128
ISBN 9781472445513, hardback

These two volumes are conceived as companion pieces, composed of essays written by African scholars and others, and seeking to fill what the editors conceive to have been a gap in the study of a nexus of subjects that has received very little academic attention: homosexuality, politics, and public religion (especially Christianity). They hope the high percentage of African scholars contributing essays will counter the observation from some Africans that the whole subject is part of a Western-driven agenda. Chitando and van Klinken see homosexuality as an issue of human rights and public health. They acknowledge, on the one hand, studies by Murray and Roscoe (1998), Epprecht (2004), and Morgan and Wieringa (2005) that show how long-standing African toleration of same-sex intimacies have not necessarily completely correlated to Western designations, and on the other hand, note studies by Ekine and Abbas (2013), Snadfort et al. (2015), and Tamale (2011) that demonstrate how, in recent times, 'Western discourses and concepts of homosexuality, LGBTI identities and queer politics have been introduced to African contexts, and to a considerable extent have been adopted by local sexual minority communities and activists' (Public 9). They leave it to individual authors to enter this debate as they see fit, while agreeing with Sylvia Tamale that there is little point in reinventing the wheel if there are Western concepts or names that, with some tweaking, will do well enough as conversational starting points.

The *Public Religion* volume explores Christian (mostly Pentecostal), Islamic, and Rastafari contexts. The editors suggest that traditional African religions have contributed less directly to the politics of homosexuality. The first section, 'The Politicisation of Homosexuality', examines that topic by looking at case studies from Uganda and Nigeria, and their new legislation, focusing on Pentecostalism in Uganda and the joint mobilisation of Christians and Muslims in Nigeria to work against homosexuality. Another chapter in this section looks at Egypt, where recent fatwas encourage the growth in attacks on homosexuals. A chapter deals with Zimbabwe and Mugabe's use of religious fervour to bolster his political standing. A chapter on Kenya records how Muslims overlook 'the traditions of same-sex sexuality in coastal Muslim communities' (11) possibly because they consider themselves marginalised from Christian-dominated politics in the country. The final chapter in this section focuses on Côte d'Ivoire, where 'the legalisation of same-sex marriage in France allowed religious and political leaders ... to affirm national sovereignty over and against neo-colonial influence' (11).

The book's section on 'Global and Local Mobilisations' discusses the influence of international rights activism on analogous movements within local African communities. Various of the essayists show the nuances of 'glocalisation', and the influence of external actors even in actions that are described by participants as completely home-grown (whether this is anti- or pro-homosexuality), but other essayists point to examples of 'indigenous anti-LGBTI organizing', for example in the context of the New Citizens Movement in Liberia (11) and the mobilisation against homosexuality in Senegal in response to the concerns over HIV (12).

The book's third section, 'Contestation, Subversion and Resistance', details African action in opposition to homophobia. Several essays discuss the role of African fiction and autobiographies in providing this resistance; others try to debunk the notion of a monolithic African anti-homosexual position by describing 'an alternative form of queer worldmaking within the very heteronormative public spaces of Christianity' (13). The volume ends with the African LGBTI manifesto, which was written in Nairobi in 2010 and 'sets out clearly the foundation of the LGBTI movement and its connection to the broader Pan-African struggle for liberation' (273).

This points to the need for the second volume, *Christianity and Controversies over Homosexuality in Contemporary Africa*, which focuses more insistently on the one religion. The first section offers four essays dealing with 'Pentecostalism as a public religion', and analysing recent activities in Nigeria, Uganda, Cameroon and Kenya. The second section of the book, 'Broader Christian case studies and perspectives', presents four essays that deal with Zambia, the Anglican Church in Zimbabwe, the politics of the Catholic Church in Cameroon and the interpolation of Christian social ethics and queer fragility, and the Dutch Reformed Church in South Africa as it addresses the question: 'Is "being right" more important than "being together"?' The third and final section, 'Christian subversions and transformations', much like the final section of the prior volume, seeks to demonstrate 'how Christian discourses and practices are mobilised not only by those opposing homosexuality, but also by advocates of gay and lesbian human rights, LGBT activists, and by gay and lesbian people themselves when they negotiate their sexual identity and faith' (13). This volume ends with the Elmina Consultation Statement. This resulted from a years-long discussion between the Chicago Consultation (USA) and the Ujamaa Centre (South Africa), held in Durban (South Africa) in 2011, in Limuru (Kenya) in 2013, and in Elmina (Ghana) in 2015. These discussions were 'cross-sectoral, involving clergy, academics and activists' (199). It calls upon Episcopalians to 'curb anti-gay and anti-transgender violence, discrimination, and marginalization; to build relationships with and learn from African Anglican scholars who are already offering biblical interpretations that affirm the dignity and humanity of LGBTI people; and "to pray for the safety of our LGBTI sisters and brothers, their families and communities, and for the scholars and activists who tirelessly work on their behalf"' (200).

In short, the Elmina statement provides the mandate for these two volumes, which together lay out in stark but hopeful terms the present condition of those within Africa who identify with same-sex sexuality.

WORKS CITED

Ekine, Sokari and Hakina Abbas (eds). *The Queer African Reader*. Dakar: Pambazuka Press, 2013.

Epprecht, Marc. *Hungochani: The History of a Dissident Sexuality in Southern Africa*. Montreal: McGill-Queen's University Press, 2004.
Morgan, Ruth and Saskia Wieringa (eds). *Tommy Boys, Lesbian Men, and Ancestral Wives: Female Same-Sex Practices in Africa*. Johannesburg: Jacana Media, 2005.
Murray, Stephen O. and Will Roscoe (eds). *Boy-Wives and Female Husbands: Studies in African Homosexualities*. New York: St. Martin's Press, 1998.
Snadfort, Theo, Fabierne Simenel, Kevin Mwachiro and Vasu Reddy. *Boldly Queer: African Perspectives on Same-Sex Sexuality and Gender Diversity*. The Hague: Hivos, 2015.
Tamale, Sylvia. 'Researching and Theorising Sexualities in Africa'. In *African Sexualities: A Reader*, S. Tamale (ed.). Cape Town: Pambazuka Press, 2011: 11-36.

JOHN C. HAWLEY
Santa Clara University,
Santa Clara, CA, USA

Chantal Zabus. *Out in Africa: Same-Sex Desire in Sub-Saharan Literatures & Cultures.*
James Currey: Woodbridge, UK and Rochester, NY, 2013, 298 pp, $80
ISBN 9781847010827, hardback

Chantal Zabus begins her interesting study by noting that she hopes to do for Sub-Saharan Africa what Jarrod Hayes, in *Queer Nations* (2000), did for the Maghreb: that is, to demonstrate that 'the African Continent has always been more *queer* than generally acknowledged' (1). Her study attempts this task in six broadly historical chapters.

In the first, 'Anthropological Wormholes: From Pederasts to Female Husbands', Zabus provides 'cautionary tales around the instabilities and at times the inappropriateness of terminology around Sub-Saharan African same-sex relations' (16). Although expressions and phrases describing same-sex activities appear in at least 50 Sub-Saharan African languages, these are not procrustean in their designations; and although imported words like 'gay', 'lesbian', 'homosexual', and 'queer', are employed, they 'come with a hurtling conglomerate of indigenous and other designations and their corollary practices' (16). Zabus further notes that 'the imported words are not always understood or are construed differently' (16), so that non-Africans must tread cautiously when encountering terms that they might consider comfortingly accessible. Naming a thing does not make it so, and Zabus exposes 'discourse-as-event' while showing that 'relationships such as those between female husbands and their partners and between boy-wives and their boss-boys in various Sub-Saharan African societies reach back to ancestral nexuses prior to the European colonization of Africa' (50) – before, as Marc Epprecht argues, 'Europeans introduced homophobia, not homosexuality, to Africa' (20).

The second chapter, 'The Text that Dare not Speak its Name: Forging Male Colonial Intimacies', tries with some success to imply an implicit shifting (emerging) of agency in colonised subjects through same-sex relations with the European, unequal though it basically remained. She notes that 'in the second half of the nineteenth century, a true cult developed [in European writing] around brotherly companionship and the overall buddiness of mateship' (53). She briefly notes Roger Casement's *Black Diaries* (not fully available till 1997), but focuses principally on Julien Viaud (aka Pierre Loti) and his notion of 'situational homosexuality' (61), and Henry Morton Stanley's *My Kalulu, Prince, King and Slave: A Story of Central Africa* (1873), suggesting Stanley's bisexuality. Along the way, Zabus demonstrates 'the gradual shift [in European writing] from a discourse about the 'act' of sodomy to 'the homosexual', from a rhetoric of 'vice' to the identity politics of same-sex behaviour' (65). The emphasis in the chapter is on Europeans, but Zabus looks at the local subjects described by Loti and Stanley as vectors pointing to an 'inchoate' (74) form of African same-sex desire.

The third chapter, 'The School for Scandal: Missionary Positions and African Sexual Initiations,' analyses francophone and anglophone African novels of the 1960s and 1970s all the way up to the early twenty-first century, showing a 'church-and-state pincer plot around the issue of male homosexuality' (75), including a state-sponsored anti-clerical existentialist humanism in the more recent works. Building on the studies by Neville Hoad and Chris Dunton, Zabus analyses early novels that portray corrupt clerics corrupting young African men and more recent novels in which zealous conservative priests try to straighten out, as it were, homosexual Africans: Dillibe Onyeama's *Nigger at Eton* (1972), Yulisa Amadu Maddy's *No Past, No Present, No Future* (1973), Biyi Bandele's *The Street* (1999) and Jude Dibia's *Walking with Shadows* (2006). Uche Peter Umez's short story, 'A Night So Damp' (2005), uses the misogyny of it characters to suggest a more complex reading of same-sex relations in contemporary Nigeria.

Zabus reviews francophone novels to demonstrate the comparatively liberating influences of visits to Paris by characters, or the complex entanglements of Frenchmen with visiting Africans: Abdoul Doukouré's *Le déboussolé* (1978), Bernard Nanga's *La Trahison de Marianne* (1984), and Saïdou Bokoum's *Chaîne* (1974). She notes the controversy over the authorship of Camara Laye's *L'enfant noir* (1953) and *Le Regard du roi* (1954) and his relationship with Francis Soulié.

She notes that 'with few exceptions ... homosexuality continues to be construed as essentially male' (122) but, in chapter four, 'The Stuff of Desire: Boarding School Girls, Plain Lesbians and Teenage Dykes', Zabus proceeds to describe a few of those exceptions. Offering her examples chronologically, she begins with the 'implicit "queer" gesturing by African women novelists' in the 1970s (Rebeka Njau, Ama Ata Aidoo), then on to more explicit and self-confident assertion of same-sex desire in the 1990s (Unoma Azuah, Lola Shoneyin, Temilola Abioye) and the 2010s (Helen Oyeyemi). Zabus suggests that the work of the more daring of these writers, such as Unoma Azuah and Monica Arac de Nyeko, 'disturbs and dismantles' (159) structures of heteronormativity.

The fifth chapter, 'Apartheid, Queerness, and Diaspora', dealing with southern Africa, valorises the female writers outside South Africa (Bessie Head, Sheila Kohler, and Shamim Sarif) for forging 'their own reconstructions of female same-sex desire against not only the canvas of Apartheid law but also the Afrikaner grain of [what Michael Heyns calls] an "erotic patriarchy"' (160). The bulk of the chapter, though, deals with white writers like Mark Behr and Stephen Gray and the complicated relationship of their opposition to Apartheid and inescapable complicity with it. She writes that, in Behr's *The Smell of Apples* (1995), 'queerness is shown to be the very skeleton in Apartheid's closet' (187). Referring to the critique offered from a diasporic position by Head, Kohler and Sarif, Zabus concludes by noting that 'it remains to be seen whether the African "home" rather than its diasporic counterpart can truly host same-sex desire for both men and women in post-Apartheid South Africa and in other African nation-states' (216).

Following directly from that question, the sixth chapter, 'Male and Female Mythologies', argues that 'queerness is still seen as a way of being in the world that is in need of being validated and "justified" by what I have called a "mythology" harking back to ancestral African foundations' (216). Using recent writers like K. Sello Duiker, Doumbi Fakoly and Calixthe Beyala, Zabus argues that they are reinvigorating ancient myths to subliminally suggest a rootedness to queerness before the imposition of Victorian morality and Freudian definitions. 'The presence of ancestors ... connects past and present; ancestral myths and the contemporary right to gender variance' (249).

Her conclusion, 'Trans Africa', rehearses the structure of the book: the identification of 'those texts by a handful of colonial writers and some thirty African postcolonial writers that present homosexuality-as-an-identity, however nebulous, rather than an occasional or ritualized practice' (251). Zabus has performed a revisionist historical task of reshaping the archive of same-sex writing for Sub-Saharan Africa, and produced an argument that cannot be ignored.

JOHN C. HAWLEY
Santa Clara University,
Santa Clara, CA, USA

Unoma Azuah. *Blessed Body: The Secret Lives of Nigerian Lesbian, Gay, Bisexual & Transgender.*
Jackson, TN: Cooking Pot Publishing, 2016, 257 pp. $15
ISBN 9780996546072, paperback

Unoma Azuah's *Blessed Body: The Secret Lives of Nigerian Lesbian, Gay, Bisexual and Transgender* is a collection of 37 stories, largely autobiographical, by Nigerians from ages 20 to 50 years residing in Nigeria and various parts of the world. The stories are batched into eight sections that have different significations. The stories constitute not just a means for the writers to present their experiences as lesbians, gays, bisexuals and transgenders, but also a reaction to the diverse debilitating experiences, isolation, condemnation, rejection and humiliating treatments that people of these sexual orientations have suffered in private and public contexts over the ages.

Several of the stories portray the experiences of young people who are inclined to homosexuality. The authors recount their attractions to same sex, their traumas in sustaining passion for same sex in families or environments that repudiate homosexuality. Often times, in pursuit of suitable strategies to deploy to fulfil their eroticism, which is largely despised by their parents, siblings and others, they tend to develop some deviant tendencies, and get pulled deeper into homosexuality.

The first section of the book, titled 'Discovery: Coming of Age', has five stories that depict homosexual tendencies among teenagers. Prominently, the children's play of 'mummy and daddy' serves as a platform for some of the children to demonstrate their affection for same sex, especially where the actors are of the same sex, since one will inevitably perform the role of the opposite sex. The same actors also narrate their attractions often times to the opposite sex, even though this context of relationship is hardly as vibrant, exciting, motivating or enduring as the same-sex relationship. There is a high degree of pretence and endurance in the former – the person involved in a heterosexual relationship is unsure if what he/she feels is true love. The female often pretends to reach orgasm when making love with a man, and feigns several sounds and expressions to deceive him that she is enjoying the sex act. Essentially, there is an underlying desire among the narrators to be 'normal' and meet societal and family expectations of getting married to the opposite sex, and having families. They also recognise the oddity in their sexual inclination to same sex, and their lack of interest for the opposite sex. Consequently, they endure the reactions from the people around them. These reactions include forms of verbal abuse, physical abuse, taunts, mistreatment, isolation and rejection. These combine to generate discovery and coming of age among the narrators.

The second section with five stories is titled 'Blurring Lines'. The stories are written by more mature people – a university student, a career lady, and other mature and maturing people. The writers portray the abnormality versus the sexual orientation that the society recognises and accepts as normal. The bisexual lady attains adequate spiritual mettle from lesbianism to create an equilibrium that sustains her marriage to her husband. She surrenders to her husband and tries to meet his emotional needs in a mechanical way – she feels nothing with and for him – neither love nor hate, but she is sure of her active inclination to lesbianism, which actually accounts for her stability and sanity. The writers in this section stress the distinction between the two genders. By implication, the line of gender distinction is blurred. Someone is first a person, a human being before the gender is considered. One can be male physically, but he is female spiritually, mentally and psychologically, and vice versa. Sadly, the Nigerian culture makes no provision for such a personality, and consequently he/she often faces different forms of abuse and mistreatment because he is too 'soft' for manhood. The abuses and poor treatment coalesce to create negative complexes, and sometimes, suicidal tendencies.

The frequent rejection of the homosexual or transgender is as intense within the family as it is in the public. When a man exhibits female traits, he feels that he is a woman in the wrong body, and when a woman exhibits male attributes, she feels that she is a man in the wrong body. These imply an inherent defect that the person suffers because he/she will fail to perform the expected gender roles in both private and public spheres; he/she will be inclined to things that are at variance with his/her physical personality; his/her modes of thinking and action will be considered dysfunctional and he/she will be torn between being male/female to correspond with his/her physique and the expectations of his/her family and the society, and being female/male which is what gives him/her joy and satisfaction and makes him/her a full-rounded person. Correspondingly, in 'The Down-Low Glow', James, one of the contributors, admits to his mother that he is gay, after a long period of denial. His disclosure of his sexual orientation is a means of surmounting self-resentment and depression that have plagued him for a long time. To him, living in denial of who he is amounts to attempting to change God's design. That is a subtle challenge of his mother's constant declarations that as a homosexual, he is hell-bound. But James feels better informed as he is conscious that life is diverse and full of complexities, which are beyond human understanding. Thus, one should not judge another. James becomes empowered by the knowledge that God Himself is a complex entity that is more profound than human imaginations, expectations and speculations.

Unlike James, who admits and firmly sticks to his sexual orientation, there are some homosexuals who succumb to the pressures of culture that are imposed on them by their families and the society. They accept that one cannot successfully and happily live as lesbian or gay, but must marry and have children to fit into the cultural mould of the society. However, they try to sustain their lesbian or gay relationships that seem to offer the impetus needed to keep their respective marriages. In 'Damie was Her Name', Damie explains to Halima that you 'do know that we can't get married here [in Nigeria]. It's just fantasy. Let's not waste a good thing by talking about things that can't be ... We can't marry each other and have a life together' (73-4). She also declares that as her mother's only daughter, 'no matter what, she had to do the right thing: marry a man' (74). This concept of what is right always conflicts with what are the desires of gays, lesbians, bisexuals and transgenders, and instills a fundamental contradiction in their lives, tendencies and expectations.

'Facebook Fantasies', the third section of the collection, comprises four short stories that are largely based on experiences derived from diverse electronic and print devices and Facebook. While Lexy Woku is chasing phantoms in the story of the same title as he makes friends with the elusive but dangerous Max who gets him severely battered for declining his amorous invitations, Niyi Baaki in 'Jump' is attracted to the men in the porn magazine – their big muscles and amorous physique. As he sees his dimpled school mate, he visualises a lot of the things that the men do in the porn magazines. He is also fascinated by the gay community that he discovers on Facebook. That serves as the platform for him to assert himself, socialise and really be at peace with himself.

Kennedy Tchidi in 'We Met, Had Hot Sex, and Then He Preached', explores Facebook and several other social network platforms to make friends with other gays. He is shocked by his partner who is sexually very vibrant and resilient, but who also spends time preaching to him on the evils of homosexuality. Seun Don in 'Feeding the Ghost' is also an active explorer of the internet and a regular visitor to cybercafés that connect him with several other homosexuals in Nigeria and abroad. Strangely, he is only fifteen years old, but he has affairs with Jason, who is 28 years old, PD, an English man who is resident in France, and others. Don admits 'I had a lot of sex. I was having sex with virtually everyone in the community – careless unprotected sex. It was how "they" wanted me' (93). Yet he also suffers rejection from many of his sex partners. Don ends up testing positive to HIV, and registers at the Nigerian Institute of Medical Research (NIMR) in Lagos where he receives free counselling and treatment. He uses the period of his illness to recondition his mind and check the intensity of his homosexual activities. His conviction is that 'God listens. He doesn't promise us easy life, but he promised that his hand and heart in our lives will always see us through' (103-4).

The next section, 'Homo-sexing', comprises five stories, which reveal the intricacies of homosexuality. These are portrayed among young male students in the school dormitory. The stories demonstrate how the rich and influential are so powerful as to manipulate the system, evade every form of disciplinary action, and achieve their unwholesome desires through corrupt means. As a transgender, Stephanie is denied entry into the Public Library by security men who see her as an aberration and tell her that she is indecent. But as she argues against such a label and an identity, she is physically attacked by a security man with a long whip and baton. She is also verbally attacked and described as an animal, or worse than an animal. Stephanie suffers enormous scorn and intense animosity among the people around her, including her contemporaries. She finds herself alone, often crying because of the taunts and derision that she confronts from her friends and other people around her.

The fifth section, with the caption 'Unwanted Marriage', presents three stories. 'Resurrection' is the story by Bee Kenny on her escapades as a bisexual. She displays recklessness in her search for partners, and she changes them often. Starting from her secondary school to the university, Kenny demonstrates audacious adventure. She gets pregnant at age 24, and her education is interrupted; she has neither a job nor a skill, she has no friends, and depression and mood swings set in. After having two children, she drifts back to lesbianism. Her bisexual nature compels her husband to complain to her family and then move out of their home. Even though she is warned and urged to stop the same-sex relationship, she refuses to budge, because she feels that being a lesbian has enabled her to get resurrected and to attain freedom in a very oppressive environment.

The women in marriages in the stories 'Benign Tumor' and 'Bent: Not Broken' are bisexuals: while in marriage, they deny their husbands sex, and practise lesbianism, which causes tremendous rancour and desperation from their husbands. The man moves out of the home in disgust, but the woman is not deterred. The section, 'Secret Lives' comprises four stories that expound the secret lives of homosexuals – how a gay patron facilitates the successful relocation of the partner to Canada, how Nigerian homosexuals are versatile and interested in the interface of their sexual preference and HIV/AIDS, how homosexuality as a practice is always under cover in Nigeria, how the fact of being gay implies the failure of a parent, how homosexuality means a mission to occupy oneself and be fully present in one's life.

'The Church' is a section with six stories that narrate the place of homosexuality in Christianity. In 'Holy Anger', the Preacher Boy, the fervent assistant of Sister Odolo, the Great Prophetess, becomes gay. He faces the challenge of reconciling the desires of his body with the desires of his mind. His mind is ready and happy to obey and serve the Lord, but his body is reprobate. This section generally demonstrates the contradiction between the Christian faith and homosexuality. The thrust of the contradiction is in the fact as stated in Ephesians chapter 6 verse 12 that 'we wrestle not against flesh and blood, but against principalities, against powers, against the rulers of the darkness of this world, against spiritual wickedness in high places'

(King James Version). The battle is consistently against homosexuality, the seemingly abominable spirit that plagues the ardent child of God. Reverend Rowland Jide Macaulay narrates in 'This Spiritual Wickedness in High Places' that the Christian faith made him know that his being gay means that he is unclean and, as a person of faith and deep spirituality, he resorts to offering secret prayers of cleansing. Sadly, the more he prays the more he feels gay and is drawn to sexual encounters even with church members. Ebele Dimi in 'Deliverance' fails to get delivered from the spirit of lesbianism despite every effort of her parents and the pastor. She is seen as demon-possessed but the Holy Ghost fire cannot burn out the lesbian spirit. She is neither able to relate with men and marry one, nor has she any plans of having children, yet she is convinced that she has a good relationship with God.

The last section, 'Unapologetic' consists of five stories that stress that to have a different sexual orientation does not make a person abnormal: if a woman is a lesbian, she actually appreciates men, but she cannot form an emotional bond with them as she does with women. If a man is gay, he appreciates women but he is more easily emotionally bonded with men than women. If a person is bisexual, he/she is able to balance the physical and emotional attractions that he/she feels towards both men and women. The person who is transgender has an intrinsic desire to be, live and be accepted as the opposite sex. At the core of the above categories is love. Each of the members of the different groups sees beyond the physical presentation of a person – male or female – whatever can accord the feeling of loving and being loved. This transcendence is captured by J. T. Okoni in 'Find Your Joy' as 'I love my parents. I love my family, but I love me more' (226). By implication, each person should get to terms with his/her sexual preference – gay, lesbian, bisexual or transgender – and be confident and consistent in it. Confidence within this context is the force that helps the person to deal with the hatred, persecutions and rejection that emerge from the family and the society.

The 37 stories in *Blessed Body* highlight certain commonalities that generate diverse degrees of curiosity, interest, query, agitation, apprehension and concern towards the future of authentic social living, marriage and true personal integrity among Nigerians. The issue of homosexuality is always concealed, and regarded as a secretive and shameful act. There is the factor of fear along with guilt that characterises the mind of the gays, lesbians, bisexuals and transgenders. They seem to fear how people will respond to their sexual orientation, how they will justify their sexual preference within the context of their traditional expectations and Christian faith, how they are likely to be condemned for deviating from the norm. They also feel guilty for choosing what the society and the Bible abhor. Consequently, the parents get agitated in their efforts to deliver their children from the homosexual spirit. They display resentment and sometimes brutality towards their homosexual children as a way of correcting their erroneous choice of a dysfunctional life style. The rejection that they often face generates a sense of loneliness which sometimes pushes the homosexual into deviance.

In the stories, there is a prominent incongruity between homosexuality and sin. The homosexuals actually refer to the Bible passages in Genesis and Leviticus which condemn the act and practice of homosexuality. They strive to justify homosexuality, bisexuality and transgender by arguing that they who practise them are truly enjoying freedom – freedom to love the way they choose, freedom to be unique, and to be different from the crowd, etc. Significantly, this paradoxical freedom seems to be always shrouded in the fear, self-loathing, betrayal, distrust, deceit and a general sense of inadequacy that characterise the world of the homosexuals, bisexuals and transgenders, as portrayed in the stories.

Nigeria is a highly religious and conservative society that considers homosexuality an unacceptable deviation. Nigeria's 2013 Same Sex Marriage Prohibition Act (SSMPA), makes it illegal for gay people to hold meetings. The Act also criminalises homosexual clubs, associations and organisations with penalties of up to 14 years jail term. As one of 38 African countries that have laws against gay people. In that connection, there are widespread stigmas and discriminations based on sexual orientation and gender identity along with high levels of physical, psychological or sexual violence against lesbians, gays, bisexuals and transgenders (LGBT). These create fear among members of the LGBT community, and make their activities largely clandestine. The fear deters them from seeking proper medical attention or support services when necessary. Within the above context, there seems to be very little hope that members of the LGBT community in Nigeria will be really free, or be accepted, or be able to publicly admit their sexual disposition, and cease being victims of violence from State and non-State actors. This interface of what is desired by the LGBT community and what is accepted by the State is likely to progress into more complex structures since homosexuality seems to be prevalent among the Nigerian youth, as portrayed in many of the stories in Azuah's *Blessed Body*. This potential promises to challenge the authenticity of the age-long traditional value of the marriage institution and other trends and practices in Nigeria. Even though members of LGBT community in Nigeria may not easily consider same-sex marriage, they are able to form associations and relationships that operate at variance with the norms of the tradition and the Christian faith. This potentiality is what the people, the State and its surrogates often find repulsive, and then react against by attacking and rejecting as reflected in the tensions, conflicts, scorns and isolation that members of the LGBT community experience at micro and macro levels, as portrayed in Azuah's *Blessed Body*.

INIOBONG UKO
English Department, University of Uyo
Akwa Ibom State, Nigeria

Chimamanda Ngozi Adichie. *Dear Ijeawele, or a Feminist Manifesto in Fifteen Suggestions.*
London: Harper Collins Publishers, 2017, 66 pp, £10
ISBN 9780008241032, hardback

Chimamanda Ngozi Adichie is a bold feminist who is not afraid to express her opinions and position on the issues of feminism. Her passion for the liberation of women is evident in her novels: *Purple Hibiscus* and *Americanah*. In the latter, she incorporates some of the ideas that she develops in *Dear Ijeawele*. One such idea is the creation of a female character (Ifemelu) who subverts the notion that it is male prerogative to initiate physical intimacy in a heterosexual relationship:

> Aren't we going to kiss? She asked.
> He seemed startled. Where did that come from?
> I'm just asking. We've been sitting here for so long.
> I don't want you to think that is all I want.
> What about what I want?
> What do you want? (62)

Though the young man at first is shocked at her boldness, he accepts her proposal and they kiss for the first time. A traditional man would see Ifemelu as morally lax, and may not want to continue the relationship with her. Adichie here is saying that women also are human beings with flesh and blood and feel the same things that men feel, so that it should not matter who initiates the move for the expression of physical love. This is a significant paradigm shift in gender matters.

It is still in her bid to create more awareness for gender equality that she wrote *Dear Ijeawele* which one can see as a sequel to her famous speech entitled: 'We should all be Feminists'. Indeed, it *is* a sequel to the foregoing because it reinforces the basic ideas about gender inequality especially as women in Nigeria experience it. Her text therefore develops and discusses in details many of the points made in that speech. This sequel is a continuation of her famous speech because she believes that, though 'we have evolved ... our ideas about gender had not evolved' (*We Should All Be Feminists*).

Dear Ijeawele is Adichie's response to some of the critical gender issues in Igbo (Nigerian) culture that the literary feminist movement in Nigeria has not been able to fully address. The text questions the presentation of marriage as the ultimate prize for every woman:

> We condition girls to aspire to marriage, and so there is already a terrible imbalance at the start. The girls will grow up to be women preoccupied with marriage. The boys will grow up to be men who are not preoccupied with marriage. The women marry those men. The relationship is automatically uneven because the institution matters more to one than the other'(30).

Adichie laments about the effect of this uneven relationship in the lives of women, especially when one considers that the aspiration towards marriage of the female gender compels them to spend their entire youthful years preparing for marriage yet when they eventually get into it, they have less or no power in the relationship. One of the instances of their lack of power is seen in the giving of the right of proposing marriage basically to men. Thus women's lot is just to wait patiently in every relationship and hope that the man will eventually come round to popping the question. Adichie sees this as a great injustice and speaks out: 'Marriage is such a major step in your life and yet you cannot take charge of it; it depends on a man asking you. So many women are in long-term relationships and want to get married but have to wait for the man to propose' (56). Thus, Adichie looks forward to a society where things will be equal such that any of the parties in a relationship can make the marriage proposal without any impediment.

Another example of the imbalance in the relationship between men and women / husbands and wives is seen in the basic title that is given to men and women in society. An adult male member of a society is addressed as 'Mr' whether married or unmarried whereas their female counterparts are addressed as 'Miss' and 'Mrs' respectively for the unmarried and married ones. Thus a man is not embarrassed or harassed at any point in his unmarried state because the title 'Mr' does not indicate marital status whereas the 'importance' attached to marriage for women is revealed in the change from 'Miss' to 'Mrs' after marriage for women. Thus at some point in a woman's life, the use of 'Miss' for her becomes discriminatory and even accusatory while the title of 'Mrs' is used as though the married woman has achieved a great feat. This social change is uneven because it does not affect a man. He is addressed as 'M.' whether married or unmarried. Adichie expresses this disturbing situation thus:

> I dislike the title of 'Mrs.' is because I think Nigerian society gives it too much value – I have observed too many cases of men and women who loudly and proudly speak of the title of Mrs. as though those who are not Mrs. have somehow failed at something. Mrs. can be a choice, but to infuse it with so much value as our culture does is disturbing. The value we give to Mrs. means that marriage changes the social status of a woman but not of a man. (34)

Thus in order to correct this anomaly, Adichie asserts: 'Never speak of marriage as an achievement.' (34). Basically, she focuses on the need to create equal spaces for men and women. She draws on a lot of illustrations – to portray the uneven power relations between men and women – from the marriage institution where many of the injustices against women are perpetrated. She lays emphasis on how the verb 'allow' is used in marriages to show power imbalance. Dominantly, the husbands are the ones who use 'allow' to talk about permissions given to their wives to engage in an activity or do something. Adichie argues that this is injustice and promotes inequality because it is one-sided. If the verb should operate in a marriage, it should be used by both spouses. This is how to ensure an equal marriage. She asserts: 'A husband is not a headmaster. A wife is not a schoolgirl. Permission and being allowed, when used one-sidedly – and they are nearly only used that way – should never be the language of an equal marriage'(22).

Adichie also argues that gender roles are not static. In her words, 'culture does not make people. People make culture' (TEDX Euston, London, December 2012). She elaborates that gender roles change because people make the roles. Thus if Ijeawele wants to raise her daughter a feminist, Adichie says: 'Do not ever tell her that she should or should not do something because she is a girl' (15), and her responses in life to any challenge should not be shaped by gender inequality. Thus, in her relationship with people, the girl must embrace the belief in giving and taking. If she gives emotionally, morally, etc., she should also expect to receive such attention in return.

Also the inequality in the treatment of men and women is seen in the different attitudes that are exhibited towards powerful men and women. Accordingly, powerful men are accepted for who they are and nobody questions their motives or ways of behaving or their decisions in public places. However, this is not the same for women. Adichie asserts: 'We have been so conditioned to think of power as male that a powerful woman is an aberration. We judge powerful women more harshly than we judge powerful men.' Adichie's position in this matter is that what is good for the goose is also good for the gander. Thus the unequal power relations that exist between men and women, which society expresses in the giving of ample spaces and freedom to men while providing women with little spaces and multiple rules, should be abolished.

The text also draws attention to the need for early sex education, the teaching of self-reliance to girls, the instilling of self-dignity, respect for others, and the need to divorce moral laxity from radical dress-code sense.

The language of the text is direct and bold; for instance, her blunt calling of sexual organs by their known names instead of ambivalent references.

> I remember people used 'ike' when I was a child to mean both 'anus' and 'vagina'; 'anus' was the easier meaning but it left everything vague and I never quite knew how to say, for example, that I had an itch in my vagina. (51)

This directness demonstrates Adichie's refusal to endorse and perpetuate that Igbo tradition of vagueness in speaking about these matters. In the Igbo tradition, proverbs are used to capture experiences that people find embarrassing to openly talk about. Thus, taking the lead in her injunction: 'Tell her that if anything ever makes her uncomfortable, to speak up, to say it, to shout,'(38), she vehemently rejects the attitude that encourages vagueness in discussing sexual matters since sexual matters must necessarily come up sometime in a person's life.

Dear Ijeawele is a must-read for all parents and potential parents and for all who truly believe in and fight for the true liberation of humanity. Even though the letter basically captures the realities and experiences of Igbo women in Nigeria, the text is useful beyond Nigerian borders because it addresses the challenges of women and society in ways that men and women from other contexts can relate to.

NONYE C. AHUMIBE
Department of English, Imo State University
Owerri, Nigeria

Razinat T. Mohammed. *The Travails of a First Wife.*
Lagos: Origami Books, 2015, 222 pp, $22
ISBN 9789785342567, paperback

> A man was beating his wife and the wife was screaming for help when one of their neighbours rushed in and yelled at the husband: 'No, no, no, Peter! I am highly disappointed in you; you don't beat a woman! What you do is, ignore her, and marry a new wife.' The woman immediately stopped crying and turned to her husband and said: 'Peter, don't mind this stupid man, just continue beating me!!' (Anonymous joke)

The novel explores the stifling nature of polygamous marriage for women in a Muslim society. Here, marriage is seen as a Freudian prison. Society is highly stratified and conservative, and husbands are seen as lords and masters over their wives who must be subject to them according to Quaranic injunctions. Women aspire to marriage as the ultimate goal in their lives and they expend so much energy to keep it because marriage seems to be the only way by which they can earn respect and affirmation in their societies. Thus, the dream of every young woman is to get married at all costs and their greatest fear is to be divorced by their husbands.

This is a great malady, and it is portrayed in the lives of the wives, especially the first two wives of the central male figure, Ibrahim, in Razinat Mohammed's novel, *The Travails of a First Wife*. The title of the novel is unpretentious; perhaps in fact, even too literal. But it makes its point directly, unencumbered by needless artifice. Zarah, the first wife, from all indications is long suffering and should long have left her marriage. Her husband treats her badly, and ignores her deepest emotional and sexual needs. To make the situation even direr, Ibrahim marries two new and younger wives and brings them into their home. He has robust sexual relations with them to the dismay and anguish of Zarah. Unfortunately for Zarah she is also a barren and childless woman. The truth however is that she has a son for her husband that both of them for certain reasons refuse to identify with, and her womb has also been destroyed through several abortions that she does to save Ibrahim's name before their marriage such that now they have a marriage in which she is unable to conceive any more children. Zarah sacrifices a lot for Ibrahim, yet instead of gratitude, her husband treats her with contempt. Having lost all, rather than walk away from the marriage, she stays put and endures a great deal more mental and psychological torture.

The second wife Kellu dates Ibrahim for eight years. Kellu wants their relationship to quickly morph into marriage because she feels the haunting presence of time. She gets older. Her love for Ibrahim makes her to turn down other offers of marriage. However, Ibrahim insensitive to the plight of Kellu always makes her feel inadequate when she brings up the issue of their prolonged courtship. Eventually, a date is fixed for the marriage and four days to the big event, amidst all the excitement of preparation, Ibrahim announces to Kellu that he is also going to take another wife in addition to Kellu on the same day. Just like Zarah, Kellu's joy and hopes of being the centre of her husband's life and desire are dashed. However, in spite of this great betrayal, Kellu is unwilling to postpone or cancel the marriage. The weight of the shame that will follow in the wake of her rejection will be colossal and devastating. Society will not sympathise with her and Ibrahim will not be judged by society for making such an insensitive decision. Since Kellu is not strong enough to rebel against her society, she takes to the false consolations of marriage just to safeguard her interest against her rival. As she muses:

> It is a man's world my dear. What do you want us to do about this now? Postpone the marriage so that that man of yours will have reasons to change his mind and his other woman have the joy of thinking she has defeated you? No, the marriage must go on. (46)

Thus, she goes into the new marriage with great misgiving and sadness. The elderly women who bless her before she finally leaves her maiden home are equally sad, not because they will miss her but because from their own experience, they anticipate the many sad experiences of marriage that she will eventually have to live with:

> We will always put you in our prayers my child. As she said the last words, she again wiped the tears from her face. For a while, they all sat still, weeping silently into the tips of their Laffayas. The older women wept as they remembered their own marital experiences. Some of which could have

been horrific telling from the passion stitched into the blowing of noses or the subdued but rhythmic rise and fall of their heaving chests. (84)

This is a poignant and telling moment in the novel, and it underscores its very moral project. Again, Kellu's response on hearing that she has a new and younger rival accords with Zarah's response when she hears she will soon have co-wives; one sees the compulsory mourning and torture that first, second and so on wives go through in the wake of their displacement. For the older wives, the coming of the new wives becomes a period of mourning rather than of celebration and affirmation. Their relatives spend several days with them trying to comfort them just as it is done for a woman whose husband is dead. The act of mourning is itself symbolic and powerful in this instance. While the new bride comes in with pomp and ceremony, the old wife hides in her room in shame and despair. We hear Zarah's sister try to console her:

> You have to be strong. It was as if the newcomers heard her for at that particular moment, they let out a long shrill ululating that cracked the silent walls built in Zarah's room. Her stomach churned ... You want people to think you have gone insane at the mention of a mate? Do you really want your mate to conclude you are a weak woman that she can trample upon? Get hold of yourself my sister. (87-8)

Razinat Mohammed uses the arrival of Kellu's retinue in the novel and the coming of her new rival, Fantere and her own party at the exact time to stage the central conflict of the novel, and in a sense, situate the consequence or implication of contemporary polygyny. It is a form of civil war staged inside the battlegrounds of conjugal domesticity:

> Rama ran to Kellu's side and asked in a whisper if she knew about the other woman and failed to inform her. Kellu merely smiled and said nothing. She quickly remembered the advice from home, to keep her pains to her chest. As the other group joyously and triumphantly made their entrance, Kellu's group was humbled to a tangible, depressive silence ... Everyone in the room assumed a mournful look. Kellu herself didn't want her friends and relations think she was getting inwardly devastated by what she found herself faced by. (106-7)

Marrying a second, third and so forth wife for the man in the African world where these practices are still valued invariably suggests the inadequacy of the woman; its sets up a power struggle and a problematic hierarchy, and creates unhealthy rivalry among the wives, in ways that suggest that women, particularly the older they get in the marriage, are dispensable. This is the sum in itself of the devaluation of womanhood which feminists insist is at the very heart of patriarchy and patriarchal societies.

Again, in a world where various governments and organisations are spending huge sums of money setting up forums and facilities for conflict resolution in the face of religious, socio-political and cultural disagreements and conflicts, a particular culture diligently and consciously cultivates and nurtures a tradition that promotes hatred, rancour and disputes amongst the female gender and, by extension, the family unit. Here, the husband becomes a referee in a wrestling competition while his wives are the wrestlers who spend considerable time and energy thinking of how to outdo each other in the scramble and fight for the man's attention. In addition, these women have to contend with verbal violence, diabolical manipulation, fear and outright accusations, etc. from one another.

Apart from these challenges from their co-wives, they also have to endure the contempt and scorn of their husbands. One of the humiliating instances of this in Razinat Mohammed's novel is when Kellu and Fantere argue over who should share their husband's bed on a particular night. The narrator tells us:

> The two women had made so much noise about it that Ibrahim came out tired from a long journey to listen to the frivolity of the two. Zarah had laughed behind her curtains at them, heavily pregnant and yet quarrelling over whom to sleep with Ibrahim that night. She had watched as he went back into his room and returned with a piece of paper and began drawing lines and dates to ascertain the rightful owner of his bed. After drawing lines from top to bottom on the paper, he came up with a final solution that Kellu had the right of occupation for the day. Fantere screamed and rejected that verdict. (188-9)

In a polygamous setting, it is understood that there is some kind of arrangement on how and when each wife shares her husband's bed, but the literal drawing of lines and dates before two quarrelling co-wives to ascertain this by a husband is the height of contempt and humiliation; it trivialises the powerful intimacy associated with marital union, and in a sense fetishises the needs of the women in question. Furthermore, the weak nature of the women allows no space for them outside the institution of marriage. The novel suggests the helplessness of married women in the face of betrayals and oppressions from their husbands and husbands- to-be. They never consider separation or divorce as an option. They would rather die battered and tortured bearing their husband's names than live in peace and quiet without a husband's name.

The first wife, Zarah, from whom the title of the novel is constructed, meditates on her powerlessness, and contemplates rebellion against the system, but eventually chooses not to opt out of the marriage even when her husband directly tells her that their marriage is over. One gets hopeful that the woman eventually will try other options. However, the last chapter of the novel, 'A New Day' feels unsatisfying because it turns out to be Zarah's joy that her husband accepts to have her back (I mean to tolerate her presence in his house) after her uncle's intervention. Thus, the 'new day' entails the continuation of the woman's dehumanisation, and the suppression of her rights at her husband's hands. One begins to wonder at the myriad figurative meanings that the phrase 'new day' entails in this instance. What is Zarah's justification of her acceptance of this 'new day?'

> But as it was, she was in no position to disagree for she was glad that Ibrahim had even agreed to her return to the house. Her fear was more about the shame she was going to face if she lost out on her marriage. The feeling sent painful shivers through her spine. She was scared because the society was a conservative one that still did not recognize a woman if she was not appended to a man, as wife. (220)

Evidently, her musings reveal she wants a change but is too handicapped to initiate it. She then hides her lack of moral strength behind the mask of conformity and society's conservatisms. Zarah facilitates society's conspiracy against her and provides the chains for her own imprisonment. This underscores the novelist's central claim in her work; that women themselves are complicit in their own situation; in their own powerlessness because they enable the conditions that continue to humiliate and commodify them. She makes her characters docile and without agency. Deliberately so.

In terms of language the novel is bare-boned and uncluttered. There is a quality of directness to it that does not condone misinterpretation. However, there are a lot of errors in spelling, concord, and tense use that a proper editing can remedy. Yet, it is in spite of it all, a very interesting read; more so because it opens a powerful, insider look into the Islamic culture of the North of Nigeria, which might seem opaque and mysterious to outsiders. The anonymous joke about the abused wife at the beginning of this review, though derogatory to women, situates the sad irony of women as their own banes; as it captures the responses of the wives in this novel towards the tyranny and abuse of their husbands, and by extension, the majority of responses that women in patriarchal societies give towards domestic violence and all manners of injustices meted against them by their husbands in order to simply stay married. Razinat Mohammed's detailed and unamused look at women's suppression and women's passive response to such humiliation in her society is her indirect way of questioning women's silence and quiet acceptance of their dehumanisation by such a society. This resonates with Hélène Cixous' position in her essay: 'The Laugh of the Medusa' that, 'It is ... by taking up challenge of speech which has been governed by the phallus, that women will confirm women in a place other than that which is reserved in and by the symbolic, that is, in a place other than silence. They shouldn't be conned into accepting a domain which is the margin or the harem'(quoted in Richter *The Critical Tradition*: 1094) Thus, the novel seems to suggest itself as a wake-up call for women in such contexts to rise and take the lead in dismantling structures that impede their growth. It is a valuable addition to the narrative on this question of polygamous culture in many African societies, and seems to continue with such works as Lola Shoneyin's *The Secret Lives of Baba Segi's Wives*, to raise questions of its values and complexity in contemporary Nigerian and African society. It is superb storytelling, for the narrative unfolds with hardly a boring moment.

WORK CITED

Richter, David H. (ed.), *The Critical Tradition: Classic Texts and Contemporary Trends*. Boston, MA: Bedford/St. Martin's, 1989.

NONYE C. AHUMIBE
Imo State University
Owerri, Nigeria

Efe Farinre. *Folktales are Forever,* Vol. 1
Lagos: Narrative Landscape Press, 2017, 161pp, $10, £8
ISBN 9789789579204, paperback

Folktales are timeless and appeal to people of all ages. This timeless quality is found basically in its shunning of any particular historical context and in portraying characters who fit into ancient and modern times. Again, the philosophies of life explored in folktales are relevant for all times, for they give insights into how best to move in a world teeming with human beings from all walks of life. Part of the universal appeal of folktale is the simple nature of its language, which makes it accessible to both young and old people. Most folktales have satire built into their structures such that these stories are spiced with humour, ridicule and exaggeration and, like many double-voiced narratives, entertain as well as teach morals to their consumers.

In this collection by Efe Farinre, we are entertained with 15 freshly-told familiar and not-too-familiar folktales, with such memorable titles as 'Why Pigs Sniff the Earth', 'The Race', etc. Though these stories are familiar, the story-teller's knack for injecting freshness into them is quite remarkable, and we enjoy them as fresh, delectable inventions with new twists. In 'Why Pigs Sniff the Earth', for instance, one might raise the moral question of why the pig should be the loser at the end when actually he is the upright one. However, these stories – like some of the questions that philosophy raises about life – have no answers. Sometimes the just are winners; at other times they are losers. Likewise, in some cases, the unjust clever person 'wins' and sometimes he receives his comeuppance. Thus, the lesson here is that tact and cleverness are virtues that must be upheld in the real world, for living is like a game of cards: sometimes one wins, at other times one loses. One's triumph or defeat most times is not determined by uprightness or how virtuous one might be, but by a pragmatic engagement with reality. Idealists may of course question these conclusions, and perhaps that too is the point of the stories: to compel us to reflect and question existential conundrums.

In the story, 'The Race', the narrative subscribes to the abiding belief that a successful man needs to be tactful in the way he relates with other people so as not to arouse jealousy in the less successful people. Antelope is humiliated in this story because he rubs the inabilities of others on their faces by constantly boasting about his own abilities. The notoriously tardy Frog outsmarts him in the race by surreptitiously using the assistance of his folks. Furthermore, in the stories 'How Tortoise Became Bald', 'How Lion Became the King of the Jungle', 'Monkey and the Couple's Child' and 'Tortoise and the Drum', one notices a general philosophy that runs through them all: when a cunning man dies, a cunning man buries him. Here these narratives endorse the law of retributive justice, where greedy, power-drunk and cunning people receive just desserts for their plans to undo other people. In these stories, the fair aspect of the world is portrayed and people are consoled and reassured by the fact that the law of planting and reaping is still at work.

In the tale entitled: 'Why Chicken is served at Celebrations', the narrative endorses collective responsibility. Every member of a community has a responsibility towards sustaining the growth and development of the community, and shying away from collective responsibility has grave consequences. Because the Hen fails to contribute her quota to societal development, her interests are not represented at the meeting and this affects her whole life. Thus, this story through the guise of simplicity and entertainment, reveals great insights into human relations and collective responsibility. Lessons on how to apportion priorities to private and public matters are clearly relayed.

Again in 'Chimpanzee and its Human Features', one's attention is drawn to the need to promote and reinforce individual identity and uniqueness, for in such diversity is embedded the myriad skills and qualities that make for growth and development. No one individual has it all. A tree cannot make a forest as the saying now goes, and having only one identity is equal to having just a tree; hence, the need to encourage people to build on their unique qualities. An apt illustration of the importance of this is pointed out by Chimpanzee:

> It dawned on Chimpanzee that the only reason he got to the meeting point first was because he could swing from tree to tree. If I didn't have my long arms and limbs, I would have had to walk, he thought. His thoughts drifted his fellow animals: His dear friend, Tortoise, never got hurt while playing because of his hard shell. Cock's crow woke them up each morning and them to emergencies. Lion's roar scared away hunters. (25)

Also in 'Tortoise and the Gourd of Wisdom', the story equally lays emphasis on the need for unity in diversity. No one person can be the 'be-all' and 'know-all' in a particular place. Because of human limitations, no person can have knowledge of all things. No matter how knowledgeable a person is, there are still matters in which s/he will seek the advice and insights of other people.

In 'Why Tortoise has a Small Nose', attention is drawn to the fate that befalls individuals who meddle in other people's affairs. Most often the victims are ruled by their impulsive and uninformed actions but cannot turn back the hand of the clock as harm or evil has already befallen them. Folktales therefore are universal and belong to all peoples, and the values they reflect and their impacts are enduring. Furthermore, the adage says, 'Never throw a stone into the market place because you can never tell who it will fall on' – a truism from the ancient lore, which aptly captures the lesson drawn from the story, 'The Slave Sister'. The Queen maltreats her maid for no reason other than she is not her equal and eventually realises that her maid is her long-lost younger sister. She upbraids herself as her conscience chastises her for her cruelty towards a helpless person. Thus, the promotion of fairness and justice is endorsed by the story. The story 'Why Monkeys Live in the Forest', subscribes to the upstanding argument that certain positions of authority should be given to mature people who are scrupulous, diligent and disciplined. Roles should be given based on certain conditions that one must meet. Thus, nurturing and reinforcing sanity and order in society.

Efe Fanrire's folktale collection is very accessible to all because of the nature of the language employed. The font size used is a kind of middle ground joining the font size typical of nursery rhymes and the font size of adult texts. This middle ground makes the text attractive to kids and adults alike. The illustrations in the book will also appeal to children as they love books with pictures, and even to adults as a kind of pleasurable change from the monotony of reading texts with dense fonts and no pictures. The packaging of the story does not limit the readership of this simple, joyous work to children alone. Efe Fanrire is able to build a meeting point that will make the book a favourite of both children and adults and, possibly re-awaken those moments when our grandmothers told us on moonlit nights many of these tales now captured in print.

NONYE C. AHUMIBE
Imo State University
Owerri, Nigeria

M. J. Simms-Maddox. *Priscilla: Engaging in the Game of Politics.*
Prospect, KY: Professional Woman Publishing, 2016, $20
ISBN 9780578178998, paperback

There are some great stories in whose form we identify an elevated piece of creative writing fundamentally as the sole conception of a writer's innovative mind, premeditated through a meticulous attention to craft and solemn devotion to her muse. Such stories do not only make readers reconsider their recognition of a well-tailored narrative as basically the triumph of talent, they also reveal who tells them and how they are told. This is a clear manifestation of a laborious but conscious attempt of the stories to reclaim their selfhood. There are also other authentic, and striking ways that stories make us aware of their promise and fervour – they decidedly lead by the hands into and through the beautifully decorated alleys of their plots, ensuring, because it is their elementary concern, that we do not only meet the characters – humans, animals and plants – but also perceive their smell, penetrate into their multi-layered psyche, explore the horizon of their thoughts, trace the militant forces that attempt to stifle their breath, and acknowledge their spontaneous revolutionary reckoning, even as we touch their scars. M. J. Simms-Maddox's book, *Priscilla: Engaging in the Game of Politics*, the prequel of the Priscilla trilogy, has managed very admirably to attain such elemental aesthetic heights.

It seems like autobiographical fiction, an intriguing and impressionistic political saga about the shenanigans of power. Simms-Maddox's novel bristles with action captured in a controlled touch of personal details. It could also be seen as a nostalgic story of many triumphs that astonishingly casts no shadow of darkness on the present but rises to a yarn whose dialectics examines the unbalanced human condition of American society, especially regarding race, colour, status and gender. This novel does not pull punches; it simply plucks the strings of power and looks at its underbelly in ways that helps to crystallise the enormous political hopes of black America as it reflects on the inconcealable prejudice of white America. It is a novel that looks into the falsity of America's claim of upholding human rights as a land of freedom. This book is emotionally charged, stylistically elliptic but a daringly omniscient tale about the Austins, through whose many generations bound by unfailing love and loyalty we are endeared to the power of the black family and its long memory of survival. It echoes both the connections to an African ancestry, as well as that longing for home in Africa we experience in Black America. It is a coherent and fearless account of modern day American politics too. It begins its journey from the contrived place of Priscilla Austin as a political observer, and later as a participant, evolving in the complicated and dangerously heated arena of Ohio Senate, where Priscilla, first as a graduate intern and later as a legislative aide witnesses the perplexing political intrigues, and a plot she eventually rises against; an attempt which threatens at the outset to compromise her existence. We are, ourselves as readers, to contend with the intense political atmosphere as we observe the controversial and competing sides: the Democratic and Republican parties, struggling to define and twist the destiny of their constituencies. Sadly, self-aggrandisement is the tragic flaw of politicians who prey on the condition of the people to stoke their selfish political ambitions. Politicians often dream about immortality, for they do not only design to perpetuate themselves in power, but they also hope, even against hope, to be deified and eventually worshipped as political ancestors. The narrator, just like some of the characters, and despite the swarming issues that power the plot of the story, recognises this as the incontrovertible pitfall of politics, which shapes the fate of the bewitched and the marginalised, the ones Fanon calls the 'wretched of the earth'. The narrator says,

> Priscilla felt as if she has taken a job in the belly of political treachery. Some lawmakers, she thought, would make characters in *The Godfather* look meek, for they would actually 'step over their ailing mothers for political gain', as senator Callahen had once told her. The senator had also shared a story with her about one of his colleagues who had used his own wife's virtue to get something he wanted. (184)

The acuity of the narrative, especially in its subtle representation of racial injustice is remarkable. Gradually, but surely, the atavistic horror of black slavery is shown to us; the historical uprooting of Africans from their native homes, the result of the murderous colonial empire of Europe, is subtly highlighted through the story. This past of slavery is, at least through the lived lives of the characters, re-echoed in the menacing condition of the black Americans. The Austins' experience with James Peterson, one of Nelson Austin's megalomaniac Rotary friends, the white man's foolishness. The author's apt capturing of Priscilla's memory in this signal moment is vital to the essential meaning of the story. It underscores the racial climate of America. There is a wall of racial separation, and it feels almost elemental. It is clear in the encounter between James Peterson and Nelson Austin; in the segregation of their lives. Once while visiting Nelson, James Peterson refuses to enter his home in spite of their 'friendship':

> 'Come inside, James. It's good to see you, friend.' Nelson had called out [when James arrived]. But with reserve, James had answered, 'Ah, come on, Nelson, you know I can't be seen entering your house. Folks around here'll never let me live that down.' (184)

Priscilla herself bears the double burden of race and gender. She has to learn to raise her voice just to make her point in a society built on white supremacy, unkind to blacks, and especially frustrating to black women. One would be mistaken to take Nelson's account of racial discrimination as a thing that belongs to the past. Nelson tells his grandchildren: 'Even when I was a young man, white people used to mistreat people who looked like us.' Here, however hard one tries, one is imbricated by this reality. We are forced to look hard at the new subtle forms of racism in America and its constant reification of otherness. 'One way to humiliate us or to put us down', Priscilla's father reveals further, 'was to call us without using our names or to call grown men [boy].' At this moment, the reality of blackness must have fully revealed itself to the children. Nelson Austin assumes the role of a sanitiser when he says apologetically: 'I'm sorry, kids, but that's just the way life used to be for us' (286-7). But the underlying truth, the heart-wringing danger is that nothing has changed after all.

Despite the few (risky) attempts of the writer to forcefully make judgements that interfered with the flow of the narrative, M. J. Simms-Maddox has done an impressive job in her effort at creating for us a story built around a family tied by love. But the more remarkable aspect of this love is that it also gestures its affinities inexorably to Africa, which is at the very core, the essential meaning of this story. That beneath the unresolved question of Priscilla's political quest, and reflections on race, is a gesture to the sublime motherland. The novel also questions the values of integrationist politics in much the same way as Harold Cruce does in his *The Crisis of the Negro Intellectual*, but in this case of the novel, by using the experience of a generation of blacks who have had to negotiate the politics and reality of a post-integration America and its contradictions. Maddox-Simm's novel is an essential prequel to her series based on the adventures of Priscilla which is eventually set in Zimbabwe and South Africa in the early post-apartheid years.

PETROLINA IFEOMA KPANAH
Imo State University
Owerri, Nigeria

Uzodinma Iweala. *Speak No Evil.*
New York: Harper Collins, 2018, 214 pp, $26
ISBN 9780061284922, hardback

The trouble with Uzodinma Iweala's first novel, *Beast of No Nation* is the problem of authenticity. The language of the novel is far too contrived to register a correct West African speech, whose rhetoric of the creolised, the broken Pidgin English was thoroughly insulted by Iweala, in his attempt to appropriate it in *Beast of No Nation* and echo its long-tenured insouciance. He failed. But Iweala's debut novel was praised roundly in the best of the metropolitan press beyond its value and, one suspects, for the wrong reasons. It was even turned into a movie with Idris Elba acting the role of a warlord. Iweala's debut was about war in Africa; topical and hot, and feeding into the unquenchable voyeurism of an audience quickly, and routinely titillated by gore in Africa. It is the kind of story by which, as the novelist Achebe once noted, Europe saw Africa and Africans as 'a foil' of its true self. *Beast of No Nation* is about child-soldiers who became victims as well as perpetrators of violence, in a war imagined as a cross between Biafra and the civil wars in Sierra Leone. The image of Africa in Iweala's novel is Conradian. It serves the kinds of imaginary fault lines that particular kinds of audiences expect of stories about Africa: war, pestilence, disease, hunger, brutality; children sent to wars by barbaric war lords who become thus evidence of the irremediable 'bastardy' of civilisation in postcolonial Africa. There are hints here of what I call the 'Richburg disease' – a condition which I ascribe to Keith Richburg, one-time African correspondent for the *Washington Post*, whose book *Out of America: A Black man confronts Africa* (2009), now one of the great classics of the genre of Afro-pessimism, details with pure outrage, the historical and moral failures of Africa and its great poverty and violence, to the point that he thanked his God that his African ancestors were captured as slaves and taken out of Africa; otherwise, he suggested, 'I would have been one of them, now'. But he is not. 'Thank God I am an American.' As Richburg wrote in the prelude of his book:

> And so it was that I came to be born in Detroit and that thirty-five years later, a black man born in white America, I was in Africa, birthplace of my ancestors, standing at the edge of the river not as an African, but as an American journalist – a mere spectator – watching the bloated bodies of black Africans cascading down a waterfall. And that's when I thought about how, if things had been different, I might have been one of them – or might have met some similarly anonymous fate in one of the countless on-going civil wars or tribal clashes on this brutal continent. And so I thank God my ancestors survived that voyage. (xxii)

Of course Richburg ignores the on-going civil wars on the streets of Chicago, and the brutal and routine massacres of black men and women on his American streets, or the profound poverty and collapse of his own city Detroit, in Michigan, or the mass incarceration of black men in his own backyard, but writes of Africa from Somalia, in one of those ways that eclipse and flatten Africa into a one-dimensional object.

Of course, Richburg is not 'one of them' Africans. He was a reporter for the *Washington Post*, a tourist writing in the sensational tradition of the nineteenth-century European travel writer, on whose meditations, the immediacy of whose 'truths', came to be framed the image of the African continent in the European mind. Keith Richburg was far too removed from the reality, and far more enclosed by the veil of his double consciousness to comprehend the reality and values, and condition of a complex continent, and was also unlikely to understand or even truly see Africa, or the Africans, until he solves his fundamental problem of a deep-seething self-hatred and antipathy for a continent and her people, among whom he stood, just 'a mere spectator', unresolved by his journey from Michigan to Nairobi.

But this is not about Keith Richburg. It is about another alienated African – Uzodinma Iweala – and his unresolved (dis)connections to Africa and his ancestral linkages to it. Iweala writes of Africa from the perch of a *différance*. His new novel, *Speak No Evil*, has again attracted very eloquent praise in reviews in New York, London, Paris, and Berlin. The problem is that Iweala speaks to a particularly narrow audience: a highly westernised, cosmopolitan, affluent class of Africans and a western audience exercised by the problems of homophobia and same-sex relationship. It is a hot and topical issue but far too constrained by its very elite discourse. The gay question in Africa is most certainly an important and evolving question. But Iweala's novel addresses it from two potentially dangerous sites: the site of privilege, of the exo-African, children of African immigrants and exiles who have difficulty of affiliations with the cultures of their ancestors and have either given up on it, or struggle to make sense of it, because it is far too alien to them; and from the site of imperial discourse: the idea that certain issues are quite frankly the result of the kind of cultural imperialism that selects, places, displaces or reticulates the African imagination to conform to metropolitan ideas rather than articulate more immediate questions of the material condition of the continent. This factor of course renders Iweala's novel inaccessible, alien, and possibly irrelevant to a wider audience of African readers. Nonetheless Uzodinma Iweala addresses that question forcefully of the traditional, and often problematic African attitude to homosexuality in his new novel. It is just that Niru, the central subject of *Speak No Evil*, lives in the *boushie* suburb of Washington DC, where the Washington elite and power brokers – Congressmen, lobbyists, diplomats, the 'fat cats' of the powerful capital of the 'new empire' – live.

Niru is no ordinary African. His parents are successful Africans – the kind of Africans Iweala himself represents: wealthy, alienated, cosmopolitan. Niru's father, a Nigerian immigrant, is a bit *arriviste*:

> Appearances matter to him. That's why we live in Avenel instead of Prince George's County. That's why he drives a Range Rover and wears a Rolex with his tailored suits and Ferragamos. You have to pay attention to these things, my father says, don't give the world any reason to doubt you. A gay son, what would the world think of that? (59)

For a man who loves to say he is neighbours with Ted Koppel, he also struggles to maintain that balance between home and cultural exile, by his attempts to bring his children to regularly visit their ancestral home in Nigeria. But Niru and his brother are actually not interested. They are American. They go with their parents to Nigeria only out of sheer ennui and obligation. Moreover, Niru and his brother OJ are highflying scholars, and when we meet him, Niru is eighteen years, a track star in his very posh private school, and bound for Harvard, where he had been offered early admission. He is following in the distinguished footsteps of his brother who is already in Medical school. Niru is not only remarkable in that regard of his social place as a child of affluent African immigrants, he is remarkable in his solitude and loneliness, surrounded with white privilege and cushioned by his own privilege. Behind that cocoon of privilege nothing is actually real, or true, except his one true friendship with Meredith. Niru is living a lie because he feels ambiguous; he is fighting the image of his more 'normal' elder brother, and his attraction to the masculine, and possibly a Freudian struggle with his father over the love of his mother.

All these come to a dramatic head one sultry night, when he is forced by the terrible weather to seek shelter in his friend Meredith's house also in that same affluent suburb of Washington. Meredith's parents – power couples themselves – are not home. Meredith wants to make love. But the truth is forced out. Niru is not attracted to her in that way. He is gay. This revelation does change their relationship. First it imposes a burden of secrecy on Meredith, a little distancing, and a deeper sense of guilt on Niru. In her attempt to help him come to terms with his truth, Meredith loads hook-up apps to his phone where gay men meet online. It is her way of helping Niru accept himself, but it is also in a sense, an act of perfect love, and surrender, to the truths of her friend:

But you've probably always been gay and if no one has said anything for the last eighteen years then why would they say anything now, Meredith said. It just feels different now, Meredith. Before I said it out loud, I could pretend I didn't know, I said, but speaking the words out loud, I feel like I've let something loose that I can't control. You definitely need an outlet, she said, if only so you'll stop asking me the same question over and over and over again, and she tossed me my phone. The lock screen was filled with Grindr alerts and Tinder notifications. What the fuck did you do, I asked as I fumbled the catch and it dropped to the grass. You're welcome, Meredith said. (21)

It is a very poignant moment in the novel. Meredith's intervention has consequences that blowback, and indeed establishes the clear conflict of the story; the sense of its deep moral fissures: that struggle between the father and the son; between the old African ways and the ways of the new world where her descendants are scattered all over, and are appropriating and creating new identities suitable for their new locations and new realities.

One day, Niru's father discovers his secrets in his phone, and confronts him violently, even to the chagrin of Niru's mother. 'You want to go and do gay marriage, is that what you want, you want to go and carry man, put your thing for his *nyansh*? Abomination. A BOMI NATION' (31). A mother's love is perfect and forgiving, and Niru's mother is precisely so. Even when she is confused by her son's 'gayness', she warns her angry husband with all the force of her feminine terror, 'if you touch my child again, I will kill you myself'. It is from that point that this story takes its various detours: the visit to the pastor, Reverend Olumide, who tries spiritual counselling; a forced trip to Nigeria for more spiritual deliverance. Meredith is astonished by this move to take Niru to Nigeria, where she heard that terrible things happen to homosexuals. The spiritual pilgrimage to Nigeria, and the ceremony of deliverance by Bishop Okereke quite clearly did not work, for Niru returns to Washington DC and begins to date the boys he meets, and soon develops a relationship with Damien, further complicating his friendship and relationship with Meredith, whose hopes for college admission to Harvard are shattered, and she is in in restless limbo, until she is admitted finally by Barnard College. The implication is that Meredith and Niru are pulling rapidly apart, and the very forces, social and psychological that make this inevitable, also stage the fundamental conditions for the devastating tragedy that soon unfold. The last time we see him, Niru is running away from his father, escaping to something meaningless, and profound, and tragic.

There are two parts to this story, which is really about unrequited love. The next part is the story of Niru's friend Meredith. For as it turns out, Meredith is nursing her own searing pain. Six years later, she is in New York, dating a boy, and untangling the story of Niru's tragedy. She is back to her parent's home; moving her things. Meredith's parents are moving out; down-sizing, with a new life in Cambridge, Massachusetts, where her father has been appointed to a Professorship. Meredith's life is contained, unresolved: 'Ever since I left Washington', she muses,

> I have tried to contain my world in the smallest space possible. Don't keep anything that can't be packed into two suitcases. Don't attach yourself too strongly to people or places. My boyfriend says I have commitment issues. When we argue. I tell him attachment and commitment are two different things. Dogs are attached, humans are committed, I say. He wants to get a dog, but I'm not ready for that. Maybe that will change after they move and I'm really homeless. (148-9)

There is, in that voice, restless agony. A slippery slope of detachment from all emotional things. Meredith is very clearly existing in that numb state of shock and restlessness, and ambiguity that comes from an existential crisis. She is in a state of mourning, and her loss is still too intimate, and guilt still terribly searing that she finds herself perched at nullity, emptied of reason. We soon know the source of this restless agony: it is the death of Niru, six years ago, and Meredith has returned to Washington DC to mourn the past, and close it, except that it is very haunting and messy.

Speak No Evil, gives us the death of Niru as a form of sacrifice, from two conjoined reasons: the rejection of Niru's homosexuality by his father drives him towards extreme isolation, despair, and recklessness; and his unrequited love of a woman, the sign of his rejection of heterosexual love, leads to a symbolic struggle, a fight that ends his life, because we soon discover that at a bar, just before the end of that school year, and after his fight and escape from his father, Niru meets up with Meredith, and the tension and passion of their unresolved connections leads to a fierce fight, which leads to tragedy: a police officer, mistaking Niru for a black man, attacking or molesting a white woman, shoots and kills him. Niru is in death defamed as all things black in America's cultural imagination: he becomes a black male rapist attacking an innocent white woman, in spite of the prevailing facts. He is no longer the star athlete, Harvard-bound, gay son of affluent African immigrants who found the American dream. News reports reinvent the story and turn Niru into a monster. The subtle implication here crafted by the writer is that it is not only his sexuality that is framed as monstrous, but his black masculinity. Meredith is shocked from the moment the shot is heard, through the hospital where she is taken, and through counselling, where she is told, 'but you did not pull the trigger', she is silent, and it is that silence that she feels inside, that is awakened at the discovery of Niru's old jacket among her things when she returns six years later, that pushes her to make her final ablution, and come to terms with her powerful sense of loss and silence. She had once come to Niru's home to say, 'I'm sorry' to his family. Niru's brother OJ, still mourning his brother tries to drive her away, but Niru's father prevails, and welcomes her. Later, we see them again, a father dishevelled and haunted by loss, and a woman haunted by unfinished love, as they both recognise, and acknowledge the power of their loss. Meredith returns Niru's jacket as a final act of detachment – a breaking of the silence of her spirit:

> Then the door behind me opens and I spin around to face Niru's father with his unkempt hair, wrinkled gray slacks and wrinkled blue dress shirt rolled up at the sleeves. He smells sweet like whiskey and sour like he hasn't bathed. He sways a little as he squints through the half-light at my face. I want to say good morning, but my tongue refuses to move and my mouth is dry. I want to say I'm sorry. Instead, I stretch my arm forward so Niru' windbreaker hangs from my fingertips. He looks at me and then at the jacket. For a moment, he is completely confused. He says, you've been here before, haven't you? He takes the jacket from me and holds it up. He says, we've been here before, haven't we? He stares at me for a long while and says nothing. Then he says, well, go on now, speak. (206-7)

We have seen this before: Niru's father at this very point is crafted in the archetypal image of Chinua Achebe's Ezeulu, at the shattering of his mind, and the loss of his favourite son Obika at the end of *Arrow of God*, except that he is not as memorable. We have also seen his image before: he is like that savage and tyrannical patriarch, Eugene, of Chimamanda Adichie's novel, *Purple Hibiscus*, who is supposed to reflect all the failures of contemporary African man, and the evils of his attachments to the power of patriarchy, and his mindless intolerance of change, and the fragility of his subaltern ego in the face of a world impervious of his fixity.

I did begin this review with a point about the 'Richburg disease' and, in my reading of Uzodinma Iweala, the trouble is not that he has chosen to explore a taboo subject, a very brave, and splendid gesture indeed, of situating the question of homosexuality in the discourse of African ideas and reality, but the trouble is the status and location of his discourse. It is about the slippery relationship between Niru and Nigeria, which hints at a rejection of the self – connected to an ancestral place and its values – in that scene of his problematic return to Nigeria. Niru's alienation disrupts the value of his experience, and makes his homosexuality alien and refutable. *Speak No Evil* is not the subaltern speaking, nor does it speak for the subaltern. The novel itself – its movements and construction – feel brittle, and flat in many instances. The characters are more symbolic than true: they feel one-dimensional, except in perhaps Niru's father, who is a little more developed. There is therefore a strange, propagandist feel to this novel that makes it unlikely to enter into the ages, in spite of the wide, familiar accolades currently trailing its publication.

OBI NWAKANMA
English Department, University of Central Florida
Orlando, FL, USA

www.ingramcontent.com/pod-product-compliance
Lightning Source LLC
Chambersburg PA
CBHW051604230426
43668CB00013B/1971